GRUBER'S
COMPLETE
SAT*
READING
WORKBOOK

*SAT is a registered trademark of the College Entrance Examination Board. The College Entrance Examination Board is not associated with and does not endorse this book.

GARY R. GRUBER, PhD

SOURCEBOOKS, INC.
NAPERVILLE, ILLINOIS

Published by Sourcebooks, Inc.
P.O. Box 4410, Naperville, Illinois 60567-4410
(630) 961-3900
Fax: (630) 961-2168
www.sourcebooks.com

Library of Congress Cataloging-in-Publication Data

Gruber, Gary R.
  Gruber's complete SAT reading workbook / Gary R. Gruber.
      p. cm.
  1. SAT (Educational test)—Study guides. 2. Reading comprehension—Examinations—Study guides. 3. Reading—Ability testing. 4. Test-taking skills. I. Title.
II. Title: Complete SAT reading workbook. III. Title: SAT reading workbook.
  LB2353.57.G779 2009
  378.1'662—dc22

                                       2009002542

          Printed and bound in the United States of America.
              DR 10 9 8 7 6 5 4 3 2 1

Recent and Forthcoming Study Aids From Dr. Gary Gruber

Gruber's Essential Guide to Test Taking: Grades 3–5

Gruber's Essential Guide to Test Taking: Grades 6–9

Gruber's Complete SAT Guide 2009 (12th Edition)

Gruber's SAT 2400

Gruber's Complete SAT Math Workbook

Gruber's Complete SAT Writing Workbook

Gruber's SAT Word Master

Gruber's Complete SAT Guide 2010 (13th Edition)

Gruber's Complete ACT Guide 2010

www.sourcebooks.com

www.drgarygruber.com

Contents

PART I

SIXTEEN VERBAL (CRITICAL READING) STRATEGIES   1

PART II

FIFTEEN READING QUIZZES   49

PART III

VOCABULARY BUILDING THAT IS GUARANTEED TO RAISE YOUR SAT SCORE   67

TWO SAT CRITICAL READING PRACTICE TESTS

Purpose of This Book

The Critical Reading questions on the SAT test contain reading passages with questions and sentence completion questions. The reading questions test your ability to read and understand a passage and get involved with what the writer is saying. The sentence completion questions test whether you can fill in one or two words in the sentence so that the sentence is meaningful. All these questions also indirectly test your vocabulary skills. The purpose of this book is to get you to master the methods of answering these questions and enable you to quickly answer them. You don't necessarily have to know the meaning of the words if you can figure them out in the context of the rest of the sentence or passage, the process that is described in this book. You may also figure out the meaning of words or how to use them in the sentence through Dr. Gruber's strategies, which are all in this book.

Dr. Gruber has developed powerful, time-tested strategies for the Critical Reading questions on the SAT. He is the originator of the critical thinking skills used on standardized tests, and he is the leading authority on test preparation.

Note that this book can be used effectively for learning shortcuts and strategies, and practice for all reading and sentence completion questions on any test.

How to Use This Book Most Effectively

1. Read through the Introduction to familiarize yourself with the SAT and construction of the Critical Reading part.
2. Read Part I to learn all the strategies necessary for the Critical Reading parts of the SAT.
3. Take the Reading Quizzes in Part II to see how you are doing with reading comprehension.
4. If you want to further increase your vocabulary, read Part III and perhaps take the Vocabulary Practice Tests.
5. Take the two SAT Critical Reading practice tests (Part IV) and look at the explanatory answers to see the best approach. When the answer refers to a strategy, make sure that you've learned it.

Important Note about This Book and Its Author

This book was written by Dr. Gary Gruber, the leading authority on the SAT, who knows more than anyone else in the test-prep market exactly what is being tested for in the SAT. In fact, the procedures to answer the SAT questions rely more heavily on the Gruber Critical Thinking Strategies than ever before, and this is the only book that has the exact thinking strategies you need to use to maximize your SAT score. Gruber's SAT books are used more than any other books by the nation's school districts, and they are proven to get the highest documented school district SAT scores.

Dr. Gruber has published more than thirty books with major publishers on test-taking and critical thinking methods, with more than seven million copies sold. He has also authored more than 1,000 articles on his work in scholarly journals and nationally syndicated newspapers, has appeared on numerous television and radio shows, and has been interviewed in hundreds of magazines and newspapers. He has developed major programs for school districts and for city and state educational agencies for improving and restructuring curriculum, increasing learning ability and test scores, increasing motivation, developing a "passion" for learning and problem solving, and decreasing the student dropout rate. For example, PBS (Public Broadcasting System) chose Dr. Gruber to train the nation's teachers on how to prepare students for the SAT through a national satellite teleconference and videotape. His results have been lauded by people throughout the country from all walks of life.

Dr. Gruber is recognized nationally as the leading expert on standardized tests. It is said that no one in the nation is better at assessing the thinking patterns of how a person answers questions and providing the mechanism to improve faulty thinking approaches. SAT score improvements by students using Dr. Gruber's techniques have been the highest in the nation.

Gruber's unique methods have been and are being used by PBS, the nation's learning centers, international encyclopedias, school districts throughout the country, homes and workplaces across the nation, and a host of other entities.

His goal and mission is to get people's potential realized and the nation "impassioned" with learning and problem solving so that they don't merely try to get a "fast" uncritical answer, but actually enjoy and look forward to solving the problem and learning.

For more information on Gruber courses and additional Gruber products, visit www.drgarygruber.com.

INTRODUCTION

I. Important Facts about the SAT

What Is on the Critical Reading Part of the SAT?

It will include a test with some long and shorter reading passages, a long paired passage, a short paired passage, and sentence completion questions.

How Will the Critical Reading Test Be Scored?

There will be a range of scores, each from 200–800.

How Long Will the Critical Reading Test Be?

The total time of the Critical Reading test will be 70 minutes. There may be an experimental critical reading section of 25 minutes that will not count toward your score.

What Verbal Background Must I Have?

The reading and vocabulary level is at the 10th- to 12th-grade level, but strategies presented in this book will help you even if you are at a lower grade level.

Is Guessing Still Advisable?

Although there is a small penalty for wrong answers ($\frac{1}{4}$ point for 5-choice questions), in the long run, you *break even* if you guess *or* leave the answer blank. So it really will not affect your score in the long run if you guess or leave answers out. And, if you can eliminate an incorrect choice, it is imperative that you do not leave the answer blank.

Should I Take an Administered Actual SAT for Practice?

Yes, but only if you will learn from your mistakes by seeing what strategies you should have used on your exam. Taking the SAT merely for its own sake is a waste of time and may in fact reinforce bad methods and habits. Note that the SAT is released to students on their *Question and Answer Service* three times a year, usually in the January, May, and October administrations. It is wise to take exams on these dates if you wish to see your mistakes and correct them.

A Table of What's on the SAT Critical Reading Parts

Critical Reading	
Time	70 min. (Two 25 min. sections, one 20 min. section)
Content	Sentence Completion Critical Reading: Short and Long Reading Passages with one Double Long Passage and one Double Short Passage
Score	CR 200–800

Note: There is an experimental section that does not count toward your SAT score. This section can contain any of the SAT item types (writing [multiple-choice], critical reading, or math) and can appear in any part of the test. Do not try to outguess the test maker by trying to figure out which of the sections is experimental on the actual test (believe me, you won't be able to)—treat every section as if it counts toward your SAT score.

A Table of What's on the PSAT Critical Reading Parts

Critical Reading	
Time	50 min. (Two 25 min. sections)
Content	Sentence Completion Critical Reading: Short and Long Reading Passages, with one Double Long Passage and one Double Short Passage
Score	20–80

Can I Get Back the SAT with My Answers and the Correct Ones after I Take It? How Can I Make Use of This Service?

The SAT is disclosed (sent back to the student on request with a $16 payment) three of the seven times it is given through the year. You can also order a copy of your answer sheet for an additional $25 fee. Very few people take advantage of this fact or use the disclosed SAT to see what mistakes they've made and what strategies they could have used on the questions.

Check your SAT information bulletin or log on to www.collegeboard.com for the dates this Question and Answer Service is available.

Should I Use Scrap Paper to Write On?

Always use your test booklet (not your answer sheet) to write on. Many of my strategies direct you to circle important words and sentences, etc., so feel free to write anything in your booklet. The booklets aren't graded—only the answer sheets are.

Should I Be Familiar with the Directions to the Various Items on the SAT Before Taking the SAT?

Make sure you are completely familiar with the directions to each of the item types on the Critical Reading part of the SAT—the directions for answering the Sentence Completions and for the Reading questions.

How Should a Student Pace Himself/Herself on the Exam? How Much Time Should One Spend on Each Question?

Calculate the time allowed for the particular section. For example, 25 minutes. Divide by the number of questions. For example, 20. That gives you an average of 1¼ minutes per question in this example. However, the first set of questions within an item type in a section is easier, so spend less than a minute on the first set of questions and perhaps more than a minute on the last set. For the reading passages, give yourself only about 30 seconds for each question and spend the extra time reading the passage. The more difficult reading questions may take more time.

How Is the Exam Scored? Are Some Questions Worth More Points?

Each question is worth the same number of points. After getting a raw score—the number of questions right minus a penalty for wrong answers—this is equated to a "scaled" score from 200 to 800. A scaled score of 500 in each part is considered "average."

It's Three Days Until the SAT; What Can a Student Do to Prepare for the Critical Reading Part?

Make sure you are completely familiar with the structure of the test (page xvi), the basic verbal skills, such as prefixes and roots (pages 70–89). Take the practice tests and refresh your understanding of the strategies used to answer the questions.

What Is the Most Challenging Type of Question on the Exam and How Does One Attack It?

Many questions on the test, especially those at the end of a section, can be challenging. You should always attack challenging questions by using a specific strategy or strategies and common sense.

What Should a Student Do to Prepare on Friday Night before the Test? Cram? Watch TV? Relax?

On Friday night, I would just refresh my knowledge of the structure of the test, some strategies, and some basic verbal skills. You want to do this to keep the thinking going so that it is continual right up to the exam. Don't overdo it; just do enough so that your thinking is somewhat continuous. This will also relieve some anxiety, so that you won't feel you are forgetting things before the exam.

The Test Is Given in One Booklet. Can a Student Skip between Sections?

No—you cannot skip between the sections. You have to work on the section until the time is called. If you get caught skipping sections or going back to earlier sections, then you risk being asked to leave the exam.

Should a Student Answer All Easy Questions First and Save Difficult Ones for Last?

The easy questions usually appear at the beginning of the section, the middle difficulty ones in the middle, and the hard ones toward the end. So I would answer the questions as they are presented to you, and if you find you are spending more than 30 seconds on a question and not getting anywhere, go to the next question. You may, however, find that the more difficult questions toward the end are actually easy for you because you have learned the strategies in this book.

What Is the Recommended Course of Study for Those Retaking the Exam?

Try to get a copy of the exam that you took if it was a disclosed one—the disclosed ones, which you have to send a payment for, are usually given in October, January, and May. Try to learn from your mistakes by seeing what strategies you could have used to get questions right. Certainly learn the specific strategies for taking your next exam.

What Are the Most Crucial Critical Reading Strategies for Students?

All specific Verbal (Critical Reading) Strategies are crucial, as are writing and drawing in your test booklet and being familiar with question-type directions. The key Reading Strategy is to know the four general types of questions that are asked in reading—main idea, inference, specific details, and tone or mood.

I Know There Is an Experimental Section on the Exam That Is Not Scored. How Do I Know Which Section It Is?

The SAT people have now made it so difficult to tell which is the experimental section, I would not take a chance at second-guessing them and leaving it out. It will look like any of the other sections. It is true that if there are, for example, two of the same sections, such as two sections that both deal with grid questions, one of them is experimental—but you won't know which one it is. Also, if there are two sections with a long double reading passage, one of those sections is experimental, but again you won't know which one it is.

Can I Take the Test More Than Once, and if So, How Will the Scores Be Reported to the Schools of My Choice? Will All Scores Be Reported to the School, and How Will They Be Used?

Check with the schools to which you are applying to see how they use the reported scores, e.g., whether they average them, whether they take the highest. Ask the schools whether they see unreported scores; if they do, find out how the individual school deals with single and multiple unreported scores.

How Do Other Exams Compare with the SAT? Can I Use the Strategies and Examples in This Book for Them?

Most other exams are modeled after the SAT, so the strategies used here are definitely useful when taking them. For example, the GRE (Graduate Records Examination, for entrance into graduate school) has questions that use the identical strategies used on the SAT. The questions are just worded at a slightly higher level. The ACT (American College Testing Program), another college entrance exam, reflects more than ever strategies that are used on the SAT.

How Does the Gruber Preparation Method Differ from Other Programs and SAT Books?

Many other SAT programs try to use "quick fix" methods or subscribe to memorization. "Quick fix" methods can be detrimental to effective preparation because the SAT people constantly change questions to prevent "gimmick" approaches. Rote memorization methods do not enable you to answer a variety of questions that appear on the SAT exam. In more than thirty years of experience writing preparation books for the SAT, Dr. Gruber has developed and honed the Critical Thinking Skills and Strategies that are based on all standardized tests' construction. So, while his method immediately improves your performance on the SAT, it also provides you with the confidence to tackle problems in all areas of study for the rest of your life. He remarkably enables you to be able to, without panic, look at a problem or question, extract something curious or useful from the problem, and move to the next step and finally to a solution, without rushing into a wrong answer or getting lured into a wrong choice. It has been said that test taking through his methodology becomes enjoyable rather than a pain.

II. What Are Critical Thinking Skills?

Critical Thinking Skills, a current buzz phrase, are generic skills for the creative and most effective way of solving a problem or evaluating a situation. The most effective way of solving a problem is to extract some piece of information or observe something curious from the problem, and then use one or more of the specific strategies or Critical Thinking Skills (together with basic skills or information you already know) to get to the next step in the problem. This next step will catapult you toward a solution with further use of the specific strategies or thinking skills.

> 1. EXTRACT OR OBSERVE SOMETHING CURIOUS
>
> 2. USE SPECIFIC STRATEGIES TOGETHER WITH BASIC SKILLS

These specific strategies will enable you to "process" think rather than just be concerned with the end result, the latter of which usually results in a fast, rushed, and wrong answer. The Gruber strategies have been shown to make one more comfortable with problem solving and make the process enjoyable. The skills will last a lifetime, and you will develop a passion for problem solving. These Critical Thinking Skills show that conventional "drill and practice" is a waste of time unless the practice is based on these generic thinking skills.

Here's a simple example of how Critical Thinking Skills can be used for a Verbal problem:

If you see a word such as DELUDE in a sentence or in a reading passage, you can assume that the word DELUDE is negative and probably means "taking away from something" or "distracting," since the prefix DE means "away from" and thus has a negative connotation. Although you may not get the exact meaning of the word (in this case the meaning is to "deceive" or "mislead"), you can see how the word may be used in the context of the sentence it appears in, and thus get the flavor or feeling of the sentence, paragraph, or sentence completion. I have researched and developed more than fifty prefixes and roots (present in this book) that can help you make use of this context strategy.

Notice that the Critical Thinking approach gives you a fail-safe and exact way to find the solution without superficially trying to answer the question or merely guessing at it. This book contains all the Critical Thinking Strategies you need to know for the Critical Reading part of the SAT test.

Dr. Gruber has researched hundreds of SAT tests (thousands of SAT questions) and documented the Critical Thinking Strategies for Reading Completion questions (all found in this book) coursing through every test. These strategies can be used for any Verbal problem.

In short, you can learn how to answer a specific question and thus find the answer to that specific question, or you can learn a powerful strategy that will enable you to answer hundreds of questions.

III. Format of the Critical Reading Part of the SAT

Total time for "counted" (not experimental) CRITICAL READING: 70 minutes—67 questions
Total time for experimental, pre-test items: 25 minutes—number of questions varies

Note: The following represents a form of the Critical Reading sections. The SAT has many different forms, so the order of the sections may vary and the experimental section* may not be the third section as we have here. However, the first section will always be the *Essay*, and the last section will be a 10- minute Multiple-Choice *Writing* section.

10 Sections of the SAT	*Number of Questions*	*Number of Minutes*
		5-minute break
Section 3: EXPERIMENTAL* Could be Writing, Critical Reading, or Math	varies	25
Section 4: CRITICAL READING	24	25
Sentence Completions	8	
1 short passage (60–125 wds)	2	
1 short passage (60–125 wds)	2	
1 passage (650–850 wds)	11–13	
OR		
Double reading passage (350–450 wds each)	11–13	
		1-minute break
		5-minute break
Section 7: CRITICAL READING	24	25
Sentence Completions	5	
1 paired short passage (about 130 wds each)	4	
1 passage (400–550 wds)	5–7	
1 passage (550–700 wds)	8–10	
Section 9: CRITICAL READING	19	20
Sentence Completions	6	
Double reading passage (350–450 wds each)	13	
OR		
1 passage (650–850 wds)	13	

*The order of the sections on the actual test varies since the SAT has several different forms. There will be passages on Humanities, Social Sciences, Natural Sciences, and Narrative (fiction or non-fiction). Total number of counted reading questions will be 48.
Note: One of the sections is experimental. An experimental section does not count in your SAT score. You cannot tell which of the sections of the test is experimental.

ABOUT READING COMPREHENSION TESTS

Reading comprehension tests are becoming ever more important in all kinds of examinations. Their purpose is to test your ability to read and understand passages that are typical of the kinds of material you would read at your level of education. The questions on these exams test seven major skills. These are the ability to (1) find errors in logic, (2) draw conclusions from information given, (3) develop generalizations, (4) search out hidden meanings, (5) form value judgments, (6) detect bias in writing, and (7) think critically.

The reading materials given and the types of questions asked throughout the examination vary in difficulty. The easiest kind of question simply tests your understanding of what you have read by asking you to list facts or explain the meaning of words.

At the next stage of difficulty the questions call for you to interpret materials by giving the central thought of the passage or noting contradictions.

The third stage of difficulty consists of questions in which you must apply principles or opinions expressed in the reading passage to other situations.

The final and most difficult kind of question asks you to evaluate what you have read and to agree or differ with the point of view of the author.

Because all these levels of questions appear on the reading sections of the examination, your study tests include many questions of each type.

Understanding Passages

In your high school studies, you have learned many things about reading for comprehension. To help you review what you know, here is a summary of the important features of written passages and some suggestions for approaching passages critically.

Any written passage contains two main elements: main ideas and supporting details. A main idea is the subject of a passage—what the passage is about. Details support, expand, or limit the main idea.

The placement of main ideas and details in a passage is important. In fact, the placement of these elements often makes the difference between an interesting, effective passage and a dull, unimaginative one.

Sometimes the writer states his main idea first and then goes on to support it with details; sometimes he presents a series of details and concludes with a main summarizing statement. In still other cases, the main idea is stated somewhere in the middle of the passage. In others, the main idea may not be stated at all and the reader will have to infer it.

The design the writer uses depends on his purpose and on the effect he wants his words to have. As a reader, it is important for you to understand the main idea, whether stated or implied.

It is also important for you to understand the writer's vocabulary. In your reading, you may encounter words with which you are not familiar. For example, you may read a sentence such as this: "At first, Muller refused to accept the new interpretation of events, but later he succumbed to the scholars' opposing arguments and wrote in support of them." The word *succumbed* means "gave in" or "yielded." You can readily determine its meaning by looking for clues or hints in the context—that is, in the words and phrases surrounding the unfamiliar word. One context clue in the example above is the word *but*, which signals a contrast between the unfamiliar word *succumbed* and a phrase you do know—*refused to accept*. Another context clue is the supporting detail—"and wrote in support of them"—which follows the word *succumbed*. These modifying words, together with the signal *but*, help you figure out the meaning of *succumbed*.

Writers often provide other kinds of context clues. One kind involves the use of examples. Notice how examples are used to help you understand the meaning of *artifact* in the following sentence: "Next to the bones of animals were artifacts such as arrowheads, spears, pottery, and tools." Artifacts are man-made objects, as you can infer from the sentence.

Another important context clue is restatement—repetition of the meaning of the unfamiliar words in other words. This technique is used to help you understand the meaning of *hyperbole* in the following passage:

> The story was filled with many metaphors and similes. It also contained several hyperboles, or exaggerations, such as "He was centuries old" and "He ran with the speed of lightning."

As you understand the writer's meaning, it will often become clear to you that he is expressing a particular opinion or arguing for a certain point of view. Note the writer's argument. Is it sound? Do his statements support his opinion or point of view?

Sometimes you will have to go one step further and tell, on the basis of the author's stated opinions, how he would probably feel about a situation other than the one he writes about. Imagine, for example, that a writer argues that the United States should increasingly withdraw from international affairs, devoting its time and resources to solving domestic problems. How would this writer probably feel if the United States began arming a South American country and supplying it with troops to protect itself against a neighboring country? He would probably oppose this action.

As you read, try to keep in mind more than just the words on the page. Look for the writer's point of view, his arguments, and the implications in the passage. Before you begin taking the Reading Comprehension Tests, you can get additional hints in the Dos and Don'ts for Answering Reading Comprehension Tests on the following page.

Developing Reading Speed

In addition to understanding passages thoroughly, it is important for you to be able to read with reasonable speed and efficiency. The SAT, as you know, is a timed test, so it is to your advantage to be able to do the work well in as short a time as possible.

Many people are poor readers. They look at each word on each line and say it to themselves as they cover the reading material. Good readers do not look at each word. They take in phrases and ideas as their eyes skim the lines. They do not spend time vocalizing, or saying words to themselves, as they go.

You can improve your reading speed by being aware of your reading habits and consciously improving them. You can practice every day as you read magazines, newspapers, or fiction.

For practice, find a newspaper story with narrow columns. Your first goal will be to read each line in two "fixations" of your eyes. That is, you will try to stop your eyes just twice on each line and make your eyes pick up the rest of the line without looking directly at all the words. To do this, use your hand or a pencil as a marker underneath the words you are reading. First move it to a spot about one-fourth of the way along the first line. That will be the point of your first fixation. Then move it to a spot about three-fourths of the way along. That will be the point of your second fixation. Continue in the same way with each line, pushing yourself to keep up a steady speed. Do not allow yourself to "back up" to pick up words you think you missed. Concentrate on moving forward, taking in ideas rather than words.

At first, you may feel that you are missing a lot of material. With practice, however, you will probably find not only your speed improving but your comprehension, too.

Next try to take in each line of a newspaper column with just one fixation. Again, use your hand or a pencil underneath each line and concentrate on moving forward steadily. Continue practicing whenever you read.

Your reading speed depends, of course, on the kind of material you are reading. You can probably cover newspaper stories and light fiction very quickly. Science or history textbooks, on the other hand, require slower speed and more careful attention, since they are often packed with names, terms, dates, and other details that you must learn.

You will find reading materials of many kinds on the different parts of the SAT. Read everything as quickly as you can with understanding. Answer the questions carefully, referring back to the passages when necessary.

Dos and Don'ts for Answering Reading Comprehension Tests

DO follow these three steps in beginning a reading comprehension test: *First*, scan the passage quickly to get the general idea. *Second*, read the passage carefully and critically, *underlining leading phrases and ideas. Third*, read each question carefully, then look for the answer in the text, if you cannot answer the question directly.

DO be sure to answer the questions only on the basis of the information given to you in the passage and not from outside information you may happen to know.

DO notice whether a question refers to a specific line, sentence, or quotation from the reading passage. The answer to such a question is almost certain to be found in or near this reference in the passage.

DO be suspicious of words such as *never, always, wholly, forever* in the answer choices. Usually, answers that use such categorical terms are incorrect.

DO watch out for the too-easy answer. Be especially on your guard when the question seems to follow word-for-word the reference in the text.

DO leave the more dfficult questions for last. Try to answer the easier ones first so that you have time to spend thinking about the harder ones.

DON'T expect the answers to follow the order of the text. In most cases, you have to skip from one part of the passage to another to find an answer.

DON'T look in just one sentence or paragraph for an answer. Often the thread of an answer flows through the whole passage.

DON'T give your opinion in an answer unless specifically asked to do so. If a question asks you to choose the writer's opinion from a list of choices, make sure it is his opinion.

DON'T be disturbed if none of the passages deals with your subject field or areas of interest. Even if you have no familiarity with the subject matter in a passage, you should be able to read through it and work out the answers.

DON'T waste time by worrying about sections or questions you do not understand. Just work as quickly and methodically as you can.

DON'T read the questions before reading the passage. If you do, you may destroy a true understanding of the passage by fixating and trying to memorize those questions. You may also destroy any interest you may develop while reading the passage. If you truly grasp the meaning of the passage, you'll in fact anticipate many of the questions. Research finds that most people get a decreased score on the reading if they read the questions before reading through the passage.

ABOUT SENTENCE COMPLETION TESTS

√21/11

Sentence completion questions are probably the best test of your ability to understand and use words. In them, you are tested on your understanding of words in sentences and paragraphs. Because you are expected to be able to reason out the meaning of words in context, many of the words used in sentence completion tests are more difficult than the test words used in the reading tests.

Sentence completion questions consist of a sentence in which one word or two words are missing. It is your job to fill in the missing words from among a number of choices given. To do so, you have to read and understand the section of the sentence given and then choose the word or words that best complete the thought expressed in the sentence. The answer you choose must be idiomatically suited to the rest of the sentence. It also must be grammatically correct and in keeping with the mood of the sentence.

Key Words in Sentence Completion Questions

It is very important to watch for key words in the sentence completion questions. Here are some examples of typical SAT sentence completion questions that you can answer rapidly, once you are aware of these key words.

1. It is important that you envision the correct approach to the problem, as that will _____ you to solve the problem correctly.
   (A) entice
   (B) enable
   (C) convince
   (D) believe
   (E) make

The *key word* is "as" because this word links the two ideas—"that you envision the correct approach to the problem" and "that will _____ you to solve the problem correctly." The first idea *implies* the second idea (because of the word "as.") It is then obvious that *enable* is the missing word. Therefore Choice B is correct.

2. Let us not _____ the students as being childish, even though they are very _____ in their behavior.
   (A) classify—compulsive
   (B) assess—calm
   (C) dedicate—presumptuous
   (D) categorize—systematic
   (E) discuss—simple

The *key words* are "even though" and "as being." The words "as being" refer to some type of *classification*. The words "even though" represent a contrast to the first idea, "Let us not (classify) the students as being childish." Therefore, let's look for something that contrasts with or contradicts the students *not* being childish. This would be the students' compulsive behavior. Thus, the correct choices are *classify* and *compulsive*. Therefore, Choice A is correct.

3. The government is trying to _____ with the energy crisis, but it is going to be quite some time before real _____ is made.
   (A) deal—effort
   (B) cease—energy
   (C) coordinate—efforts
   (D) cope—progress
   (E) contend—acknowledgement

Here the *key words* are "trying" and "but." The word "but" shows that something will happen that is contrary to the first idea. The words "cope" and "progress" are the best choices. Thus Choice D is correct.

4. Even a _____ pianist has many hours of practicing to do in order to perform well.
   (A) clever
   (B) poor
   (C) knowledgeable
   (D) tired
   (E) talented

The *key word* is "Even." The word "Even" is introducing something that you may not usually think is correct. Normally, one might think that a "talented" pianist is so good that he or she doesn't have to practice much to perform well. So the word "Even" is essentially telling you that that is not altogether true. "Even a talented pianist has many hours of practicing to do in order to perform well" is like saying "You might not think that a talented pianist must practice many hours, but he or she really does have to." Thus Choice E is correct.

Notice that it is not always necessary to completely analyze every choice. If you get the jist of the sentence completion and see the key words, you may immediately spot the correct word or word set, without looking closely at every other choice.

Dos and Don'ts for Answering Sentence Completion Tests

DO consider three things when choosing a fill-in for a sentence completion question: *First*, the answer you choose must make sense in the sentence. *Second*, the answer must help carry out the meaning of the sentence. *Third*, the answer must be idiomatic and grammatically correct.

DO be especially careful of sentences that call for conjunctions in the answer. The conjunction must be just the right one to connect the various elements of the sentence.

DO be alert for paired words that cancel each other in meaning or content. Such words can be discarded at once from among the choices given.

DO make sure that the words you choose to fill a two-blank sentence appear in the same order that the blank spaces occur in the sentence. If the order of the words is wrong, that choice is incorrect in the sentence.

DO choose words that fit the tone or style of the sentence.

DON'T—in answering two-blank questions—choose answers in which only one of the words really fits the sentence. Both words in an answer pair should be meaningful within the sentence.

DON'T use up all your time on two-blank questions. The one-blank questions are usually easier to answer. When possible, answer these questions first and then go on to the two-blank questions.

DON'T ponder each answer choice. Read the sentence carefully, then scan through the possible answers. Choose the answer that *best* completes the sentence . If you cannot decide on an answer, go on to the next question and come back to the harder questions later.

Study the Following Samples   1/21/11

Directions: The following question consists of a sentence in which one word is missing. Beneath the sentence are five words lettered (A) through (E). Choose the word that *best* completes the sentence. Then mark the appropriate space in the answer column.

A strike, like a war, should be resorted to only when less _____ measures have failed.

    (A) drastic
    (B) important
    (C) derogatory
    (D) objective
    (E) eventful

                    A B C D E

Answer: (A) drastic. Drastic is the correct answer, so you would mark space A in the answer column.

                    A B C D E

Explanation: This question tests your ability to distinguish between words in order to choose the very best word for the sentence. Choice (B), *important,* and choice (E), *eventful*, might have been used. But on careful examination you can see that *drastic* (extreme in effect) is most suitable. Choice (C), *derogatory*, and choice (D), *objective*, have little meaning within the sentence.

Directions: The following question consists of a sentence in which two words are missing. Beneath the sentence are five pairs of words lettered (A) through (E). Choose the word that *best* completes the sentence. Then mark the appropriate space in the answer column.

Hannibal's efforts came to _____ when he was defeated by Scipio, principally because he was too hot-headed to agree with those who counseled _____ while he hastened to engage in battle.

    (A) wisdom—defeat
    (B) victory—speed
    (C) discretion—nothing
    (D) naught—circumspection
    (E) nirvana—prudence

                    A B C D E

Answer: (D) naught—circumspection. Naught—circumspection is the correct answer, so you would mark space D in the answer column.

                    A B C D E

Explanation: *Naught* means *nothing* or *failure. Circumspection* means *caution, prudence,* or *wariness.* This combination of words best suits the meaning of the sentence. Choice (A), *wisdom—defeat,* and choice (C), *discretion—nothing*, invert the order of words and, therefore, must be discarded immediately. Choice (B), *victory—speed*, is incorrect because the word *victory* makes no sense in the sentence. Choice (E), *nirvana— prudence*, must be discarded because the word *nirvana* (bliss) is very positive.

Part I
Sixteen Verbal (Critical Reading) Strategies

Using Critical Thinking Skills in Verbal
Questions (Critical Reading Section)

Sixteen Easy-to-Learn Strategies

Sixteen Verbal (Critical Reading) Strategies

Critical thinking is the ability to think clearly in order to solve problems and answer questions of all types—SAT questions, for example, Verbal!

Educators who are deeply involved in research on Critical Thinking Skills tell us that such skills are straightforward, practical, teachable, and learnable.

The 16 Verbal Strategies in this section are Critical Thinking Skills. These strategies have the potential to raise your SAT scores dramatically. A realistic estimate is anywhere from approximately 50 points to 300 points for the Critical Reading. Since each correct SAT question gives you an additional 10 points on average, it is reasonable to assume that if you can learn and then use these valuable SAT strategies, you can boost your SAT scores phenomenally!

BE SURE TO LEARN AND USE THE STRATEGIES THAT FOLLOW!

How to Learn the Strategies

1. For each strategy, look at the heading describing the strategy.

2. Try to answer the first example without looking at the EXPLANATORY ANSWER.

3. Then look at the EXPLANATORY ANSWER and if you got the right answer, see if the method described would enable you to solve the question in a better way with a faster approach.

4. Then try each of the next EXAMPLES without looking at the EXPLANATORY ANSWERS.

5. Use the same procedure as in (3) for each of the EXAMPLES.

The VERBAL STRATEGIES start on page 1.

Four Sentence Completion Strategies

For a Sentence with Only One Blank, Fill the Blank with Each Choice to See the Best Fit*

Before you decide which is the best choice, fill the blank with each of the five answer choices to see which word will fit best into the sentence as a whole.

EXAMPLE 1

He believed that while there is serious unemployment in our auto industry, we should not _____ foreign cars.

(A) discuss
(B) regulate
(C) research
(D) import
(E) disallow

EXPLANATORY ANSWER

Choice D is correct. The word "import" means to bring in from another country or place. The sentence now makes good sense. The competition resulting from importation of foreign cars reduces the demand for American-made cars. This throws many American auto workers out of jobs.

EXAMPLE 2

His attempt to _____ his guilt was betrayed by the tremor of his hand as he picked up the paper.

(A) extenuate
(B) determine
(C) conceal
(D) intensify
(E) display

EXPLANATORY ANSWER

Choice C is correct. The word "conceal" means to keep secret or to hide. The sentence now makes good sense. The nervousness caused by his guilty conscience is shown by the shaking of his hand. He is thus prevented in his attempt to hide his guilt.

EXAMPLE 3

In large cities, the number of family-owned grocery stores has fallen so sharply that the opportunity to shop in such a place is _____ occasion.

(A) a celebrated
(B) an old
(C) a fanciful
(D) a rare
(E) an avid

EXPLANATORY ANSWER

Choice D is correct. A rare occasion is one that you seldom have the opportunity to participate in. Shopping in a family-owned grocery store in a large city today is, indeed, a rare occasion.

EXAMPLE 4

Legal _____ initiated by the government necessitate that manufacturers use _____ in choosing food additives.

(A) entanglements . . knowledge
(B) devices . . intensification
(C) talents . . decretion
(D) proclivities . . moderation
(E) restraints . . caution

EXPLANATORY ANSWER

Choice E is correct. Although this is a two-blank question, we should use Sentence Completion Strategy 1. Try the words in each of the choices in the blanks in the sentence.

Another possibility is Choice A. But the point of the sentence evidently is that government prohibitions of certain food additives necessitate care by manufacturers in choosing food additives that are permitted. Thus Choice A is not as good as Choice E.

---

*Strategy 1 is considered the Master Strategy for *one-blank* Sentence Completion questions because it can be used effectively to answer every *one-blank* Sentence Completion question. However, it is important that you learn all of the other Sentence Completion Strategies because they can be used to double-check your answers.

1/21/11

EXAMPLE 5

It is unthinkable for a prestigious conductor to agree to include _____ musicians in his orchestra.

(A) capable
(B) seasoned
(C) mediocre
(D) recommended
(E) professional

EXPLANATORY ANSWER

Choice C is correct. The word "mediocre" (meaning average, ordinary) completes the sentence so that it makes good sense. The other choices do *not* do that.

EXAMPLE 6

A desire to be applauded by those in attendance, not his sensitivity to the plight of the underprivileged, was the reason for his _____ at the charity affair.

(A) shyness
(B) discomfort
(C) surprise
(D) arrogance
(E) generosity

EXPLANATORY ANSWER

Choice E is correct. No other choice makes sense in the sentence. It is clear that the person was primarily interested in being appreciated for his donation.

SENT. COMPL. STRATEGY 2

For a Sentence with Two Blanks, Begin by Eliminating the Initial Words That Don't Make Sense in the Sentence*

This strategy consists of two steps.

Step 1. Find out which "first words" of the choices make sense in the first blank of the sentence. Don't consider the second word of each pair yet. *Eliminate those choices that contain "first words" that don't make sense in the sentence.*

Step 2. Now consider the *remaining* choices by filling in the pair of words for each choice.

EXAMPLE 1

The salesmen in that clothing store are so _____ that it is impossible to even look at a garment without being _____ by their efforts to convince you to purchase.

(A) offensive . . considerate
(B) persistent . . harassed
(C) extensive . . induced
(D) immune . . aided
(E) intriguing . . evaluated

EXPLANATORY ANSWER

Choice B is correct.

STEP 1 [ELIMINATION]

We have eliminated Choice (C) extensive . . induced because saying salesmen who are "extensive" does not make sense here. We have eliminated Choice (D) immune . . aided because salesmen who are "immune" does not make sense here.

STEP 2 [REMAINING CHOICES]

This leaves us with these remaining choices to be considered. Choice (A) offensive . . considerate. The sentence *does not* make sense. Choice (B) persistent . . harassed. The sentence *does* make sense. Choice (E) intriguing . . evaluated. The sentence *does not* make sense.

*Strategy 2 is considered the Master Strategy for *two-blank* Sentence Completion questions because it can be used effectively to answer *every two-blank* Sentence Completion question. However, it is important to learn all of the other Sentence Completion Strategies because they can be used to double-check your answers.

1/21/11

EXAMPLE 2

Television in our society is watched so _____ that intellectuals who detest the "tube" are _____.

(A) reluctantly . . offended
(B) stealthily . . ashamed
(C) frequently . . revolted
(D) intensely . . exultant
(E) noisily . . amazed

EXPLANATORY ANSWER

Choice C is correct. We have eliminated Choice A because television is not watched reluctantly in our society. We have eliminated Choice B because television is not watched stealthily in our society. We have eliminated Choice E because it is not common for the viewer to watch television noisily. This leaves us with these remaining choices to be considered. Choice D—intensely . . exultant. The sentence does *not* make sense. Choice C—frequently . . revolted. The sentence *does* make sense.

EXAMPLE 3

In view of the company's _____ claims that its scalp treatment would grow hair on bald heads, the newspaper _____ its advertising.

(A) unproved . . banned
(B) interesting . . canceled
(C) unreasonable . . welcomed
(D) innocent . . settled
(E) immune . . questioned

EXPLANATORY ANSWER

Choice A is correct. The first step is to examine the first words of each choice. We eliminate Choice (D) innocent . . and Choice (E) immune . . because "claims" are not innocent or immune. Now we go on to the remaining choices. When you fill in the two blanks of Choice B and of Choice C, the sentence does *not* make sense. So these two choices are also incorrect. Filling in the two blanks of Choice A makes the sentence meaningful.

EXAMPLE 4

The renowned behaviorist B. F. Skinner believed that those colleges set up to train teachers should _____ change their training philosophy, or else be _____.

(A) inconsistently . . supervised
(B) drastically . . abolished
(C) haphazardly . . refined
(D) secretly . . dedicated
(E) doubtlessly . . destroyed

EXPLANATORY ANSWER

Choice B is correct. We can first eliminate Choice (A) inconsistently, Choice (C) haphazardly, and Choice (D) secretly because these first blank words do *not* make sense in the sentence. This leaves us with Choice (B) drastically and Choice (E) doubtlessly. But Choice (E) doubtlessly . . destroyed does *not* make sense. Choice (B) drastically . . abolished *does* make sense.

EXAMPLE 5

The report indicates that the crime rate in the United States remains _____ and that one in every three households _____ some form of major crime in any year.

(A) incredible . . visualizes
(B) astronomical . . experiences
(C) simultaneous . . welcomes
(D) unsuccessful . . initiates
(E) constant . . anticipates

EXPLANATORY ANSWER

Choice B is correct. Examine the first word of each choice. We eliminate Choice (C) simultaneous and Choice (D) unsuccessful because it does not make sense to say that the crime rate remains simultaneous or successful. Now we consider Choice (A), which does *not* make sense in the sentence; Choice B *does* make sense; and Choice E does *not* make sense.

EXAMPLE 6

The discouragement and _____ that so often plague perfectionists can lead to decreases in _____ and production.

(A) pressure . . creativity
(B) uplift . . motivation
(C) enthusiasm . . efficiency
(D) boredom . . idleness
(E) involvement . . laziness

EXPLANATORY ANSWER

Choice A is correct. Examine the first word of each choice. Choice (B) uplift and Choice (C) enthusiasm do not make sense because "uplift" and "enthusiasm" are not likely to plague any person. Now consider the other choices. Choice (D) boredom . . idleness and Choice (E) involvement . . laziness do *not* make sense in the sentence as a whole. Choice (A) pressure . . creativity *does* make sense.

1/21/11

SENT. COMPL. STRATEGY 3

Try to Complete the Sentence in Your Own Words before Looking at the Choices

This strategy often works well, especially with one-blank sentences. You may be able to fill in the blank with a word of your own that makes good sense. Then look at the answer choices to see whether any of the choices has the same meaning as your own word.

EXAMPLE 1

Many buildings with historical significance are now being _____ instead of being torn down.

(A) built
(B) forgotten
(C) destroyed
(D) praised
(E) repaired

EXPLANATORY ANSWER

Choice E is correct. The key words "instead of" constitute an *opposite indicator*. The words give us a good clue—we should fill the blank with an antonym (opposite) for "torn down." If you used the strategy of trying to complete the sentence *before* looking at the five choices, you might have come up with any of the following appropriate words:

remodeled
reconstructed
remade
renovated

These words all mean the same as the correct Choice E word, "repaired."

EXAMPLE 2

Wishing to _____ the upset passenger who found a nail in his steak, the flight attendant offered him a complimentary bottle of champagne.

(A) appease
(B) berate
(C) disregard
(D) reinstate
(E) acknowledge

EXPLANATORY ANSWER

Choice A is correct. Since the passenger was upset, the flight attendant wished to do something to make him feel better. If you used the strategy of trying to complete the

sentence *before* looking at the five choices, you might have come up with the following words that would have the meaning of "to make someone feel better":

pacify
soothe
satisfy
conciliate
relieve

These words all mean the same as the Choice A word, "appease."

EXAMPLE 3

Just as the person who is kind brings happiness to others, so does he bring _____ to himself.

(A) wisdom
(B) guidance
(C) satisfaction
(D) stinginess
(E) insecurity

EXPLANATORY ANSWER

Choice C is correct. You must look for a word that balances with "happiness." Here are some of the words:

joy
goodness
satisfaction
enjoyment

All these words can be linked to Choice C.

EXAMPLE 4

Actors are sometimes very _____ since they must believe strongly in their own worth and talents.

(A) laconic
(B) unequivocal
(C) tedious
(D) egotistic
(E) reticent

1/21/11

EXPLANATORY ANSWER

Choice D is correct. "Since" signifies *result*. So the second clause of the sentence, starting with "since," really tells us that the missing word or words must be

boastful
very much interested in one's own self
egotistic
self-centered

Thus, Choice D is correct.

EXAMPLE 5

Hunger has reached epidemic proportions nationwide, leaving up to 20 million people _____ to illness and fear.

(A) agreeable
(B) vulnerable
(C) obvious
(D) acclimated
(E) sensitive

EXPLANATORY ANSWER

Choice B is correct. You might have come up with any of the following words:

susceptible (to)
open (to)
unprotected (from)

These words all mean about the same as the correct one, Choice B: "vulnerable."

SENT. COMPL. STRATEGY 4

Pay Close Attention to the Key Words in the Sentence

A key word may indicate what is happening in the sentence. Here are some examples of key words and what these words may indicate.

Key Word	Indicating
although however in spite of rather than nevertheless on the other hand but	OPPOSITION
Key Word	*Indicating*
moreover besides additionally furthermore in fact	SUPPORT
Key Word	*Indicating*
therefore consequently accordingly because when so	RESULT

1/21/11

There are many other words—in addition to these—that can act as key words to help you considerably in getting the right answer. A key word frequently appears in the sentence. Watch for it!

EXAMPLE 1

Richard Wagner was frequently intolerant; moreover, his strange behavior caused most of his acquaintances to _____ the composer whenever possible.

(A) contradict
(B) interrogate
(C) shun
(D) revere
(E) tolerate

EXPLANATORY ANSWER

Choice C is correct. The word "moreover" is a *support indicator* in this sentence. As we try each choice word in the blank, we find that "shun" (avoid) is the only logical word that fits. You might have selected Choice A ("contradict"), but very few would seek to contradict Wagner because most of his acquaintances tried to avoid him.

EXAMPLE 2

Until we are able to improve substantially the _____ status of the underprivileged in our country, a substantial _____ in our crime rate is remote.

(A) burdensome . . harmony
(B) beneficial . . gloom
(C) financial . . reduction
(D) remarkable . . puzzle
(E) questionable . . disappointment

EXPLANATORY ANSWER

Choice C is correct. The word "Until" is a *result indicator.* As we try the first word of each choice in the first blank, we find that "burdensome," "financial," and "questionable" all make sense up until the second part of the sentence except "beneficial" and "remarkable." We therefore eliminate Choices B and D. Now let us try both words in Choices A, C, and E. We then find that we can eliminate Choices A and E as not making sense in the entire sentence. This leaves us with the correct Choice C, which *does* bring out the result of what is stated in the first part of the sentence.

EXAMPLE 3

All of the efforts of the teachers will bring about no _____ changes in the scores of the students because the books and other _____ educational materials are not available.

(A) impartial . . worthwhile
(B) unique . . reflected
(C) spiritual . . inspiring
(D) marked . . necessary
(E) effective . . interrupted

EXPLANATORY ANSWER

Choice D is correct. First see **Sentence Completion Strategy 2.** Let us first eliminate Choices (A) impartial . . and (C) spiritual . . because we do not speak of "impartial" or "spiritual" changes. Now note that we have a *result* situation here as indicated by the presence of the conjunction "because" in the sentence. Choices B and E do not make sense because "unique" changes have nothing to do with "reflected" educational materials, and "effective" changes have nothing to do with "interrupted" educational materials. Choices B and E certainly do not meet the *result* requirement. Choice D is the only correct choice because it makes sense to say that there will be no "marked" changes in the scores because the books and other "necessary" educational materials are not available.

EXAMPLE 4

Being _____ person, he insisted at the conference that when he spoke he was not to be interrupted.

(A) a successful
(B) a delightful
(C) a headstrong
(D) an understanding
(E) a solitary

EXPLANATORY ANSWER

Choice C is correct. The main clause of the sentence— "he insisted . . not be interrupted"—*supports* the idea expressed in the first three words of the sentence. Accordingly, Choice C "headstrong" (meaning stubborn) is the only correct choice.

1/21/11

EXAMPLE 5

Although Grete Waitz is a celebrated female marathon runner, she is noted for her _____.

(A) vigor
(B) indecision
(C) modesty
(D) speed
(E) endurance

EXPLANATORY ANSWER

Choice C is correct. The beginning word "Although" constitutes an *opposition indicator*. We can then expect the second part of the sentence to indicate an idea that is opposite to what is said in the first part of the sentence. Choice C "modesty" provides the word that gives us the closest to an opposite idea. Since Waitz is celebrated, we expect her to be immodest. The words in the other choices do *not* give us that opposite idea.

For two-blank sentences, look for contrasts or opposition in the two parts of the sentence—then look for opposite relationships in the choices.

EXAMPLE 6

In spite of the ___+/p___ of his presentation, many people were ___+/n___ with the speaker's concepts and ideas.

(A) interest . . enthralled
(B) power . . taken
(C) intensity . . shocked
(D) greatness . . gratified
(E) strength . . bored

EXPLANATORY ANSWER

Choice E is correct. The words *in spite of* at the beginning of the sentence tell you that the two blanks have an *opposite* flavor. Watch for opposites in the choices:

(A) interest . . enthralled—NOT OPPOSITE
(B) power . . taken—NOT OPPOSITE
(C) intensity . . shocked—NOT OPPOSITE
(D) greatness . . gratified—NOT OPPOSITE
(E) strength . . bored—OPPOSITE

Practice Your Sentence Completion Strategies

This set of questions will test your skill in handling sentence completion questions.

1. STRATEGY No. 1, 3, 4

Since we have many cornfields in this city, we do not have to ____corn.

(A) distribute
(B) develop
(C) contain
(D) import
(E) eat

2. STRATEGY No. 1, 3, 4

Unfortunately, many times insurance companies do not insure the person who really may ____ the insurance.

(A) sanctify
(B) appeal
(C) consider
(D) renege
(E) need

3. STRATEGY No. 1, 3, 4

I never can tolerate a situation which is ____, in other words, where nothing seems to go anywhere.

(A) abrupt
(B) uncomfortable
(C) uncontrollable
(D) static
(E) pliant

4. STRATEGY No. 2, 4

While a television course is not able to ____ a live course, it is still able to teach the ____ aspects of the subject.

(A) develop . . necessary
(B) replace . . important
(C) manage . . relevant
(D) create . . negative
(E) anticipate . . inconsequential

5. STRATEGY No. 2, 4

This is a poem which elicits great ____, unlike many which give the impression of utter ____ .

(A) chaos . . confusion
(B) understanding . . happiness

(C) joy . . sorrow
(D) knowledge . . intelligence
(E) hatred . . solemnity

6. STRATEGY No. 1, 3, 4

By realizing how much ____ the author had, we can see how he created so many books on different subjects.

(A) intensity
(B) knowledge
(C) enthusiasm
(D) intelligence
(E) time

7. STRATEGY No. 1, 3, 4

Although some ____ the performance, most either thought that it was mediocre or actually disliked it.

(A) enjoyed
(B) ignored
(C) belittled
(D) scrutinized
(E) considered

8. STRATEGY No. 2, 4

If there is no ____ for the product, ____ promotion alone will not convince people to buy it.

(A) precursor . . lackadaisical
(B) despondency . . superficial
(C) need . . extensive
(D) development . . stringent
(E) contract . . expeditious

9. STRATEGY No. 1, 3

Dr. Paul's clear and ____ analysis of the subject won her great literary acclaim.

(A) esoteric
(B) superficial
(C) jaundiced
(D) vestigial
(E) precise

Answers to Sentence Completion Questions

1. D. Key words: *since, have*. We don't have to import corn since we have cornfields.

2. E. Key words: *unfortunately, really*

3. D. Key words: *in other words*. Translate the words following the key-word phrase: "where nothing seems to go anywhere" into the word *static*.

4. B. Use the positive-negative approach. Key words: *while* (meaning "although"), *still*. The key words tell you that the two clauses of the sentence are being contrasted. The first clause is negative, with a *not* in it. The second clause must therefore be positive. Choice B makes the best sense with this construction.

5. C. Also a sentence with two contrasting parts, as shown by the key word *unlike*. Choice C, with two words that are antonyms, fits the bill.

6. B. Work backwards from the second part of the sentence. The key words *we can see how* show that the second part of the sentence must follow logically from the first. Since the author created books on many different subjects, he must have had a lot of *knowledge*.

7. A. Again, work backwards. Key words: *although, most, mediocre, disliked*. If most people disliked the performance, the obvious contrast is that some *enjoyed* it.

8. C. Don't be scared or led astray by difficult words in choices, like *lackadaisical, stringent*, and *expeditious*. They may not be correct. The sentence seems to make most sense using the easy words *need* and *extensive*.

9. E. Again, don't be scared by difficult words like *esoteric, jaundiced, vestigial. Precise* is correct (since the missing word is joined by *and* to the word *clear*, the word is probably a near-synonym of *clear*). *Precise* fits the bill.

Critical Reading Strategies

Introduction

Before getting into the detailed strategies, I want to say that the most important way to really understand what you're reading is to **get involved** with the passage—as if a friend of yours were reading the passage to you and you had to be interested so you wouldn't slight your friend. When you see the passage on paper it is also a good idea to **underline** important parts of the passage—which we'll also go over later in one of the strategies.

So many students ask, How do I answer reading comprehension questions? How do I read the passage effectively? Do I look at the questions before reading the passage? Do I underline things in the passage? Do I have to memorize details and dates? How do I get interested and involved in the passage?

All these are good questions. They will be answered carefully and in the right sequence.

What Reading Comprehension Questions Ask

First of all it is important to know that most reading comprehension questions ask about one of four things:

1. the MAIN IDEA of the passage
2. INFORMATION SPECIFICALLY MENTIONED in the passage
3. INFORMATION IMPLIED (not directly stated) in the passage
4. the TONE or MOOD of the passage

For example, following are some typical question stems. Each lets you immediately know which of the above four things is being asked about.

1. It can be inferred from the passage that . . . (IMPLIED INFORMATION)

2. According to the author . . . (MAIN IDEA)

3. The passage is primarily concerned with . . . (MAIN IDEA)

4. The author's statement that . . . (SPECIFIC INFORMATION)

5. Which of the following describes the mood of the passage? (TONE or MOOD)

6. The author implies that . . . (IMPLIED INFORMATION)

7. The use of paper is described in lines 14–16 . . . (SPECIFIC INFORMATION)

8. The main purpose of the passage . . . (MAIN IDEA)

9. The author's tone is best described as . . . (TONE or MOOD)

10. One could easily see the author as . . . (IMPLIED INFORMATION)

Getting Involved with the Passage

Now, let's first put aside the burning question, Should I read the questions first, before reading the passage? The answer is NO! If you have in mind the four main question types given above, you will not likely be in for any big surprises. Many questions, when you get to them, will be reassuringly familiar in the way they're framed and in their intent. You can best answer them by reading the passage first, allowing yourself to become involved with it.

To give you an idea of what I mean, look over the following passage. When you have finished, I'll show you how you might read it so as to get involved with it and with the author's intent.

Introductory Passage 1

We should also know that "greed" has little to do with the environmental crisis. The two main causes are population pressures, especially the pressures of large metropolitan populations, and
5 the desire—a highly commendable one—to bring a decent living at the lowest possible cost to the largest possible number of people.

The environmental crisis is the result of success—success in cutting down the mortality of
10 infants (which has given us the population explosion), success in raising farm output sufficiently to prevent mass famine (which has given us contamination by pesticides and chemical fertilizers), success in getting the people out of the tenements

15 of the 19th-century cities and into the greenery and privacy of the single-family home in the suburbs (which has given us urban sprawl and traffic jams). The environmental crisis, in other words, is largely the result of doing too much of the right sort
20 of thing.

To overcome the problems that success always creates, one must build on it. But where to start? Cleaning up the environment requires determined, sustained effort with clear targets and deadlines. It
25 requires, above all, concentration of effort. Up to now we have tried to do a little bit of everything— and tried to do it in the headlines—when what we ought to do first is draw up a list of priorities.

Breakdown and Underlining of Passage

Before going over the passage with you, I want to suggest some underlining you might want to make and to show what different parts of the passage refer to.

We should also know that "greed" has little to do with the environmental crisis. The two main causes are <u>population pressures</u>, especially the pressures of large metropolitan populations, and
5 the <u>desire</u>—a highly commendable one—<u>to bring a decent living at the lowest possible cost</u> to the largest possible number of people.

Sets stage.

<u>The environmental crisis is the result of success</u>—success in cutting down the mortality of
10 infants (which has given us the population explosion), success in raising farm output sufficiently to prevent mass famine (which has given us contamination by pesticides and chemical fertilizers), success in getting the people out of the tenements

This should interest and surprise you.

15 of the 19th-century cities and into the greenery and privacy of the single-family home in the suburbs (which has given us urban sprawl and traffic jams). The environmental crisis, in other words, is largely the result of doing <u>too much of the right sort</u>
20 <u>of thing</u>.

Examples of success.

Summary of the success examples.

To overcome the problems that success always creates, <u>one must build on it</u>. But where to start? Cleaning up the environment requires determined, <u>sustained effort with clear targets and deadlines</u>. It
25 requires above all, <u>concentration of effort</u>. Up to now we have tried to do a little bit of everything— and tried to do it in the headlines—when what we ought to do first is <u>draw up a list of priorities</u>.

Solutions.

Now I'll go over the passage with you, showing you what might go through your mind as you read. This will let you see how to get involved with the passage, and how this involvement facilitates answering the questions that follow the passage. In many cases, you'll actually be able to anticipate the questions. Of course, when you are preparing for the SAT, you'll have to develop this skill so that you do it rapidly and almost automatically.

Let's look at the first sentence:
We should also know that "greed" has little to do with the environmental crisis.

Immediately you should say to yourself, "So something else must be involved with the environmental crisis." Read on:

The two main causes are population pressures, especially the pressures of large metropolitan populations, and the desire—a highly commendable one—to bring a decent living at the lowest possible cost to the largest possible number of people.

Now you can say to yourself, "Oh, so population pressures and the desire to help the people in the community caused the environmental crisis." You should also get a feeling that the author is not really against these causes of the environmental crisis, and that he or she believes that the crisis is in part a side effect of worthwhile efforts and enterprises. Read on:

The environmental crisis is the result of success—success in cutting down the mortality of infants (which has given us the population explosion), success in raising farm output sufficiently to prevent mass famine (which has given us contamination by pesticides and chemical fertilizers), success in getting the people out of the tenements of the 19th-century city and into the greenery and privacy of the single-family home in the suburbs (which has given us urban sprawl and traffic jams).

Now you should say to yourself, "It seems that for every positive thing that the author mentions, there is a negative occurrence that leads to the environmental crisis."

Now read the last sentence of this paragraph:

The environmental crisis, in other words, is largely the result of doing too much of the right sort of thing.

Now you can say to yourself, "Gee, we wanted to do the right thing, but we created something bad. It looks like you can't have your cake and eat it, too!"

Now you should anticipate that in the next and final paragraph, the author will discuss what may be done to reduce the bad effects that come from the good. Look at the first sentence of the third paragraph:

To overcome the problem that success always creates, one must build on it.

Now you can say to yourself, "Well, how?" In fact, in the next sentence the author asks the very question you just asked: *But where to start?* Read on to find out the author's answer.

Cleaning up the environment requires determined, sustained effort with clear targets and deadlines. It requires, above all, concentration and effort.

So now you can say to yourself, "Oh, so that's what we need—definite goals, deadlines for reaching those goals, and genuine effort to achieve the goals."

The author then discusses what you may have already thought about:

Up to now we have tried to do a little bit of everything . . .

What the author is saying (and you should realize this) is that up to now, we haven't concentrated on one particular problem at a time. We used "buckshot instead of bullets." Read on:

—and tried to do it in the headlines—when what we ought to do first is to draw up a list of priorities.

So you can now see that, in the author's opinion, making a list of priorities and working on them one at a time, with a target in mind, may get us out of the environmental crisis and still preserve our quality of life.

How to Answer Reading Comprehension Questions Most Effectively

Before we start to answer the questions, let me tell you the best and most effective way of answering passage questions. You should read the question and proceed to look at the choices in the order of Choice A, Choice B, etc. If a choice (such as Choice A) doesn't give you the definite feeling that it is correct, don't try to analyze it further. Go on to Choice B. Again, if that choice (Choice B) doesn't make you feel that it's the right one, and you really have to think carefully about the choice, go on to Choice C and the rest of the choices and choose the best one.

Suppose you have gone through all five choices, and you don't know which one is correct, or you don't see any one that stands out as obviously being correct. Then quickly guess or leave the question blank if you wish and go on to the next question. You can go back after you have answered the other questions relating to the passage. But remember, when you return to the questions you weren't sure of, don't spend too much time on them. Try to forge ahead on the test.

Let's proceed to answer the questions now. Look at the first question:

This passage assumes the desirability of

    (A) using atomic energy to conserve fuel
    (B) living in comfortable family lifestyles
    (C) settling disputes peacefully
    (D) combating cancer and heart disease with energetic research
    (E) having greater government involvement in people's daily lives

Look at Choice A. That doesn't seem correct. Now look at Choice B. Do you remember that the author claimed that the environmental crisis is the result of the successful attempt to get people out of their tenements into a better environment? We can only feel that the author *assumes* this desirability of *living in comfortable family lifestyles* (Choice B) since the author uses the word *success* in describing the transition from living in tenements to living in single-family homes. Therefore, Choice B is correct. You don't need to analyze or even consider the other choices, since we have zeroed in on Choice B.

Let's look at Question 2:

2. According to this passage, one early step in any effort to improve the environment would be to

(A) return to the exclusive use of natural fertilizers
(B) put a high tax on profiteering industries
(C) ban the use of automobiles in the cities
(D) study successful efforts in other countries
(E) set up a timetable for corrective actions

Again let's go through the choices in the order Choice A, Choice B, etc., until we come up with the right choice. Choices A, B, C, and D seem unlikely to be correct. So look at Choice E. We remember that the author said that we should establish clear targets and deadlines to improve the environment. That makes Choice E look like the correct answer.

Let's look at Question 3:

3. The passage indicates that the conditions which led to overcrowded roads also brought about

(A) more attractive living conditions for many people
(B) a healthier younger generation
(C) greater occupational opportunities
(D) the population explosion
(E) greater concentration of population pressures

Here we would go back to the part of the passage that discussed overcrowded roads. This is where (second paragraph) the author says that urban sprawl and traffic jams are one result of success in getting people out of tenements to single-family homes. So you can see that Choice A is correct. Again, there is no need to consider other choices, since you should be fairly comfortable with Choice A.

Let's look at Question 4:

4. It could logically be assumed that the author of this passage would support legislation to

(A) ban the use of all pesticides
(B) prevent the use of automobiles in the cities
(C) build additional conventional power plants immediately
(D) organize an agency to coordinate efforts to cope with environmental problems
(E) restrict the press coverage of protests led by environmental groups

This is the type of question that asks you to determine what the author would feel about something else, when you already know something about the author's sentiments on one particular subject.

Choices A, B, and C do not seem correct. But look at Choice D. The author said that the way to get out of the energy crisis is to set targets and deadlines in order

to cope with specific problems. The author would therefore probably organize an agency to do this. Choice D is correct.

Let's look at another passage, and what I'm going to tell you is what would be going through my mind as I'm reading it. The more you can get involved with the passage in an "active" and not "passive" way, the faster you'll read it, and the more you'll get out of it.

Introductory Passage 2

Some scraps of evidence bear out those who hold a very high opinion of the average level of culture among the Athenians of the great age. The funeral speech of Pericles is the most famous indication
5 from Athenian literature that its level was indeed high. Pericles was, however, a politician, and he may have been flattering his audience. We know that thousands of Athenians sat hour after hour in the theater listening to the plays of the great Greek
10 dramatists. These plays, especially the tragedies, are at a very high intellectual level throughout. There are no letdowns, no concessions to the lowbrows or to the demands of "realism," such as the scene of the gravediggers in *Hamlet*. The music and dancing
15 woven into these plays were almost certainly at an equally high level. Our opera—not Italian opera, not even Wagner, but the restrained, difficult opera of the 18th century—is probably the best modern parallel. The comparison is no doubt dangerous, but
20 can you imagine almost the entire population of an American city (in suitable installments, of course) sitting through performances of Mozart's *Don Giovanni* or Gluck's *Orpheus*? Perhaps the Athenian masses went to these plays because of a lack of
25 other amusements. They could at least understand something of what went on, since the subjects were part of their folklore. For the American people, the subjects of grand opera are not part of their folklore.

Let's start reading the passage:

Some scraps of evidence bear out those who hold a very high opinion of the average level of culture among the Athenians of the great age.

Now this tells you that the author is going to talk about the culture of the Athenians. Thus the stage is set. Go on reading now:

The funeral speech of Pericles is the most famous indication from Athenian literature that its level was indeed high.

At this point you should say to yourself: "That's interesting, and there was an example of the high level of culture."

Read on:

Pericles was, however, a politician, and he may have been flattering his audience.

Now you can say, "So that's why those people were so attentive in listening—they were being flattered."

Read on:

We know that thousands of Athenians sat hour after hour in the theater listening to the plays of the great Greek dramatists. These plays, especially the tragedies, are at a very high intellectual level throughout. There are no letdowns, no concessions to the lowbrows or to the demands of "realism"...

At this point you should say to yourself, "That's strange—it could not have been just flattery that kept them listening hour after hour. How did they do it?" You can almost anticipate that the author will now give examples and contrast what he is saying to our plays and our audiences.

Read on:

The music and dancing woven into these plays were almost certainly at an equally high level. Our opera, not Italian opera . . . is probably the best modern parallel. The comparison is no doubt dangerous, but can you imagine almost the entire population of an American city . . . sitting through performances of . . .

Your feeling at this point should be, "No, I cannot imagine that. Why is that so?" So you should certainly be interested to find out.

Read on:

Perhaps the Athenian masses went to these plays because of a lack of other amusements. They could at least understand something of what went on, since the subjects were part of their folklore.

Now you can say, "So that's why those people were able to listen hour after hour—the material was all part of their folklore!"

Read on:

For the American people, the subjects . . . are not part of their folklore.

Now you can conclude, "So that's why the Americans cannot sit through these plays and perhaps cannot understand them—they were not part of their folklore!"

Here are the questions that follow the passage:

1. The author seems to question the sincerity of

   (A) politicians
   (B) playwrights
   (C) opera goers
   (D) "low brows"
   (E) gravediggers

2. The author implies that the average American

   (A) enjoys *Hamlet*
   (B) loves folklore
   (C) does not understand grand opera
   (D) seeks a high cultural level
   (E) lacks entertainment

3. The author's attitude toward Greek plays is one of

   (A) qualified approval
   (B) grudging admiration
   (C) studied indifference
   (D) partial hostility
   (E) great respect

4. The author suggests that Greek plays

   (A) made great demands upon their actors
   (B) flattered their audiences
   (C) were written for a limited audience
   (D) were dominated by music and dancing
   (E) stimulated their audiences

Let's try to answer them.

Question 1: Remember the statement about Pericles? This statement was almost unrelated to the passage since it was not discussed or referred to again. And here we have a question about it. Usually, if you see something that you think is irrelevant in a passage you may be pretty sure that a question will be based on that irrelevancy. It is apparent that the author seems to question the sincerity of politicians (*not* playwrights) since Pericles was a politician. Therefore Choice A is correct.

Question 2: We know that it was implied that the average American does not understand grand opera. Therefore Choice C is correct.

Question 3: From the passage, we see that the author is very positive about the Greek plays. Thus the author must have great respect for the plays. Note that the author may not have respect for Pericles, but Pericles was not a playwright; he was a politician. Therefore Choice E (not Choice A) is correct.

Question 4: It is certainly true that the author suggests that the Greek plays stimulated their audiences. They didn't necessarily flatter their audiences—there was only one indication of flattery, and that was by Pericles, who was not a playwright, but a politician. Therefore Choice E (not Choice B) is correct.

Example of Underlining

Some scraps of evidence bear out those who hold ← *sets stage*
a very high opinion of the average level of culture
among the Athenians of the great age. The funeral
speech of Pericles is the most famous indication
5 from Athenian literature that its level was indeed
high. Pericles was, however, a politician, and he ← *example*
may have been flattering his audience. We know
that thousands of Athenians sat hour after hour in
the theater listening to the plays of the great Greek ← *qualification*
10 dramatists. These plays, especially the tragedies, are
at a very high intellectual level throughout. There
are no letdowns, no concessions to the lowbrows or
to the demands of "realism," such as the scene of ← *further*
the gravediggers in *Hamlet*. The music and dancing
15 woven into these plays were almost certainly at an *examples*
equally high level. Our opera—not Italian opera, not
even Wagner, but the restrained, difficult opera of the
18th century—is probably the best modern paral- ← *comparison*
lel. The comparison is no doubt dangerous, but
20 can you imagine almost the entire population of an
American city (in suitable installments, of course)
sitting through performances of Mozart's *Don
Giovanni* or Gluck's *Orpheus*? Perhaps the Athenian
masses went to these plays because of a lack of
25 other amusements. They could at least understand
something of what went on, since the subjects were ← *explanation*
part of their folklore. For the American people, the *of previous*
subjects of grand opera are not part of their folklore. *statements*

Now the whole purpose of analyzing this passage the way I did was to show you that if you get involved and interested in the passage, you will not only anticipate many of the questions, but when you answer them you can zero in on the right question choice without having to necessarily analyze or eliminate the wrong choices first. That's a great time-saver on a standardized test such as the SAT.

Now here's a short passage from which four questions were derived. Let's see if you can answer them after you've read the passage.

Introductory Passage 3

Sometimes the meaning of glowing water is ominous. Off the Pacific Coast of North America, it may mean that the sea is filled with a minute plant that contains a poison of strange and terrible virulence.
5 About four days after this minute plant comes to alter the coastal plankton, some of the fishes and shellfish in the vicinity become toxic. This is because in their normal feeding, they have strained the poisonous plankton out of the water.

1. Fish and shellfish become toxic when they

   (A) swim in poisonous water
   (B) feed on poisonous plants
   (C) change their feeding habits
   (D) give off a strange glow
   (E) take strychnine into their systems

2. One can most reasonably conclude that plankton are

   (A) minute organisms
   (B) mussels
   (C) poisonous fish
   (D) shellfish
   (E) fluids

3. In the context of the passage, the word "virulence" in line 4 means

   (A) strangeness
   (B) color
   (C) calamity
   (D) potency
   (E) powerful odor

4. The paragraph preceding this one most probably discussed

(A) phenomena of the Pacific coastline
(B) poisons that affect man
(C) the culture of the early Indians
(D) characteristics of plankton
(E) phenomena of the sea

EXPLANATORY ANSWER

1. Choice B is correct. See the last three sentences. Fish become toxic when they feed on poisonous plants. Don't be fooled by using the first sentence, which seemingly leads to Choice A.

2. Choice A is correct. Since we are talking about *minute* plants (second sentence), it is reasonable to assume that plankton are *minute* organisms.

3. Choice D is correct. We understand that the poison is very strong and toxic. Thus it is "potent," virulent.

4. Choice E is correct. Since the second and not the first sentence was about the Pacific Coast, the paragraph preceding this one probably didn't discuss the phenomena of the Pacific coastline. It would have, if the first sentence—the sentence that links the ideas in the preceding paragraph—were about the Pacific coastline. Now, since we are talking about glowing water being ominous (first sentence), the paragraph preceding the passage is probably about the sea or the phenomena of the sea.

Summary

So in summary:

1. Make sure that you get involved with the passage. You may even want to select first the passage that interests you most. For example, if you're interested in science, you may want to choose the science passage first. Just make sure that you make some notation so that you don't mismark your answer sheet by putting the answers in the wrong answer boxes.

2. Pay attention to material that seems unrelated in the passage—there will probably be a question or two based on that material.

3. Pay attention to the mood created in the passage or the tone of the passage. Here again, especially if the mood is striking, there will probably be a question relating to mood.

4. Don't waste valuable time looking at the questions before reading the passage.

5. When attempting to answer the questions (after reading the passage) it is sometimes wise to try to figure out the answer before going through the choices. This will enable you to zero in on the correct answer without wasting time with all of the choices.

6. You may want to underline any information in the passages involving dates, specific names, etc., on your test to have as ready reference when you come to the questions.

7. Always try to see the overall attempt of the author of the passage or try to get the main gist of why the passage was being written. Try to get involved by asking yourself if you agree or disagree with the author, etc.

About the Double-Reading Passages

On your SAT you will be given a "double passage" (two separate passages) with about thirteen questions. You will also be given a "double paragraph" (two separate paragraphs) with about four questions. Some of the questions will be based on *only* the first passage, some will be based on *only* the second passage, and some will be based on *both* passages. Although you may want to read both passages first, then answer all the questions, some of you may find it less anxious to **read the first passage and answer those questions relating to the first passage, then read the second passage and answer those questions relating to the second passage, then finally answer the remaining questions relating to both the passages.** By using this approach, since you are reading one passage at a time, the time you would have spent on the second passage could be spent on answering the first set of questions relating to the first passage. This is in case you would have run out of time by reading both passages. The other advantage of this approach is that you do not have to keep both passages in mind at all times when answering the questions. That is, the only time you have to be aware of the content of both passages is when answering only those few questions related to both passages.

Nine Reading Comprehension Strategies

This section of Reading Comprehension Strategies includes several passages. These passages, though somewhat shorter than the passages that appear on the actual SAT and in the two SAT Practice Tests in this book, illustrate the general nature of the "real" SAT reading passages.

Each of the 9 Reading Comprehension Strategies that follow is accompanied by at least two different passages followed by questions and explanatory answers in order to explain how the strategy is used.

READ. COMP. STRATEGY 1

As You Read Each Question, Determine the Type: Main Idea, Detecting Details, Inference, Tone/Mood

---

Here are the four major abilities tested in Reading Comprehension questions:

1. **Main Idea.** Selection of the main thought of a passage; ability to judge the general significance of a passage; ability to select the best title of a passage.

2. **Detecting Details.** Ability to understand the writer's explicit statements; to get the literal meaning of what is written; to identify details.

3. **Inferential Reasoning.** Ability to weave together the ideas of a passage and to see their relationships; to draw correct inferences; to go beyond literal interpretation to the implications of the statements.

4. **Tone/Mood.** Ability to determine from the passage the tone or mood that is dominant in the passage—humorous, serious, sad, mysterious, etc.

EXAMPLE 1

The fight crowd is a beast that lurks in the darkness behind the fringe of white light shed over the first six rows by the incandescents atop the ring, and is not to be trusted with pop bottles or other hardware.
5 People who go to prize fights are sadistic.

When two prominent pugilists are scheduled to pummel one another in public on a summer's evening, men and women file into the stadium in the guise of human beings, and thereafter become
10 a part of a gray thing that squats in the dark until, at the conclusion of the bloodletting, they may be seen leaving the arena in the same guise they wore when they entered.

As a rule, the mob that gathers to see men fight
15 is unjust, vindictive, swept by intense, unreasoning hatreds, proud of its swift recognition of what it believes to be sportsmanship. It is quick to greet the purely phony move of the boxer who extends his gloves to his rival who has slipped or been
20 pushed to the floor, and to reward this stimulating but still baloney gesture with a pattering of hands which indicates the following: "You are a good sport. We recognize that you are a good sport, and we know a sporting gesture when we see one. Therefore we are
25 all good sports, too. Hurrah for us!"

The same crowd doesn't see the same boxer stick his thumb in his opponent's eye or try to cut him with the laces of his glove, butt him or dig him a low one when the referee isn't in a position to see.

30 It roots consistently for the smaller man, and never for a moment considers the desperate psychological dilemma of the larger of the two. It howls with glee at a good finisher making his kill. The Roman hordes were more civilized. Their gladiators asked

35 them whether the final blow should be administered or not. The main attraction at the modern prize fight is the spectacle of a man clubbing a helpless and vanquished opponent into complete insensibility. The referee who stops a bout to save

40 a slugged and punch-drunken man from the final ignominy is hissed by the assembled sportsmen.

QUESTIONS

1. The tone of the passage is chiefly

   (A) disgusted
   (B) jovial
   (C) matter-of-fact
   (D) satiric
   (E) devil-may-care

2. Which group of words from the passage best indicates the author's opinion?

   (A) "referee," "opponent," "finisher"
   (B) "gladiators," "slugged," "sporting gesture"
   (C) "stimulating," "hissing," "pattering"
   (D) "beast," "lurks," "gray thing"
   (E) "dilemma," "hordes," "spectacle"

3. Apparently, the author believes that boxing crowds find the referee both

   (A) gentlemanly and boring
   (B) entertaining and essential
   (C) blind and careless
   (D) humorous and threatening
   (E) necessary and bothersome

EXPLANATORY

1. Choice A is correct. The author is obviously much offended (disgusted) by the inhuman attitude of the crowd watching the boxing match. For example, see these lines:
   Line 1: "The crowd is a beast."
   Line 5: "People who go to prize fights are sadistic."
   Lines 14–16: ". . . the mob that gathers to see men fight is unjust, vindictive, swept by intense hatreds."
   Lines 33–34: "The Roman hordes were more civilized."

   To answer this question, you must be able to determine the tone that is dominant in the passage. Accordingly, this is a TONE/MOOD type of question.

2. Choice D is correct. The author's opinion is clearly one of disgust and discouragement because of the behavior of the fight crowd. Accordingly, you would expect the author to use words that were condemnatory, like "beast," and gloom-filled words like "lurks" and "gray thing." To answer this question, you must see relationships between words and feelings. So, we have here an INFERENTIAL REASONING question-type.

3. Choice E is correct. Lines 26–29 show that the referee is *necessary*: "The same crowd doesn't see the same boxer stick his thumb into his opponent's eye . . . when the referee isn't in a position to see." Lines 39–41 show that the referee is bothersome: "The referee who stops a bout . . . is hissed by the assembled sportsmen." To answer this question, the student must have the ability to understand the writer's specific statements. Accordingly, this is a DETECTING DETAILS type of question.

EXAMPLE 2

Mist continues to obscure the horizon, but above us the sky is suddenly awash with lavender light. At once the geese respond. Now, as well as their cries, a beating roar rolls across the water as if five

5 thousand housewives have taken it into their heads to shake out blankets all at one time. Ten thousand housewives. It keeps up—the invisible rhythmic beating of all those goose wings—for what seems a long time. Even Lonnie is held motionless

10 with suspense.

Then the geese begin to rise. One, two, three hundred—then a thousand at a time—in long horizontal lines that unfurl like pennants across the sky. The horizon actually darkens as they pass. It goes

15 on and on like that, flock after flock, for three or four minutes, each new contingent announcing its ascent with an accelerating roar of cries and wingbeats. Then gradually the intervals between flights become longer. I think the spectacle is over, until yet another

20 flock lifts up, following the others in a gradual turn toward the northeastern quadrant of the refuge.

Finally the sun emerges from the mist; the mist itself thins a little, uncovering the black line of willows on the other side of the wildlife preserve. I

25 remember to close my mouth—which has been open for some time—and inadvertently shut two or three mosquitoes inside. Only a few straggling geese oar their way across the sun's red surface. Lonnie wears an exasperated, proprietary expression, as if he had

30 produced and directed the show himself and had just received a bad review. "It would have been better with more light," he says; "I can't always guarantee just when they'll start moving." I assure him I thought it was a fantastic sight. "Well," he rumbles, "I guess it

35 wasn't too bad."

QUESTIONS

1. In the descriptive phrase "shake out blankets all at one time" (lines 5–6), the author is appealing chiefly to the reader's

   (A) background
   (B) sight
   (C) emotions
   (D) thoughts
   (E) hearing

2. The mood created by the author is one of

   (A) tranquility
   (B) excitement
   (C) sadness
   (D) bewilderment
   (E) unconcern

3. The main idea expressed by the author about the geese is that they

   (A) are spectacular to watch
   (B) are unpredictable
   (C) disturb the environment
   (D) produce a lot of noise
   (E) fly in large flocks

4. Judging from the passage, the reader can conclude that

   (A) the speaker dislikes nature's inconveniences
   (B) the geese's timing is predictable
   (C) Lonnie has had the experience before
   (D) both observers are hunters
   (E) the author and Lonnie are the same person

EXPLANATORY ANSWERS

1. Choice E is correct. See lines 4–6: ". . . a beating roar rolls across the water . . . shake out blankets all at one time." The author, with these words, is no doubt appealing to the reader's hearing. To answer this question, the reader has to identify those words dealing with sound and noise. Therefore, we have here a DETECTING DETAILS type of question. It is also an INFERENTIAL REASONING question-type in that the "sound" words such as "beating" and "roar" lead the reader to infer that the author is appealing to the auditory (hearing) sense.

2. Choice B is correct. Excitement courses right through this passage. Here are examples:
   Lines 7–8: ". . . the invisible rhythmic beating of all those goose wings."
   Line 9: "Even Lonnie is held motionless with suspense."
   Lines 11–12: "Then the geese begin to rise . . . a thousand at a time."
   Lines 15–17: ". . . flock after flock . . . roar of cries and wingbeats."

To answer this question, you must determine the dominant tone in this passage. Therefore, we have here a TONE/MOOD question type.

3. Choice A is correct. The word "spectacular" means *dramatic, thrilling, impressive.* There is considerable action expressed throughout the passage. Sometimes there is a lull—then the action begins again. See lines 19–20: "I think the spectacle is over, until yet another flock lifts up, following the others." To answer this question, you must have the ability to judge the general significance of the passage. Accordingly, we have here a MAIN IDEA type of question.

4. Choice C is correct. See lines 28–33: "Lonnie wears an exasperated, proprietary expression . . . when they'll start moving." To answer this question, you must be able to draw a correct inference. Therefore, we have here an INFERENTIAL REASONING type of question.

1/22/11

READ. COMP.
STRATEGY 2

Underline the Key Parts of the Reading Passage*

The underlinings will help you to answer questions. Reason: Practically every question will ask you to detect

a) the main idea

or

b) information that is specifically mentioned in the passage

or

c) information that is implied (not directly stated) in the passage

or

d) the tone or mood of the passage

If you find out quickly what the question is aiming for, you will more easily arrive at the correct answer by referring to your underlinings in the passage.

EXAMPLE 1

That one citizen is as good as another is a favorite American axiom, supposed to express the very essence of our Constitution and way of life. But just what do we mean when we utter that platitude? One
5 surgeon is not as good as another. One plumber is not as good as another. We soon become aware of this when we require the attention of either. Yet in political and economic matters we appear to have reached a point where knowledge and specialized training count
10 for very little. A newspaper reporter is sent out on the street to collect the views of various passers-by on such a question as "Should the United States defend El Salvador?" The answer of the barfly who doesn't even know where the country is located, or that it is a
15 country, is quoted in the next edition just as solemnly as that of the college teacher of history. With the basic tenets of democracy—that all men are born free and equal and are entitled to life, liberty, and the pursuit of happiness—no decent American can possibly take
20 issue. But that the opinion of one citizen on a technical subject is just as authoritative as that of another is manifestly absurd. And to accept the opinions of all comers as having the same value is surely to encourage a cult of mediocrity.

QUESTIONS

1. Which phrase best expresses the main idea of this passage?

   (A) the myth of equality
   (B) a distinction about equality
   (C) the essence of the Constitution
   (D) a technical subject
   (E) knowledge and specialized training

2. The author most probably included the example of the question on El Salvador (lines 12–13) in order to

   (A) move the reader to rage
   (B) show that he is opposed to opinion sampling
   (C) show that he has thoroughly researched his project
   (D) explain the kind of opinion sampling he objects to
   (E) provide a humorous but temporary diversion from his main point

3. The author would be most likely to agree that

   (A) some men are born to be masters; others are born to be servants
   (B) the Constitution has little relevance for today's world
   (C) one should never express an opinion on a specialized subject unless he is an expert in that subject
   (D) every opinion should be treated equally
   (E) all opinions should not be given equal weight

*Strategy 2 is considered the Master Reading Comprehension Strategy because it can be used effectively in every Reading Comprehension question. However, it is important that you learn the other Reading Comprehension Strategies because they can often be used to double-check your answers.

EXPLANATORY ANSWERS

1. Choice B is correct. See lines 1–7: "That one citizen . . . attention of either." These lines indicate that there is quite a distinction about equality when we are dealing with all the American people.

2. Choice D is correct. See lines 10–16: "A newspaper reporter . . . college teacher of history." These lines show that the author probably included the example of the question of El Salvador in order to explain the kind of opinion sampling he objects to.

3. Choice E is correct. See lines 20–24: "But that the opinion . . . to encourage a cult of mediocrity." Accordingly, the author would be most likely to agree that all opinions should *not* be given equal weight.

EXAMPLE 2

She walked along the river until a policeman stopped her. It was one o'clock, he said. Not the best time to be walking alone by the side of a half-frozen river. He smiled at her, then offered to walk her home. It
5 was the first day of the new year, 1946, eight and a half months after the British tanks had rumbled into Bergen-Belsen.
    That February, my mother turned twenty-six. It was difficult for strangers to believe that she
10 had ever been a concentration camp inmate. Her face was smooth and round. She wore lipstick and applied mascara to her large dark eyes. She dressed fashionably. But when she looked into the mirror in the mornings before leaving for work, my mother
15 saw a shell, a mannequin who moved and spoke but who bore only a superficial resemblance to her real self. The people closest to her had vanished. She had no proof that they were truly dead. No eye-witnesses had survived to vouch for her husband's
20 death. There was no one living who had seen her parents die. The lack of confirmation haunted her. At night before she went to sleep and during the day as she stood pinning dresses she wondered if, by some chance, her parents had gotten past the
25 Germans or had crawled out of the mass grave into which they had been shot and were living, old and helpless, somewhere in Poland. What if only one of them had died? What if they had survived and had died of cold or hunger after she had been liber-
30 ated, while she was in Celle* dancing with British officers?

She did not talk to anyone about these things. No one, she thought, wanted to hear them. She woke up in the mornings, went to work, bought groceries,
35 went to the Jewish Community Center and to the housing office like a robot.

*Celle is a small town in Germany.

QUESTIONS

1. The policeman stopped the author's mother from walking along the river because

   (A) the river was dangerous
   (B) it was the wrong time of day
   (C) it was still wartime
   (D) it was so cold
   (E) she looked suspicious

2. The author states that his mother thought about her parents when she

   (A) walked along the river
   (B) thought about death
   (C) danced with officers
   (D) arose in the morning
   (E) was at work

3. When the author mentions his mother's dancing with the British officers, he implies that his mother

   (A) compared her dancing to the suffering of her parents
   (B) had clearly put her troubles behind her
   (C) felt it was her duty to dance with them
   (D) felt guilty about dancing
   (E) regained the self-confidence she once had

EXPLANATORY ANSWERS

1. Choice B is correct. See lines 1–4: "She walked along . . . offered to walk her home." The police-man's telling her that it was not the best time to be walking alone indicates clearly that "it was the wrong time of day."

2. Choice E is correct. Refer to lines 22–31: ". . . during the day . . . dancing with the British officers."

3. Choice D is correct. See lines 28–31: "What if they had survived . . . dancing with British officers?"

1/22/11

READ. COMP.
STRATEGY 3

Look Back at the Passage When in Doubt

Sometimes while you are answering a question, you are not quite sure whether you have chosen the correct answer. Often, the underlinings that you have made in the reading passage will help you to determine whether a certain choice is the only correct choice.

EXAMPLE 1

A critic of politics finds himself driven to deprecate the power of words, while using them copiously in warning against their influence. It is indeed in politics that their influence is most dangerous, so that
5 one is almost tempted to wish that they did not exist, and that society might be managed silently, by instinct, habit and ocular perception, without this supervening Babel of reports, arguments and slogans.

QUESTION

1. Which statement is true according to the passage?

   (A) Critics of politics are often driven to take desperate measures.
   (B) Words, when used by politicians, have the greatest capacity for harm.
   (C) Politicians talk more than other people.
   (D) Society would be better managed if mutes were in charge.
   (E) Reports and slogans are not to be trusted.

EXPLANATORY ANSWER

1. Choice B is correct. An important part that you might have underlined is in the second sentence. "It is indeed in politics that their influence is most dangerous. . . ."

EXAMPLE 2

All museum adepts are familiar with examples of *ostrakoi*, the oystershells used in balloting. As a matter of fact, these "oystershells" are usually shards of pottery, conveniently glazed to enable
5 the voter to express his wishes in writing. In the Agora, a great number of these have come to light, bearing the thrilling name, Themistocles. Into rival jars were dropped the ballots for or against his banishment. On account of the huge vote taken on

10 that memorable date, it was to be expected that many ostrakoi would be found, but the interest of this collection is that a number of these ballots are inscribed in an *identical* handwriting. There is nothing mysterious about it! The Boss was on the job,
15 then as now. He prepared these ballots and voters cast them—no doubt for the consideration of an obol or two. The *ballot box was stuffed*.

How is the glory of the American boss diminished! A vile imitation, he. His methods as old
20 as Time!

QUESTION

1. The title that best expresses the ideas of this passage is

   (A) An Odd Method of Voting
   (B) Themistocles, an Early Dictator
   (C) Democracy in the Past
   (D) Political Trickery—Past and Present
   (E) The Diminishing American Politician

EXPLANATORY ANSWER

1. Choice D is correct. An important idea that you might have underlined is expressed in lines 14–15: "The Boss was on the job, then as now."

EXAMPLE 3

But the weather predictions which an almanac always contains are, we believe, mostly wasted on the farmer. He can take a squint at the moon before turning in. He can "smell" snow or tell if the wind is
5 shifting dangerously east. He can register forebodingly an extra twinge in a rheumatic shoulder. With any of these to go by, he can be reasonably sure of tomorrow's weather. He can return the almanac to the nail behind the door and put a last stick of
10 wood in the stove. For an almanac, a zero night or a morning's drifted road—none of these has changed much since Poor Richard wrote his stuff and barns were built along the Delaware.

1/22/11

QUESTION

EXPLANATORY ANSWER

1. The author implies that, in predicting weather, there is considerable value in

(A) reading the almanac
(B) placing the last stick of wood in the stove
(C) sleeping with one eye on the moon
(D) keeping an almanac behind the door
(E) noting rheumatic pains

1. Choice E is correct. Important ideas that you might have underlined are the following
   Line 3: "He can take a squint at the moon."
   Line 4: "He can 'smell' snow . . ."
   Lines 5–6: "He can register forebodingly an extra twinge in a rheumatic shoulder."

   These underlinings will reveal that, in predicting weather, the quote in lines 5–6 gives you the correct answer.

READ. COMP. STRATEGY 4

Before You Start Answering the Questions, Read the Passage *Carefully*

A great advantage of careful reading of the passage is that you will, thereby, get a very good idea of what the passage is about. If a particular sentence is not clear to you as you read, then reread that sentence to get a better idea of what the author is trying to say.

EXAMPLE 1

The American Revolution is the only one in modern history which, rather than devouring the intellectuals who prepared it, carried them to power. Most of the signatories of the Declaration of Independence
5 were intellectuals. This tradition is ingrained in America, whose greatest statesmen have been intellectuals—Jefferson and Lincoln, for example. These statesmen performed their political function, but at the same time they felt a more universal responsi-
10 bility, and they actively defined this responsibility. Thanks to them there is in America a living school of political science. In fact, it is at the moment the only one perfectly adapted to the emergencies of the contemporary world, and one which can be victoriously
15 opposed to communism. A European who follows American politics will be struck by the constant reference in the press and from the platform to this political philosophy, to the historical events through which it was best expressed, to the great statesmen
20 who were its best representatives.

[Underlining important ideas as you are reading this passage is strongly urged.]

QUESTIONS

1. The title that best expresses the ideas of this passage is

(A) Fathers of the American Revolution
(B) Jefferson and Lincoln—Ideal Statesmen
(C) The Basis of American Political Philosophy
(D) Democracy versus Communism
(E) The Responsibilities of Statesmen

2. According to the passage, intellectuals who pave the way for revolutions are usually

(A) honored
(B) misunderstood
(C) destroyed
(D) forgotten
(E) elected to office

3. Which statement is true according to the passage?

(A) America is a land of intellectuals.
(B) The signers of the Declaration of Independence were well educated.
(C) Jefferson and Lincoln were revolutionaries.
(D) Adaptability is a characteristic of American political science.
(E) Europeans are confused by American politics.

1/22/11

EXPLANATORY ANSWERS

1. Choice C is correct. Throughout this passage, the author speaks about the basis of American political philosophy. For example, see lines 5–12: "This tradition is ingrained in America, . . . a living school of political science."

2. Choice C is correct. See lines 1–3: "The American Revolution is the only one . . . carried them to power." These lines may be interpreted to mean that intellectuals who pave the way for revolutions—other than the American Revolution—are usually destroyed.

3. Choice D is correct. The word "adaptability" means the ability to adapt—to adjust to a specified use or situation. Now see lines 11–15: ". . . there is in America . . . opposed to communism."

EXAMPLE 2

The microscopic vegetables of the sea, of which the diatoms are most important, make the mineral wealth of the water available to the animals. Feeding directly on the diatoms and other groups of minute unicellu-
5 lar algae are the marine protozoa, many crustaceans, the young of crabs, barnacles, sea worms, and fishes. Hordes of small carnivores, the first link in the chain of flesh eaters, move among these peaceful grazers. There are fierce little dragons half an inch long, the
10 sharp-jawed arrowworms. There are gooseberry-like comb jellies, armed with grasping tentacles, and there are the shrimplike euphausiids that strain food from the water with their bristly appendages. Since they drift where the currents carry them, with no
15 power or will to oppose that of the sea, this strange community of creatures and the marine plants that sustain them are called plankton, a word derived from the Greek, meaning wandering.

[Underlining important ideas as you are reading this passage is strongly urged.]

QUESTIONS

1. According to the passage, diatoms are a kind of

   (A) mineral
   (B) alga
   (C) crustacean
   (D) protozoan
   (E) fish

2. Which characteristic of diatoms does the passage emphasize?

   (A) size
   (B) feeding habits
   (C) activeness
   (D) numerousness
   (E) cellular structure

EXPLANATORY ANSWERS

1. Choice B is correct. See lines 3–5: "Feeding directly on the diatoms . . . minute unicellular algae are the marine protozoa. . . ." These lines indicate that diatoms are a kind of alga.

2. Choice A is correct. See lines 1–5: "The microscopic vegetables of the sea . . . minute unicellular algae . . ." In these lines, the words "microscopic" and "minute" emphasize the small size of the diatoms.

1/22/11

READ. COMP. STRATEGY 5

Get the Meanings of "Tough" Words by Using the Context Method

Suppose you don't know the meaning of a certain word in a passage. Then try to determine the meaning of that word from the context—that is, from the words that are close in position to that word whose meaning you don't know. Knowing the meanings of difficult words in the passage will help you to better understand the passage as a whole.

EXAMPLE 1

Like all insects, it wears its skeleton on the outside—a marvelous chemical compound called chitin which sheathes the whole of its body. This flexible armor is tremendously tough, light and shatterproof, and
5 resistant to alkali and acid compounds which would eat the clothing, flesh and bones of man. To it are attached muscles so arranged around catapult-like hind legs as to enable the hopper to hop, if so diminutive a term can describe so prodigious a leap
10 as ten or twelve feet—about 150 times the length of the one-inch or so long insect. The equivalent feat for a man would be a casual jump, from a standing position, over the Washington Monument.

QUESTIONS

1. The word "sheathes" (line 3) means

(A) strips
(B) provides
(C) exposes
(D) encases
(E) excites

2. The word "prodigious" (line 9) means

(A) productive
(B) frightening
(C) criminal
(D) enjoyable
(E) enormous

EXPLANATORY ANSWERS

1. Choice D is correct. The words in lines 1–2: "it wears a skeleton on the outside" gives us the idea that "sheathes" probably means "covers" or "encases."

2. Choice E is correct. See the surrounding words in lines 8–11 "enable the hopper to hop . . . so prodigious a leap as ten or twelve feet—about 150 times the length of the one-inch or so long insect." We may easily imply that the word "prodigious" means "great in size"; "enormous."

EXAMPLE 2

Since the days when the thirteen colonies, each so jealous of its sovereignty, got together to fight the British soldiers, the American people have exhibited a tendency—a genius to maintain widely divergent
5 viewpoints in normal times, but to unite and agree in times of stress. One reason the federal system has survived is that it has demonstrated this same tendency. Most of the time the three coequal divisions of the general government tend to compete. In
10 crises they tend to cooperate. And not only during war. A singular instance of cooperation took place in the opening days of the first administration of Franklin D. Roosevelt, when the harmonious efforts of Executive and Legislature to arrest the havoc
15 of depression brought the term *rubber-stamp Congress* into the headlines. On the other hand, when in 1937 Roosevelt attempted to bend the judiciary to the will of the executive by "packing" the Supreme Court, Congress rebelled. This frequently proved
20 flexibility—this capacity of both people and government to shift from competition to cooperation and back again as circumstances warrant—suggests that the federal system will be found equal to the very real dangers of the present world situation.

1/23/11

QUESTIONS

1. The word "havoc" (line 14) means

(A) possession
(B) benefit
(C) destruction
(D) symptom
(E) enjoyment

2. The word "divergent" (line 4) means

(A) interesting
(B) discussed
(C) flexible
(D) differing
(E) appreciated

EXPLANATORY ANSWERS

1. Choice C is correct. The prepositional phrase "of depression," which modifies "havoc," should indicate that this word has an unfavorable meaning. The only choice that has an unfavorable meaning is Choice C—"destruction."

2. Choice D is correct. See lines 3–6: "... the American people ... widely divergent viewpoints ... but to unite and agree in times of stress." The word "but" in this sentence is an *opposite* indicator. We may, therefore, assume that a "divergent viewpoint" is a "differing" one from the idea expressed in the words "to unite and agree in times of stress."

READ. COMP. STRATEGY 6

Circle Transitional Words in the Passage

There are certain transitional words—also called "bridge" or "key" words—that will help you to discover logical connections in a reading passage. *Circling* these transitional words will help you to get a better understanding of the passage.

Here are examples of commonly used transitional words and what these words may indicate.

EXAMPLE 1

Key Word	Indicating
although however in spite of rather than nevertheless on the other hand but	OPPOSITION

Key Word	Indicating
moreover besides additionally furthermore in fact	SUPPORT

Key Word	Indicating
therefore consequently accordingly because when so	RESULT

Somewhere between 1860 and 1890, the dominant emphasis in American literature was radically changed. But it is obvious that this change was not necessarily a matter of conscious concern to all writers. In fact, many writers may seem to have been actually unaware of the shifting emphasis. Moreover, it is not possible to trace the steady march of the realistic emphasis from its first feeble notes to its dominant trumpet-note of unquestioned leadership. The progress of realism is, to change the figure, rather that of a small stream, receiving accessions from its tributaries at unequal points along its course, its progress now and then balked by the sand bars of opposition or the diffusing marshes of error and compromise. Again, it is apparent that any attempt to classify rigidly, as romanticists or realists, the writers of this period is doomed to failure, since it is not by virtue of the writer's conscious espousal of the romantic or realistic creed that he does much of his best work, but by virtue of that writer's sincere surrender to the atmosphere of the subject.

QUESTIONS

1. The title that best expresses the ideas of this passage is

   (A) Classifying American Writers
   (B) Leaders in American Fiction
   (C) The Sincerity of Writers
   (D) The Values of Realism
   (E) The Rise of Realism

2. Which characteristic of writers does the author praise?

   (A) their ability to compromise
   (B) their allegiance to a "school"
   (C) their opposition to change
   (D) their awareness of literary trends
   (E) their intellectual honesty

EXPLANATORY ANSWERS

1. Choice E is correct. Note some of the transitional words that will help you to interpret the passage: "but" (line 3); "in fact" (line 5); "moreover" (line 6); "again" (line 15). A better understanding of the passage should indicate to you that the main idea (title)—"The Rise of Realism"—is emphasized throughout the passage.

2. Choice E is correct. See lines 17–21: ". . . since it is not by virtue of . . . but by virtue of the writer's sincere . . . of the subject." The transitional word "but" helps us to arrive at the correct answer, which is "their intellectual honesty."

EXAMPLE 2

A humorous remark or situation is, furthermore, always a pleasure. We can go back to it and laugh at it again and again. One does not tire of the *Pickwick*

Papers, or of the humor of Mark Twain, any more
5 than the child tires of a nursery tale which he knows by heart. Humor is a feeling and feelings can be revived. But wit, being an intellectual and not an emotional impression, suffers by repetition. A witticism is really an item of knowledge. Wit, again, is
10 distinctly a gregarious quality; whereas humor may abide in the breast of a hermit. Those who live by themselves almost always have a dry humor. Wit is a city, humor a country, product. Wit is the accomplishment of persons who are busy with ideas; it is
15 the fruit of intellectual cultivation and abounds in coffeehouses, in salons, and in literary clubs. But humor is the gift of those who are concerned with persons rather than ideas, and it flourishes chiefly in the middle and lower classes.

QUESTION

1. It is probable that the paragraph preceding this one discussed the

   (A) *Pickwick Papers*
   (B) characteristics of literature
   (C) characteristics of human nature
   (D) characteristics of humor
   (E) nature of human feelings

EXPLANATORY ANSWER

1. Choice D is correct. See lines 1–2: "A humorous remark or situation is, furthermore, always a pleasure." The transitional word "furthermore" means "in addition." We may, therefore, assume that something dealing with humor has been discussed in the previous paragraph.

1/23/11

Don't Answer a Question on the Basis of Your Own Opinion

Answer each question on the basis of the information given or suggested in the passage itself. Your own views or judgments may sometimes conflict with what the author of the passage is expressing. Answer the question according to what the author believes.

EXAMPLE 1

The drama critic, on the other hand, has no such advantages. He cannot be selective; he must cover everything that is offered for public scrutiny in the principal playhouses of the city where he works.
5 The column space that seemed, yesterday, so pitifully inadequate to contain his comments on *Long Day's Journey Into Night* is roughly the same as that which yawns today for his verdict on some inane comedy that has chanced to find for itself a num-
10 skull backer with five hundred thousand dollars to lose. This state of affairs may help to explain why the New York theater reviewers are so often, and so unjustly, stigmatized as baleful and destructive fiends. They spend most of their professional lives
15 attempting to pronounce intelligent judgments on plays that have no aspiration to intelligence. It is hardly surprising that they lash out occasionally; in fact, what amazes me about them is that they do not lash out more violently and more frequently. As Shaw
20 said of his fellow-critics in the nineties, they are "a culpably indulgent body of men." Imagine the verbal excoriations that would be inflicted if Lionel Trilling, or someone of comparable eminence, were called on to review five books a month of which three were nov-
25 elettes composed of criminal confessions. The butchers of Broadway would seem lambs by comparison.

QUESTIONS

1. In writing this passage, the author's purpose seems to have been to

    (A) comment on the poor quality of our plays
    (B) show why book reviewing is easier than play reviewing
    (C) point up the opinions of Shaw
    (D) show new trends in literary criticism
    (E) defend the work of the play critic

2. The passage suggests that, as a play, *Long Day's Journey Into Night* was

    (A) inconsequential
    (B) worthwhile
    (C) poorly written
    (D) much too long
    (E) pleasant to view

EXPLANATORY ANSWERS

1. Choice E is correct. Throughout the passage, the author is defending the work of the play critic. See, for example, lines 11–16: "This state of affairs . . . plays that have no aspiration to intelligence." Be sure that you do not answer a question on the basis of your own views. You yourself may believe that the plays presented on the stage today are of poor quality (Choice A) generally. The question, however, asks about the *author's opinion*—not yours.

2. Choice B is correct. See lines 5–11: "The column space . . . dollars to lose." You yourself may believe that *Long Day's Journey Into Night* is a bad play (Choice A or C or D). But remember—the author's opinion, not yours, is asked for.

EXAMPLE 2

History has long made a point of the fact that the magnificent flowering of ancient civilization rested upon the institution of slavery, which released opportunity at the top of the art and literature which
5 became the glory of antiquity. In a way, the mechanization of the present-day world produces the condition of the ancient in that the enormous development of laborsaving devices and of contrivances which amplify the capacities of mankind affords the base
10 for the leisure necessary to widespread cultural pursuits. Mechanization is the present-day slave power, with the difference that in the mechanized society there is no group of the community which does not share in the benefits of its inventions.

1/26/11

QUESTION

1. The author's attitude toward mechanization is one of

(A) awe
(B) acceptance
(C) distrust
(D) fear
(E) devotion

EXPLANATORY ANSWER

1. Choice B is correct. Throughout the passage, the author's attitude toward mechanization is one of acceptance. Such acceptance on the part of the author is indicated particularly in lines 11–14: "Mechanization is . . . the benefits of its inventions." You yourself may have a feeling of distrust (Choice C) or fear (Choice D) toward mechanization. But the author does not have such feelings.

READ. COMP. STRATEGY 8

After Reading the Passage, Read Each Question *Carefully*

Be sure that you read *with care* not only the stem (beginning) of a question, but also *each* of the five choices. Some students select a choice just because it is a true statement—or because it answers part of a question. This can get you into trouble.

EXAMPLE 1

The modern biographer's task becomes one of discovering the "dynamics" of the personality he is studying rather than allowing the reader to deduce that personality from documents. If he achieves a
5   reasonable likeness, he need not fear too much that the unearthing of still more material will alter the picture he has drawn; it should add dimension to it, but not change its lineaments appreciably. After all, he has had more than enough material to permit him
10 to reach conclusions and to paint his portrait. With this abundance of material he can select moments of high drama and find episodes to illustrate character and make for vividness. In any event, biographers, I think, must recognize that the writing of a life may
15 not be as "scientific" or as "definitive" as we have pretended. Biography partakes of a large part of the subjective side of man; and we must remember that those who walked abroad in our time may have one appearance for us—but will seem quite different to
20 posterity.

QUESTION

1. According to the author, which is the real task of the modern biographer?

(A) interpreting the character revealed to him by study of the presently available data
(B) viewing the life of the subject in the biographer's own image
(C) leaving to the reader the task of interpreting the character from contradictory evidence
(D) collecting facts and setting them down in chronological order
(E) being willing to wait until all the facts on his subject have been uncovered

1/26/11

EXPLANATORY ANSWER

1. Choice A is correct. See lines 1–8: "The modern biographer's task . . . but not change its lineaments appreciably." The word "dynamics" is used here to refer to the physical and moral forces which exerted influence on the main character of the biography. The lines quoted indicate that the author believes that the real task of the biographer is to study the *presently available data.* Choice D may also appear to be a correct choice since a biographer is likely to consider his job to be collecting facts and setting them down in chronological order. But the passage does not directly state that a biographer has such a procedure.

EXAMPLE 2

Although patience is the most important quality a treasure hunter can have, the trade demands a certain amount of courage too. I have my share of guts, but make no boast about ignoring the hazards of div-
5 ing. As all good divers know, the business of plunging into an alien world with an artificial air supply as your only link to the world above can be as dangerous as stepping into a den of lions. Most of the danger rests within the diver himself.

10   The devil-may-care diver who shows great bravado underwater is the worst risk of all. He may lose his bearings in the glimmering dim light which penetrates the sea and become separated from his diving companions. He may dive too deep, too long and
15 suffer painful, sometimes fatal, bends.

QUESTION

1. According to the author, an underwater treasure hunter needs above all, to be

(A) self-reliant
(B) adventuresome
(C) mentally alert
(D) patient
(E) physically fit

EXPLANATORY ANSWER

1. Choice D is correct. See lines 1–3: "Although patience is the most important . . . courage too." Choice E ("physically fit") may also appear to be a correct choice since an underwater diver certainly has to be physically fit. Nevertheless, the passage nowhere states this directly.

READ. COMP. STRATEGY 9

Increase Your Vocabulary to Boost Your Reading Comprehension Score

1. You can increase your vocabulary tremendously by learning Latin and Greek roots, prefixes, and suffixes. Knowing the meanings of difficult words will thereby help you to understand a passage better.

    Sixty percent of all the words in our English language are derived from Latin and Greek. By learning certain Latin and Greek roots, prefixes, and suffixes, you will be able to understand the meanings of over 200,000 additional English words. See "Word Building with Roots, Prefixes, and Suffixes" beginning on page 70.

2. This book also includes "A List of Words Appearing More Than Once on Actual SAT Exams on page 90, and The Most Frequently Used SAT Words and Their Opposites on page 92.

    There are other steps—in addition to the two steps explained above—to increase your vocabulary. Here they are:

3. Take the Vocabulary Practice Tests beginning on page 158.
4. Read as widely as possible—novels, nonfiction, newspapers, magazines.
5. Listen to people who speak well. Many TV programs have very fine speakers. You can pick up many new words listening to such programs.
6. Get into the habit of using the dictionary often. Why not carry a pocket-size dictionary with you?
7. Play word games—crossword puzzles will really build up your vocabulary.

EXAMPLE 1

Acting, like much writing, is probably a compensation for and release from the strain of some profound maladjustment of the psyche. The actor lives most intensely by proxy. He has to be somebody
5   else to be himself. But it is all done openly and for our delight. The dangerous man, the enemy of non-attachment or any other wise way of life, is the born actor who has never found his way into the Theater, who never uses a stage door, who does not
10 take a call and then wipe the paint off his face. It is the intrusion of this temperament into political life, in which at this day it most emphatically does not belong, that works half the mischief in the world. In every country you may see them rise, the actors
15 who will not use the Theater, and always they bring down disaster from the angry gods who like to see mountebanks in their proper place.

QUESTIONS

1. The meaning of "maladjustment" (line 3) is a

    (A) replacement of one thing for another
    (B) profitable experience in business
    (C) consideration for the feelings of others
    (D) disregard of advice offered by other
    (E) poor relationship with one's environment

2. The meaning of "psyche" (line 3) is

    (A) person
    (B) mind
    (C) personality
    (D) psychology
    (E) physique

3. The meaning of "intrusion" (line 11) is

    (A) entering without being welcome
    (B) acceptance after considering the facts
    (C) interest that has developed after a period of time
    (D) fear as the result of imagination
    (E) refusing to obey a command

4. The meaning of "mountebanks" (line 17) is

    (A) mountain climbers
    (B) cashiers
    (C) high peaks
    (D) fakers
    (E) mortals

EXPLANATORY ANSWERS

1. Choice E is correct. The prefix "mal" means bad. Obviously a maladjustment is a bad adjustment—that is, a poor relationship with one's environment.

2. Choice B is correct. The root "psyche" means the mind functioning as the center of thought, feeling, and behavior.

3. Choice A is correct. The prefix "in" means "into" in this case. The root "trud, trus" means "pushing into"—or entering without being welcome.

4. Choice D is correct. The root "mont" means "to climb." The root "banc" means a "bench." A mountebank means literally "one who climbs on a bench." The actual meaning of mountebank is a quack (faker) who sells useless medicines from a platform in a public place.

EXAMPLE 2

The American Museum of Natural History has long portrayed various aspects of man. Primitive cultures have been shown through habitat groups and displays of man's tools, utensils, and art. In more recent
5   years, there has been a tendency to delineate man's place in nature, displaying his destructive and constructive activities on the earth he inhabits. Now, for the first time, the Museum has taken man apart, enlarged the delicate mechanisms that make him
10 run, and examined him as a biological phenomenon.
        In the new Hall of the Biology of Man, Museum technicians have created a series of displays that are instructive to a degree never before achieved in an exhibit hall. Using new techniques and new
15 materials, they have been able to produce movement as well as form and color. It is a human belief that beauty is only skin deep. But nature has proved to be a master designer, not only in the matter of man's bilateral symmetry but also
20 in the marvelous packaging job that has arranged all man's organs and systems within his skin-covered case. When these are taken out of the case, greatly enlarged and given color, they reveal form and design that give the lie to that old saw. Visitors
25 will be surprised to discover that man's insides, too, are beautiful.

1/26/11

1. The meaning of "bilateral" (line 19) is

   (A) biological
   (B) two-sided
   (C) natural
   (D) harmonious
   (E) technical

2. The meaning of "symmetry" (line 19) is

   (A) simplicity
   (B) obstinacy
   (C) sincerity
   (D) appearance
   (E) proportion

1. Choice B is correct. The prefix "bi" means "two." The root "latus" means "side." Therefore, "bilateral" means "two-sided."

2. Choice E is correct. The prefix "sym" means "together." The root "metr" means "measure." The word "symmetry," therefore, means "proportion," "harmonious relation of parts," "balance."

"Double Passage" Reading Questions

The two passages below are followed by questions based on their content and on the relationship between the two passages. Answer the questions on the basis of what is stated or implied in the passages and in any introductory material that may be provided.

Questions 1–13 are based on the following passages.

The following two passages describe different time periods. Passage 1 discusses the medieval time period; Passage 2 describes the present and speculates on the future.

Passage 1

To the world when it was half a thousand years younger, the outlines of all things seemed more clearly marked than to us. The contrast between suffering and joy, between adversity and happiness,
5 appeared more striking. All experience had yet to the minds of men the directness and absoluteness of the pleasure and pain of child-life. Every event, every action, was still embodied in expressive and solemn forms, which raised them to the dignity of a ritual.
10 Misfortunes and poverty were more afflicting than at present; it was more difficult to guard against them, and to find solace. Illness and health presented a more striking contrast; the cold and darkness of winter were more real evils. Honors and riches
15 were relished with greater avidity and contrasted more vividly with surrounding misery. We, at the present day, can hardly understand the keenness with which a fur coat, a good fire on the hearth, a soft bed, a glass of wine, were formerly enjoyed.
20 Then, again, all things in life were of a proud or cruel publicity. Lepers sounded their rattles and went about in processions, beggars exhibited their deformity and their misery in churches. Every order and estate, every rank and profession, was
25 distinguished by its costume. The great lords never moved about without a glorious display of arms and liveries, exciting fear and envy. Executions and other public acts of justice, hawking, marriages and funerals, were all announced by cries and processions,
30 songs and music. The lover wore the colors of his lady; companions the emblem of their brotherhood; parties and servants the badges of their lords. Between town and country, too, the contrast was very marked. A medieval town did not lose itself in
35 extensive suburbs of factories and villas; girded by its walls, it stood forth as a compact whole, bristling with innumerable turrets. However tall and threatening the houses of noblemen or merchants might be, in the aspect of the town, the lofty mass of the
40 churches always remained dominant.

The contrast between silence and sound, darkness and light, like that between summer and winter, was more strongly marked than it is in our lives. The modern town hardly knows silence or darkness
45 in their purity, nor the effect of a solitary light or a single distant cry.

All things presenting themselves to the mind in violent contrasts and impressive forms lent a tone of excitement and passion to everyday life
50 and tended to produce that perpetual oscillation between despair and distracted joy, between cruelty and pious tenderness which characterize life in the Middle Ages.

1/24/11

Passage 2

In 1575—over 400 years ago!—the French scholar
55 Louis Le Roy published a learned book in which he
voiced despair over the upheavals caused by the
social and technological innovations of his time,
what we now call the Renaissance. "All is pell-mell,
confounded, nothing goes as it should." We, also,
60 feel that our times are out of joint; we even have
reason to believe that our descendants will be worse
off than we are. The earth will soon be overcrowded
and its resources exhausted. Pollution will ruin the
environment, upset the climate, damage human
65 health. The gap in living standards between the rich
and the poor will widen and lead the angry, hungry
people of the world to acts of desperation including the use of nuclear weapons as blackmail. Such
are the inevitable consequences of population and
70 technological growth *if* present trends continue.
But what a big *if* this is! The future is never a projec-
tion of the past. Animals probably have no chance to
escape from the tyranny of biological evolution, but
human beings are blessed with the freedom of social
75 evolution. For us, trend is not destiny. The escape
from existing trends is now facilitated by the fact that
societies anticipate future dangers and take preven-
tive steps against expected upheavals.

Despite the widespread belief that the world
80 has become too complex for comprehension by
the human brain, modern societies have often
responded effectively to critical situations.
The decrease in birth rates, the partial banning
of pesticides, the rethinking of technologies for the
85 production and use of energy are but a few examples illustrating a sudden reversal of trends caused
not by political upsets or scientific breakthroughs,
but by public awareness of consequences.
Even more striking are the situations in which
90 social attitudes concerning future difficulties undergo
rapid changes before the problems have come to
pass—witness the heated controversies about the
ethics of behavior control and of genetic engineer-
ing even though there is as yet no proof that
95 effective methods can be developed to manipulate
behavior and genes on a population scale.
One of the characteristics of our times is thus
the rapidity with which steps can be taken to
change the orientation of certain trends and even
100 to reverse them. Such changes usually emerge
from grassroot movements rather than from official
directives.

QUESTIONS

1. Conditions like those described in Passage 1 would
most likely have occurred about

    (A) A.D. 55
    (B) A.D. 755
    (C) A.D. 1055
    (D) A.D. 1455
    (E) A.D. 1755

2. The phrase "with greater avidity" in line 15 is best
interpreted to mean with greater

    (A) desire
    (B) sadness
    (C) terror
    (D) silence
    (E) disappointment

3. In Passage 1, all of the following are stated or
implied about towns in the Middle Ages *except*

    (A) Towns had no suburbs.
    (B) Towns were always quite noisy.
    (C) Towns served as places of defense.
    (D) Towns always had large churches.
    (E) Merchants lived in the towns.

4. The author's main purpose in Passage 1 is to

    (A) describe the miseries of the period
    (B) show how life was centered on the town
    (C) emphasize the uncontrolled and violent course
    of life at the time
    (D) point out how the upper classes mistreated the
    lower classes
    (E) indicate how religious people were in those days

5. According to Passage 1, people at that time, as
compared with people today, were

    (A) worse off
    (B) better off
    (C) less intelligent
    (D) more subdued
    (E) more sensitive to certain events

6. In the first paragraph of Passage 2, the mood
expressed is one of

    (A) blatant despair
    (B) guarded optimism
    (C) poignant nostalgia
    (D) muted pessimism
    (E) unbridled idealism

7. According to Passage 2, if present trends continue, which one of the following situations will *not* occur?

(A) New sources of energy from vast coal deposits will be substituted for the soon-to-be-exhausted resources of oil and natural gas.
(B) The rich will become richer and the poor will become poorer.
(C) An overpopulated earth will be unable to sustain its inhabitants.
(D) Nuclear weapons will play a more prominent role in dealings among peoples.
(E) The ravages of pollution will render the earth and its atmosphere a menace to mankind.

8. Which of the following is the best illustration of the meaning of "trend is not destiny" in line 75?

(A) Urban agglomerations are in a state of crisis.
(B) Human beings are blessed with the freedom of social evolution.
(C) The world has become too complex for comprehension by the human brain.
(D) Critical processes can overshoot and cause catastrophes.
(E) The earth will soon be overcrowded and its resources exhausted.

9. According to Passage 2, evidences of the insight of the public into the dangers that surround us can be found in all of the following *except*

(A) an increase in the military budget by the president
(B) a declining birth rate
(C) picketing against expansion of nuclear plants
(D) opposition to the use of pesticides
(E) public meetings to complain about dumping chemicals

10. The author's attitude in Passage 2 is one of

(A) willing resignation
(B) definite optimism
(C) thinly veiled cynicism
(D) carefree abandon
(E) angry impatience

11. If there is a continuity in history, which of the following situations in Passage 1 is thought to lead to violence in the future of Passage 2?

(A) the overcrowding of the population
(B) the executions in public
(C) the contrast between the social classes
(D) the contrast between illness and health
(E) the contrast between religion and politics

12. One can conclude from reading both passages that the difference between the people in Passage 1 and the people in Passage 2 is that

(A) the people in Passage 2 act on their awareness in contrast to the people in Passage 1.
(B) the people in Passage 2 are more intense and colorful than the people in Passage 1.
(C) there was no controversy between sociology and science in the society in Passage 2 in contrast to the society mentioned in Passage 1.
(D) the people in Passage 1 are far more religious.
(E) sociological changes were faster and more abrupt with the people of Passage 1.

13. From a reading of both passages, one may conclude that

(A) people in both passages are equally subservient to authority.
(B) the future is a mirror to the past.
(C) the topic of biological evolution is of great importance to the scientists of both periods.
(D) the evolution of science has created great differences in the social classes.
(E) the people in Passage 1 are more involved in everyday living, whereas the people in Passage 2 are usually seeking change.

EXPLANATORY ANSWERS

1. Choice D is correct. Lines 1–2 ("To the world when it was half a thousand years younger . . .") indicate that the author is describing the world roughly five hundred years ago. Choice D—A.D. 1455—is therefore the closest date. Although Choice C is also in the Middle Ages, it is almost a thousand years ago. So it is an incorrect choice. Choices A, B, and E are obviously incorrect choices.

2. Choice A is correct. We can see that "with greater avidity" is an adverbial phrase telling the reader how "honors and riches" were enjoyed and desired. See lines 16–19: "We, at the present day . . . formerly enjoyed." The reader thus learns that even simple pleasures such as a glass of wine were more keenly enjoyed then. Choices B, C, D, and E are incorrect because the passage does *not* state or imply that "with greater avidity" means "with greater sadness *or* terror *or* silence *or* disappointment. See also **Reading Comprehension Strategy 5**.

3. Choice B is not true—therefore it is the correct choice. See lines 41–43: "The contrast between silence and sound . . . than it is in our lives." The next sentence states that the modern town hardly knows silence. These two sentences together imply that the typical town of the Middle Ages did have periods of silence.

    Choice A is true—therefore an incorrect choice. See lines 34–35: "A medieval town . . . in extensive suburbs of factories and villas."

    Choice C is true—therefore an incorrect choice. See lines 36–37: ". . . it [a medieval town] stood forth . . . with innumerable turrets."

    Choice D is true—therefore an incorrect choice. See lines 39–40: ". . . the lofty mass of the churches always remained dominant."

    Choice E is true—therefore an incorrect choice. See lines 37–39: "However tall . . . in the aspect of the town."

4. Choice C is correct. Throughout Passage 1, the author is indicating the strong, rough, uncontrolled forces that pervaded the period. See, for example, the following references. Lines 10–11: "Misfortunes and poverty were more afflicting than at present."

    Lines 20–21: "Then, again, all things in life . . . cruel publicity." Lines 27–30: "Executions . . . songs and music." Therefore, Choice C is correct. Choice A is incorrect because the passage speaks of joys as well as miseries. See lines 17–19: "We, at the present day . . . formerly enjoyed." Choice B is incorrect for this reason: Although the author contrasts town and country, he gives no indication as to which was dominant in that society. Therefore, Choice B is incorrect. Choice D is incorrect. The author contrasts how it felt to be rich or poor, but he does not indicate that the rich mistreated the poor. Choice E is incorrect because the pious nature of the people in the Middle Ages is only one of the many elements discussed in the passage.

5. Choice E is correct. See lines 5–7: "All experience . . . pain of child-life." Throughout the passage, this theme is illustrated with specific examples. Choices A and B are incorrect because they are one-sided. In the passage, many conditions that may make the Middle Ages seem worse than today are matched with conditions that may make the Middle Ages seem better than today. Choice C is incorrect because nowhere in the passage is intelligence mentioned or implied. Choice D is incorrect because the third paragraph indicates that, far from being subdued, people went about their lives with a great deal of show and pageantry.

6. Choice A is incorrect because the author stops short of outright despair in the last sentence of the first paragraph by tempering the outbursts of the Renaissance scholar with the milder "our times are out of joint." Choices B and E are incorrect because there is no positive feeling expressed in the first paragraph. Choice C is incorrect because there is no feeling of attraction toward an earlier age. Choice D is correct because the negative feeling is not quite full-bodied.

7. Choice A is correct. There is no mention of energy sources at any point in the selection. Therefore this answer is correct. Choices B, C, D, and E are mentioned in paragraph 2.

8. Choice B is correct. The positive outlook of the words "trend is not destiny" is best exemplified by Choice B, which implies that man can improve his situation. The other statements are negative or pessimistic pronouncements.

9. Choice A is correct. The author cites Choices B, C, D, and E in paragraph 5 as examples of renewed public awareness. The reference to the president's increase in the military budget does not indicate evidence of the public's insight regarding a danger.

10. Choice B is correct. Choices A and C are incorrect because the author is consistently expressing optimism in man's ability to learn from past mistakes. Choice B is the correct answer. Accordingly, Choice D contradicts the realistic tone of the essay. Choice E is not at all characteristic of the writer's attitude.

11. Choice C is correct. See lines 15–16 and lines 63–66. Note that the author of Passage B states that *if* present trends continue, the gap in living standards between the rich and the poor will lead to acts of desperation, including the use of nuclear weapons.

12. Choice A is correct. See lines 79–85. Note that Choice B is incorrect; see lines 47–53 and the descriptions in the rest of Passage 1. Choice C is incorrect; see lines 89–93. Choice E is incorrect; see lines 93–96.

13. Choice E is correct. See lines 79–98 and lines 47–53 and throughout Passage 1. Note that Choice A is incorrect; see lines 82–88.

Three Vocabulary Strategies

Introduction

Although **antonyms** (opposites of words) are not on the SAT, it is still important for you to know vocabulary and the strategies to figure out the meanings of words, since there are many questions involving difficult words in all the sections on the Verbal part of the SAT, that is the **Sentence Completions** and **Critical Reading** parts.

VOCABULARY STRATEGY 1

Use Roots, Prefixes, and Suffixes to Get the Meanings of Words

You can increase your vocabulary tremendously by learning Latin and Greek roots, prefixes, and suffixes. Sixty percent of all the words in our English language are derived from Latin and Greek. By learning certain Latin and Greek roots, prefixes, and suffixes, you will be able to understand the meanings of more than 150,000 additional English words. See "Word Building with Roots, Prefixes, and Suffixes" beginning on page 70.

EXAMPLE 1

Opposite of PROFICIENT:

(A) antiseptic
(B) unwilling
(C) inconsiderate
(D) neglectful
(E) awkward

EXPLANATORY ANSWER

Choice E is correct. The prefix PRO means *forward, for the purpose of.* The root FIC means *to make* or *to do.* Therefore, PROFICIENT literally means *doing something in a forward way.* The definition of *proficient* is *skillful, adept, capable.* The antonym of *proficient* is, accordingly, *awkward, incapable.*

EXAMPLE 2

Opposite of DELUDE:

(A) include
(B) guide
(C) reply
(D) upgrade
(E) welcome

EXPLANATORY ANSWER

Choice B is correct. The prefix DE means *downward, against.* The root LUD means *to play* (a game). Therefore, DELUDE literally means *to play a game against.* The definition of *delude* is *to deceive, to mislead.* The antonym of *delude* is accordingly *to guide.*

EXAMPLE 3

Opposite of LAUDATORY:

(A) vacating
(B) satisfactory
(C) revoking
(D) faultfinding
(E) silent

EXPLANATORY ANSWER

Choice D is correct. The root LAUD means *praise.* The suffix ORY means a *tendency toward.* Therefore, LAUDATORY means having a *tendency toward praising someone.* The definition of *laudatory* is *praising.* The antonym of laudatory is, accordingly, *faultfinding.*

1/29/11

EXAMPLE 4

Opposite of SUBSTANTIATE:

(A) reveal
(B) intimidate
(C) disprove
(D) integrate
(E) assist

EXPLANATORY ANSWER

Choice C is correct. The prefix SUB means *under*. The root STA means *to stand*. The suffix ATE is a verb form indicating *the act of*. Therefore, SUBSTANTIATE literally means *to perform the act of standing under*. The definition of *substantiate* is *to support* with proof or evidence. The antonym is, accordingly, *disprove*.

EXAMPLE 5

Opposite of TENACIOUS:

(A) changing
(B) stupid
(C) unconscious
(D) poor
(E) antagonistic

EXPLANATORY ANSWER

Choice A is correct.
TEN = to hold; TENACIOUS = holding—OPPOSITE = *changing*

EXAMPLE 6

Opposite of RECEDE:

(A) accede
(B) settle
(C) surrender
(D) advance
(E) reform

EXPLANATORY ANSWER

Choice D is correct.
RE = back; CED = to go; RECEDE = to go back—OPPOSITE = *advance*

EXAMPLE 7

Opposite of CIRCUMSPECT:

(A) suspicious
(B) overbearing
(C) listless
(D) determined
(E) careless

EXPLANATORY ANSWER

Choice E is correct.
CIRCUM = around; SPECT = to look or see; CIRCUM-SPECT = to look all around or make sure that you see everything, careful—OPPOSITE = *careless*

EXAMPLE 8

Opposite of MALEDICTION:

(A) sloppiness
(B) praise
(C) health
(D) religiousness
(E) proof

EXPLANATORY ANSWER

Choice B is correct.
MAL = bad; DICT = to speak; MALEDICTION = to speak badly about—OPPOSITE = *praise*

EXAMPLE 9

Opposite of PRECURSORY:

(A) succeeding
(B) flamboyant
(C) cautious
(D) simple
(E) cheap

EXPLANATORY ANSWER

Choice A is correct.
PRE = before; CURS = to run; PRECURSORY = run before—OPPOSITE = *succeeding*

EXAMPLE 10

Opposite of CIRCUMVENT:

(A) to go the straight route
(B) alleviate
(C) to prey on one's emotions
(D) scintillate
(E) perceive correctly

EXPLANATORY ANSWER

Choice A is correct.
CIRCUM = around (like a circle); VENT = to come; CIRCUMVENT = to come around—OPPOSITE = *to go the straight route*

V29/11

VOCABULARY STRATEGY 2

Pay Attention to the Sound or Feeling of the Word—Whether Positive or Negative, Harsh or Mild, Big or Little, Etc.

If the word sounds harsh or terrible, such as "obstreperous," the meaning probably is something harsh or terrible. If you're looking for a word opposite in meaning to "obstreperous," look for a word or words that have a softer sound, such as "pleasantly quiet or docile." The sense of "obstreperous" can also seem to be negative—so if you're looking for a synonym, look for a negative word. If you're looking for an opposite (antonym), look for a positive word.

EXAMPLE 1

Opposite of BELLIGERENCY:

(A) pain
(B) silence
(C) homeliness
(D) elegance
(E) peace

EXPLANATORY ANSWER

Choice E is correct. The word BELLIGERENCY imparts a tone of forcefulness or confusion and means warlike. The opposite would be calmness or peacefulness. The closest choices are choice B or E, with E a little closer to the opposite in tone for the capitalized word. Of course, if you knew the root BELLI means "war," you could see the opposite as (E) peace.

EXAMPLE 2

Opposite of DEGRADE:

(A) startle
(B) elevate
(C) encircle
(D) replace
(E) assemble

EXPLANATORY ANSWER

Choice B is correct. Here you can think of the DE in DEGRADE as a prefix that is negative (bad) and means *down*, and in fact DEGRADE does mean to debase or lower. So you should look for an opposite that would be a word with a *positive* (good) meaning. The best word from the choices is (B) elevate.

EXAMPLE 3

Opposite of OBFUSCATION:

(A) illumination
(B) irritation
(C) conviction
(D) minor offense
(E) stable environment

EXPLANATORY ANSWER

Choice A is correct. The prefix OB is usually negative, as in obstacle or obliterate, and in fact OBFUSCATE means darken or obscure. So since we are looking for an opposite, you would look for a *positive* word. Choices A and E are positive, and you should go for the more positive of the two, which is Choice A.

EXAMPLE 4

Opposite of MUNIFICENCE:

(A) disloyalty
(B) stinginess
(C) dispersion
(D) simplicity
(E) vehemence

EXPLANATORY ANSWER

Choice B is correct because MUNIFICENCE means generosity. Many of the words ending in ENCE, like OPULENCE, EFFERVESCENCE, LUMINESCENCE, QUINTESSENCE, etc., represent or describe something big or bright. So the opposite of one of these words would denote something small or dark.

You can associate the prefix MUNI with money, as in "municipal bonds," so the word MUNIFICENCE must deal with money and in a big way. The opposite deals with money in a small way. Choice B fits the bill.

EXAMPLE 5

Opposite of DETRIMENT:

(A) recurrence
(B) disclosure
(C) resemblance
(D) enhancement
(E) postponement

EXPLANATORY ANSWER

Choice D is correct. The prefix DE can also mean *against* and is negative, and DETRIMENT means something that causes damage or loss. So you should look for a positive word. The only one is (E) enhancement.

EXAMPLE 6

Opposite of UNDERSTATE:

(A) embroider
(B) initiate
(C) distort
(D) pacify
(E) reiterate

EXPLANATORY ANSWER

Choice A is correct. UNDERSTATE means something said in a restrained or downplayed manner. You see UNDER in UNDERSTATE so look for a choice that gives you the impression of something that is "over" as in "over-stated." The only choice is (A) embroider, which means to embellish.

EXAMPLE 7

Opposite of DISHEARTEN:

(A) engage
(B) encourage
(C) predict
(D) dismember
(E) misinform

EXPLANATORY ANSWER

Choice B is correct. You see HEART in DISHEARTEN. The DIS is negative or means "not to," or "not to have heart," and DISHEARTEN does mean to discourage. So you want to look for a *positive* word. Choice (B) encourage fits the bill.

EXAMPLE 8

Opposite of FIREBRAND:

(A) an intellect
(B) one who is charitable
(C) one who makes peace
(D) a philanthropist
(E) one who is dishonest

EXPLANATORY ANSWER

Choice C is correct. You see FIRE in FIREBRAND. So think of something fiery or dangerous. The opposite of FIREBRAND must be something that's calm or safe. The best choice is Choice C, whereas a FIREBRAND is someone who causes trouble.

1/24/11

VOCABULARY STRATEGY 3

Use Word Associations to Determine Word Meanings and Their Opposites

Looking at the root or part of any capitalized word may suggest an association with another word that looks similar and whose meaning you know. This new word's meaning may give you a clue as to the meaning of the original word or the opposite in meaning to the original word if you need an opposite. For example, *extricate* reminds us of the word "extract," the opposite of which is "to put together."

EXAMPLE 1

Opposite of STASIS:

(A) stoppage
(B) reduction
(C) depletion
(D) fluctuation
(E) completion

EXPLANATORY ANSWER

Choice D is correct. Think of STATIC or STATION-ARY. The opposite would be moving or fluctuating since STASIS means stopping or retarding movement.

EXAMPLE 2

Opposite of APPEASE:

(A) criticize
(B) analyze
(C) correct
(D) incense
(E) develop

EXPLANATORY ANSWER

Choice D is correct. APPEASE means to placate. Think of PEACE in APPEASE. The opposite would be violent or incense.

EXAMPLE 3

Opposite of COMMISERATION:

(A) undeserved reward
(B) lack of sympathy
(C) unexpected success
(D) absence of talent
(E) inexplicable danger

EXPLANATORY ANSWER

Choice B is correct. Think of MISERY in the word COMMISERATION. COMMISERATION means the sharing of misery. Choice B is the only appropriate choice.

EXAMPLE 4

Opposite of JOCULAR:

(A) unintentional
(B) exotic
(C) muscular
(D) exaggerated
(E) serious

EXPLANATORY ANSWER

Choice E is correct. Think of JOKE in the word JOCULAR, which means given to joking. The opposite would be serious.

EXAMPLE 5

Opposite of ELONGATE:

(A) melt
(B) wind
(C) confuse
(D) smooth
(E) shorten

EXPLANATORY ANSWER

Choice E is correct. Think of the word LONG in ELONGATE, which means to lengthen. The opposite would be short or shorten.

EXAMPLE 6

Opposite of SLOTHFUL:

(A) permanent
(B) ambitious
(C) average
(D) truthful
(E) plentiful

EXPLANATORY ANSWER

Choice B is correct. Think of SLOTH, a very, very slow animal. So SLOTHFUL, which means lazy or sluggish, must be slow and unambitious. The opposite would be ambitious.

EXAMPLE 7

Opposite of FORTITUDE:

(A) timidity
(B) conservatism
(C) placidity
(D) laxness
(E) ambition

EXPLANATORY ANSWER

Choice A is correct. FORTITUDE means strength in the face of adversity; you should think of FORT or FORTIFY as something strong. The opposite would be weakness or timidity.

EXAMPLE 8

Opposite of LUCID:

(A) underlying
(B) abstruse
(C) luxurious
(D) tight
(E) general

EXPLANATORY ANSWER

Choice B is correct. LUCID means easily understood or clear; you should think of LUCITE, a clear plastic. The opposite of clear is hard to see through or abstruse. *Note:* The "ab" in "abstruse" makes Choice B the only *negative* choice, which is the opposite of the positive word LUCID.

EXAMPLE 9

Opposite of POTENT:

(A) imposing
(B) pertinent
(C) feeble
(D) comparable
(E) frantic

EXPLANATORY ANSWER

Choice C is correct. Think of the word POTENTIAL or POWERFUL. To have potential is to have the ability or power to be able to do something. So the opposite would be feeble. You could also have thought of POTENT as a *positive* word. The opposite would be a negative word. The only two choices that are negative are choices C and E.

Part II
Fifteen Reading Quizzes

Here Are Fifteen Reading Quizzes.
See How You Do.

1/30/11

Quiz 1

A little over a year ago I began training to swim the English Channel this September. I will be 58 years old then.

My friends thought I had lost my mind; my wife, though not fearful for my sanity, was somewhat apprehensive. The question I was asked over and over was this: Why?

5 When a student reporter at Indiana recently asked me this question, I said, "First let me ask you a question. What are your plans for this summer?" He replied that he was going to bag groceries in a supermarket. I didn't have to say more; he understood my point.

A challenge and an element of adventure are welcome whether you are 20 or 58 and preparing to swim the Channel has it all over bagging groceries especially when you have
10 a choice.

But why did I decide to swim the Channel at 58? Perhaps the answer to it may even evade me.

The Channel has always been the supreme challenge to swimmers; a test of ability, endurance, luck and even bravery. It is this challenge that appeals to about 100 swimmers a year who
15 are willing to spend time, effort and money to try it.

One fact that contributes to my interest is that, if I succeed, I will be the oldest person ever to swim the Channel.

I don't think I'm a superman. I do think I have at least three things going for me:

First, I am training hard—presently swimming $7\frac{1}{2}$ miles a day. Prior to that time I also
20 kept physically fit by training moderately hard.

Second, I am a very goal-oriented person for whom this swim has long been a goal. I have a feeling I will be psychologically ready and won't do as one Channel swimmer did a few years ago. He trained hard for a couple of years, made the arrangements and even went to England weeks early to train in the Channel before his attempt. The great day came and he started
25 swimming toward France. After swimming only one hour, he got out of the water and climbed aboard the boat, saying that he suddenly had lost the desire to swim the Channel and it no longer meant anything to him.

On the other hand there was the young girl who was attempting to finish her swim when the ocean got rough. She was having a tough time with the rough and cold water, when her
30 trainer shouted to her from the boat that he thought she should give up and get out of the water. She shouted back, "I'm doing the swimming and I'll decide when to get out." She made it.

1. Most likely, the author of this passage decided to swim the Channel because he
   (A) enjoys a challenge
   (B) wants to upset his wife
   (C) does not recognize the difficulties involved
   (D) is basically a show-off
   (E) has made a bet that he could do so

2. The author of this passage would most readily agree with which of the following statements?
   (A) People should limit their self-expectations.
   (B) Old people lose their sense of adventure.
   (C) Only an unrealistic person would attempt the Channel.
   (D) Life's challenges can be overcome at any age.
   (E) People should recognize the dangers of physical stress.

3. According to the author,
   (A) the young girl (line 28) who swam the Channel during a storm was foolish
   (B) physical training is more important than being goal-oriented
   (C) the student reporter (line 5) was young at heart
   (D) the Channel swimmer (line 22) who did not finish needed more training
   (E) many swimmers attempt the Channel every year

4. The author of this passage can best be described as
   (A) determined
   (B) cautious
   (C) friendly
   (D) unrealistic
   (E) disappointed

1/30/11

Quiz 2

In New York, as much as in most communities in America, basketball is more religious rite than sport. Kids are at the playground as long as ten hours a day, actually playing as many as six. Seventeen- and eighteen-year-olds already have rheumatoid knees from the constant pounding of their feet on the asphalt. They play in the heat of the afternoon with not much
5   more to fuel them than a can of soda and a store-bought pastry, and they play at night in the dim illumination of nearby street lights and flashing neon. In a single summer, typical city ballplayers will wear out four or five pairs of sneakers. They play even in the dead of winter, bundled in jackets and sweaters and belching up little puffs of steam as they bang away at the netless rims.

1. When the author states that basketball is a religious rite, he is referring to the players'

(A) joy
(B) pride
(C) team spirit
(D) dedication
(E) skill

2. This passage as a whole tends to

(A) create an image
(B) defend religion
(C) ridicule basketball players
(D) uphold the American tradition of fair play
(E) describe an exception to city life

3. In writing the passage, the author points out the

(A) many advantages of playing basketball
(B) values of basketball as an escape from reality
(C) reasons basketball should be curtailed
(D) possible dangers to health of playing basketball
(E) cost of many items of basketball equipment

4. Which statement can best be defended on the basis of the passage?

(A) The basketball court is open twenty-four hours.
(B) The playground is not fenced off.
(C) The playground has a hard surface.
(D) Kids would rather play in the afternoon than at night.
(E) The kids are easily fatigued.

1/31/11

Quiz 3

I was exploring the far side of the island on the third day. I was also observing myself, an animal covering his territory. It was very quiet, even still. Suddenly a thunderous sound in the leaves and there was a pheasant, frozen in fear, three feet from my face. I wasn't sure whether I looked as scared; I certainly had been deeply frightened. The stillness had become noise,
5   and since I was alone on the island, my fantasies at that instant were elaborate. But I unfroze and the pheasant did not. The myth of man, the primitive hunter, began to unfold as I reached for a stick. But before any action, another myth took hold and there was no taking of life. The basic need of hunger; the basic force of life. I can't forget that encounter.

1. As used in line 5, the word "elaborate" most nearly means
    (A) quiet
    (B) great
    (C) groundless
    (D) expensive
    (E) unnecessary

2. In line 7, the phrase "another myth" refers to
    (A) a need for food
    (B) a respect for primitive customs
    (C) a need for action
    (D) a respect for living things
    (E) the powerlessness of animals

3. From the passage, we can most safely conclude that the
    (A) pheasant was an easy prey
    (B) narrator disliked exploring
    (C) narrator was familiar with the island
    (D) pheasant flew away
    (E) island was a noisy place

4. By the end of this episode, the narrator feels that he has
    (A) created a new myth
    (B) learned how to survive
    (C) grown in perception
    (D) become a creature of fantasy
    (E) exploded several myths

1/31/11

Quiz 4

The ancient Egyptians believed strongly in life after death. They also believed that a person would need his body to exist in this afterlife. Therefore, they carefully preserved the body by treating it with spices and oils and wrapping it in linen cloth. The wrapped body was then placed in a tomb. A body that is treated in this way is called a mummy.

5   Egyptian kings and nobles wanted to be certain that their mummies would be kept in safe places forever. They had great tombs built for themselves and their families. Many kings were buried in secret tombs carved out of solid rock in a place near Thebes called the Valley of the Kings.

About eighty kings built towering pyramid-shaped stone tombs. These pyramids have

10   become famous as one of the Seven Wonders of the Ancient World.

One of the most amazing things about these pyramids is that they were constructed without using wheels or heavy equipment to move or raise the rocks. Egypt did not learn about the wheel until long after the pyramids were built. Workmen used levers to get large blocks of stone on and off sledges and hauled them into place over long ramps built around the pyramids.

1. The term "mummy" was used to describe

(A) kings of ancient Egypt
(B) ancient Egyptian nobles
(C) the place where Egyptian kings were buried
(D) the preserved body of a dead person
(E) one of the Seven Wonders of the Ancient World

2. The pyramids were built

(A) before the Egyptians developed a sophisticated technology
(B) after the Egyptians developed a sophisticated technology
(C) to house the tombs of all ancient Egyptian kings and nobles
(D) with the use of spices, oils and linen cloth
(E) to keep mummies safe forever

3. Which of the following practices is most closely associated with ancient Egyptian belief in an afterlife?

(A) placing the dead in tombs carved out of solid rock
(B) building pyramids to house the bodies of dead kings
(C) preserving dead bodies with oils and spices
(D) creating the Valley of the Kings near Thebes
(E) constructing tombs without the use of wheels or heavy equipment

1/3/11

Quiz 5

I hear America singing, the varied carols I hear,
Those of mechanics, each one singing his as it should be blithe and strong,
The carpenter singing his as he measures his plank or beam,
The mason singing his as he makes ready for work, or leaves off work,
5   The boatman singing what belongs to him in his boat, the deckhand singing on the steamboat deck,
The shoemaker singing as he sits on his bench, the hatter singing as he stands.
The wood-cutter's song, the ploughboy's on his way in the morning, or at noon intermission or at sundown,
10   The delicious singing of the mother, or of the young wife at work, or of the girl sewing or washing,
Each singing what belongs to him or her and to none else,
The day what belongs to the day—at night the party of young fellows, robust, friendly,
Singing with open mouths their strong melodious songs.

1. Judging from this poem, it is most probable that the poet favors

(A) teachers
(B) workingmen
(C) executives
(D) singers
(E) athletes

2. The poet's main purpose in this poem is to

(A) indicate that women belong in the house
(B) criticize America's economy
(C) celebrate the American worker
(D) speak out in favor of socialism
(E) show that all work is basically the same

3. The tone of this poem can best be described as

(A) joyful
(B) humorous
(C) impatient
(D) peaceful
(E) careless

1/31/11

Quiz 6

The whole aim of good teaching is to turn the young learner, by nature a little copycat, into an independent, self-propelling creature who can work as his own boss to the limit of his powers. This is to turn pupils into students, and it can be done on any rung of the ladder of learning.

5　When I was a child, the multiplication table was taught from a printed sheet which had to be memorized one square at a time–the ones and the twos and so on up to nine. It never occurred to the teacher to show us how the answers could be arrived at also by addition, which we already knew. No one said, "Look: if four times four is sixteen, you ought to be able to figure out, without aid from memory, what five times four is, because that amounts to four more ones added to the sixteen. This would at first have been puzzling, *more* complicated and difficult

10　than memory work, but once explained and grasped, it would have been an instrument for learning and checking the whole business of multiplication. We could temporarily have dispensed with the teacher and cut loose from the printed table.

　　This is another way of saying that the only thing worth teaching anybody is a principle. Naturally, principles involve facts and some facts must be learned "bare" because they do not

15　rest on any principle. The capital of Alaska is Juneau and, so far as I know, that is all there is to it; but a European child ought not to learn that Washington is the capital of the United States without fixing firmly in his mind the relation between the city and the man who led his countrymen to freedom. That would be missing an association, which is the germ of a principle. And just as a complex athletic feat is made possible by rapid and accurate coordination, so all

20　valuable learning hangs together and *works* by associations which make sense.

1. The title that best expresses the ideas of this passage is:

   (A) How to teach arithmetic
   (B) A good memory makes a good student
   (C) Principles—the basis of learning
   (D) Using addition to teach multiplication
   (E) How to dispense with the teacher

2. The author implies that the difference between a pupil and a student is the difference between

   (A) youth and maturity
   (B) learning and knowing
   (C) beginning and ending
   (D) memorizing and understanding
   (E) learning and teaching

3. The author indicates that children are naturally

   (A) deceitful　　　(D) logical
   (B) perceptive　　 (E) imitative
   (C) independent

4. The author would be most likely to agree that the most desirable way to teach is by

   (A) relating facts to principles
   (B) stressing the importance of learning
   (C) insisting that pupils work independently
   (D) recognizing that a knowledge of facts is useless
   (E) developing pupils' ability to memorize

5. As it is used in the passage, the word "germ" (line 18) most nearly means

   (A) result　　　 (D) amage
   (B) beginning　 (E) weakness
   (C) polish

6. In this passage, the author develops his paragraphs primarily by the use of

   (A) narration　　 (D) description
   (B) comparison　 (E) examples
   (C) definitions

2/1/11

Quiz 7

Next morning I saw for the first time an animal that is rarely encountered face to face. It was a wolverine. Though relatively small, rarely weighing more than 40 pounds, he is, above all animals, the one most hated by the Indians and trappers. He is a fine tree climber and a relentless destroyer. Deer, reindeer, and even moose succumb to his attacks. We sat on a rock and
5   watched him come, a bobbing rascal in blackish-brown. Since the male wolverine occupies a very large hunting area and fights to the death any other male that intrudes on his domain, wolverines are always scarce, and in order to avoid extinction need all the protection that man can give. As a trapper, Henry wanted me to shoot him, but I refused, for this is the most fascinating and little known of all our wonderful predators. His hunchback gait was awkward
10   and ungainly, lopsided yet tireless. He advanced through all types of terrain without change of pace and with a sense of power that seemed indestructible. His course brought him directly to us, and he did not notice our immobile figures until he was ten feet away. Obviously startled, he rose up on his hind legs with paws outstretched and swayed from side to side like a bear undecided whether to charge. Then he tried to make off at top speed and watch us over his
15   shoulder at the same time, running headlong into everything in his path.

1. Wolverines are very scarce because
   (A) their food supply is limited
   (B) they are afraid of all humankind
   (C) they are seldom protected by man
   (D) trappers take their toll of them
   (E) they suffer in the survival of the fittest

2. The reason the author did not kill the wolverine seems to be that
   (A) the wolverine's ungainly gait made him miss the target
   (B) conservation laws protected the animal
   (C) the roughness of the terrain made tracking difficult
   (D) he admired the skill of the animal
   (E) he felt sorry for the animal

3. The wolverine ran headlong into everything in his path because of his
   (A) anxiety and curiosity
   (B) helplessness in the face of danger
   (C) snow blindness
   (D) ferocious courage
   (E) pursuit by the trappers

4. The author of this selection is most probably
   (A) an experienced hunter
   (B) a conscientious naturalist
   (C) an inexperienced trapper
   (D) a young Indian
   (E) a farmer

5. The author's chief purpose in writing this passage seems to be to
   (A) defend the wolverine from further attacks by man
   (B) point out the fatal weakness of the wolverine
   (C) show why the wolverine is scarce
   (D) characterize a rarely seen animal
   (E) criticize Henry's action

6. As a whole, this passage suggests that the wolverine
   (A) is every bit as awesome as his reputation
   (B) will eventually destroy the deer herds
   (C) will one day be able to outwit man
   (D) does not really need the protection of man
   (E) is too smart for other animals

2/1/11

Quiz 8

In the ordinary course of nature, the great beneficent changes come slowly and silently. The noisy changes, for the most part, mean violence and disruption. The roar of storms and tornadoes, the explosions of volcanoes, the crash of thunder, are the result of a sudden break in the equipoise of the elements; from a condition of comparative repose and silence they become
5   fearfully swift and audible. The still small voice is the voice of life and growth and perpetuity. . . . In the history of a nation it is the same.

1. The title below that best expresses the ideas of this passage is:

(A) Upsetting nature's balance
(B) Repose and silence
(C) The voice of life and growth
(D) Nature's intelligence
(E) The violent elements

2. As used in the passage, the word "equipoise" (line 4) most nearly means

(A) stress
(B) balance
(C) course
(D) slowness
(E) condition

3. The author implies that growth and perpetuity in nature and in history are the result of

(A) quiet changes
(B) a period of silence
(C) undiscovered action
(D) storms and tornadoes
(E) violence and disruptions

2/1/11

Quiz 9

It is here, perhaps, that poetry may best act nowadays as corrective and complementary to science. When science tells us that the galaxy to which our solar system belongs is so enormous that light, traveling at 186,000 miles per second, takes between 60,000 and 100,000 years to cross from one rim to the other of the galaxy, we laymen accept the statement but find it
5   meaningless—beyond the comprehension of heart or mind. When science tells us that the human eye has about 137 million separate "seeing" elements, we are no less paralyzed, intellectually and emotionally. Man is appalled by the immensities and the minuteness which science has disclosed for him. They are indeed unimaginable. But may not poetry be a possible way of mediating them to our imagination? Of scaling them down to imaginative comprehension?
10   Let us remember Perseus, who could not look directly at the nightmare Gorgon without being turned to stone, but could look at her image reflected in the shield the goddess of wisdom lent him.

1. The title below that best expresses the ideas of this passage is:
   - (A) Poetry and imagination
   - (B) A modern Gorgon
   - (C) Poetry as a mediator
   - (D) The vastness of the universe
   - (E) Imaginative man

2. According to the passage, the average man
   - (A) should have a better memory
   - (B) is impatient with science
   - (C) cannot trust the scientists
   - (D) is overwhelmed by the discoveries of science
   - (E) does not understand either science or poetry

3. Perseus was most probably
   - (A) a scientist
   - (B) a legendary hero
   - (C) an early poet
   - (D) a horrible creature
   - (E) a minor god

4. This passage is chiefly developed by means of
   - (A) examples
   - (B) cause and effect
   - (C) narration
   - (D) definition
   - (E) anecdotes

2/1/11

Quiz 10

Hail is at once the cruelest weapon in Nature's armory, and the most incalculable. It can destroy one farmer's prospects of a harvest in a matter of seconds; it can leave his neighbor's unimpaired. It can slay a flock of sheep (it has killed children before now) in one field, while the sun continues to shine in the next. To the harassed meteorologist its behavior is even more

5 Machiavellian than that of an ice storm. Difficult as it undoubtedly is for him to forecast the onset of an ice storm, he knows pretty well what its course and duration will be once it has started; just about all he can do with a hailstorm is to measure the size of the stones—and they have a habit of melting as soon as he gets his hands on them. He is not even too sure any more about the way in which hail forms—and until he knows this, of course, he isn't likely to stumble

10 upon any very satisfactory prognostic rules.

1. The title below that best expresses the ideas of this passage is:

(A) Forecasting ice storms
(B) The way that hail forms
(C) The harassed meteorologist
(D) The unpredictability of hailstorms
(E) Hail—the killer

2. As used in the passage, the word "prognostic" (last line) most nearly means

(A) restraining
(B) breakable
(C) day-by-day
(D) foretelling
(E) regular

3. The author capitalized "Nature's" (line 1) most probably because he wished to

(A) talk with nature directly
(B) contrast nature and science
(C) emphasize the power of nature
(D) show off his knowledge of figures of speech
(E) call the reader's attention to the subject of the passage

2/2/ ʌ

Quiz 11

Windstorms have recently established a record which meteorologists hope will not be equaled for many years to come. Disastrous tornadoes along with devastating typhoons and hurricanes have cost thousands of lives and left property damage totaling far into the millions. The prominence these storms have held in the news has led many people to ask about the difference
5   between the three. Is a typhoon the same as a hurricane? Is a tornado the same as a typhoon? Basically, there is no difference. All three consist of wind rotating counterclockwise (in the Northern Hemisphere) at a tremendous velocity around a low-pressure center. However, each type does have its own definite characteristics. Of the three the tornado is certainly the most treacherous. The Weather Bureau can, with some degree of accuracy, forecast the typhoon and
10   the hurricane; however, it is impossible to determine where or when the tornado will strike. And out of the three, if one had a choice, perhaps it would be safer to choose to withstand the hurricane.

1. The title below that best expresses the ideas of this passage is:

(A) Recent storms
(B) Record-breaking storms
(C) Predicting windstorms
(D) Treacherous windstorms
(E) Wind velocity and direction

2. Which is *not* common to all of the storms mentioned?

(A) fairly accurate forecasting
(B) violently rotating wind
(C) high property damage
(D) loss of human lives
(E) public interest

3. The author indicates that

(A) typhoons cannot be forecast
(B) the Southern Hemisphere is free from hurricanes
(C) typhoons are more destructive than hurricanes
(D) hurricanes are not really dangerous
(E) tornadoes occur around a low-pressure center

Quiz 12

> Stone-cutters fighting time with marble, you foredefeated
> Challengers of oblivion.
> Eat cynical earnings, knowing rock splits, records fall down,
> The square-limbed Roman letters
> 5   Scale in the thaws, wear in the rain. The poet as well
> Builds his monument mockingly;
> For man will be blotted out, the blithe earth die, the brave sun
> Die blind and blacken to the heart:
> Yet stones have stood for a thousand years, and pained thoughts found
> 10   The honey of peace in old poems.

1. The phrase "fighting time with marble" (line 1) means that the stone-cutters

   (A) despair of completing their work in a lifetime
   (B) look for recognition in the future rather than in the present
   (C) consider marble the most challenging substance to work with
   (D) take pride in working slowly and carefully
   (E) aspire to produce an imperishable monument

2. The stone-cutters are "foredefeated" (line 1) in the sense that their defeat is

   (A) undeserved
   (B) inevitable
   (C) spectacular
   (D) unsuitable
   (E) unexpected

3. The conflict presented in this poem is specifically between

   (A) stone-cutters and marble
   (B) hope and despair
   (C) poets and stone-cutters
   (D) man's creations and time
   (E) challenge and achievement

2/2/11

Quiz 13

The man who reads well is the man who thinks well, who has a background for opinions and a touchstone for judgment. He may be a Lincoln who derives wisdom from a few books or a Roosevelt who ranges from Icelandic sagas to *Penrod*. But reading makes him a full man, and out of his fullness he draws that example and precept which stand him in good stead when
5   confronted with problems which beset a chaotic universe. Mere reading, of course, is nothing. It is but the veneer of education. But wise reading is a help to action. American versatility is too frequently dilettantism, but reinforced by knowledge it becomes motive power. "Learning," as James L. Mursell says, "cashes the blank check of native versatility." And learning is a process not to be concluded with the formal teaching of schooldays or to be enriched only by the active
10 experience of later years, but to be broadened and deepened by persistent and judicious reading. "The true University of these days is a Collection of Books," said Carlyle. If that is not the whole of the truth it is enough of it for every young person to hug to this bosom.

1. The title that best expresses the ideas of this passage is:
   (A) The veneer of education
   (B) The wise reader
   (C) The reading habits of great men
   (D) The versatility of Americans
   (E) The motivation of readers

2. Which advice would the author of this passage most likely give to young people?
   (A) Develop a personal reading program.
   (B) Avoid reading too many books of the same type.
   (C) Spend more time in a library.
   (D) Read only serious books.
   (E) Learn to read more rapidly and accurately.

3. The quotation "Learning cashes the blank check of native versatility" (lines 7–8) means that
   (A) a good education is like money in the bank
   (B) to be versatile is to be learned
   (C) native intelligence has more value than acquired knowledge
   (D) education can make possible an effective use of natural capabilities
   (E) he who learns well will keep an open mind at all times

4. The author apparently believes that
   (A) the answer to the world's problems lies in a nation of learned men
   (B) America can overcome her dilettantism by broader reading programs for her citizens
   (C) people with wide reading backgrounds are likely to find right courses of action
   (D) active experience is the second-best teacher
   (E) the best book is one that is serious in tone

2/2/11

Quiz 14

Most people want to know how things are made. They frankly admit, however, that they feel completely at sea when it comes to understanding how a piece of music is made. Where a composer begins, how he manages to keep going—in fact, how and where he learns his trade—all are shrouded in impenetrable darkness. The composer, in short, is a man of mystery, and the
5 composer's workshop an unapproachable ivory tower.

One of the first things the layman wants to hear about is the part inspiration plays in composing. He finds it difficult to believe that composers are not much preoccupied with that question, that composing is as natural for the composer as eating or sleeping. Composing is something that the composer happens to have been born to do; and because of that, it loses
10 the character of a special virtue in the composer's eyes.

The composer, therefore, does not say to himself: "Do I feel inspired?" He says to himself: "Do I feel like composing today?" And if he feels like composing, he does. It is more or less like saying to himself: "Do I feel sleepy?" If you feel sleepy, you go to sleep. If you don't feel sleepy, you stay up. If the composer doesn't feel like composing, he doesn't compose. It's as
15 simple as that.

1. The author of the passage indicates that creating music is an activity that is

(A) difficult
(B) rewarding
(C) inspirational
(D) fraught with anxiety
(E) instinctive

2. When considering the work involved in composing music, the layman often

(A) exaggerates the difficulties of the composer in commencing work
(B) minimizes the mental turmoil that the composer undergoes
(C) is unaware that a creative process is involved
(D) loses the ability to enjoy the composition
(E) loses his ability to judge the work apart from the composer

3. In this passage, composing music is compared with

(A) having a feast
(B) climbing an ivory tower
(C) visualizing problems
(D) going to sleep
(E) going to sea

4. The author's approach toward his subject is

(A) highly emotional
(B) casually informative
(C) negative
(D) deeply philosophical
(E) consciously prejudiced

5. We may most safely conclude that the author is
(A) a layman
(B) a violinist
(C) a working composer
(D) an amateur musician
(E) a novelist

Quiz 15

Social Science Double Passage

Below are two excerpts from speeches that were made more than two thousand years apart and yet have much in common; both speeches address the issue of democracy and both concern those who had recently given their lives defending their government.

The first was reportedly made in 431 B.C. by the Greek general Pericles shortly after the outbreak of the Peloponnesian War; the second was delivered during the American Civil War at Gettysburg, Pennsylvania, on November 19, 1863, by President Abraham Lincoln.

PASSAGE 1—Athens, Greece

Many of those who have spoken here in the past have praised the institution of this speech at the close of our ceremony. It seemed to them a mark of honor to our soldiers who have

5 fallen in war that a speech should be made over them. I do not agree. These men have shown themselves valiant in action, and it would be enough, I think, for their glories to be proclaimed in action, as you have just seen it

10 done at this funeral organized by the state. Our belief in the courage of so many should not be hazarded on the goodness or badness of any single speech.

Let me say that our system of government

15 does not copy the institutions of our neighbors. It is more the case of our being a model to others than of our imitating anyone else. Our constitution is called a democracy because power is in the hands not of a minority but of the

20 whole people. When it is a question of settling private disputes, everyone is equal before the law; when it is a question of putting one person before another in positions of public responsibility, what counts is not membership in a particu-

25 lar class, but the actual ability that the individual possesses. No one who could be of service to the state is kept in political obscurity because of poverty. And, just as our political life is free and open, so is our day-to-day life in our rela-

30 tions with each other. We do not get into a state with our neighbors if they enjoy themselves in their own way, nor do we give anyone the kind of frowning looks that, though they do no real harm, still hurt people's feelings. We are free

35 and tolerant in our private lives; but in public affairs we keep to the law. This is because it commands our great respect . . .

They gave Athens their lives, to her and to all of us, and for their own selves they won

40 praises that never grow old, the most splendid of sepulchers—not the sepulcher in which their bodies are laid, but where their glory remains eternal in others' minds, always there on the right occasion to stir them to speech or

45 to action. For the famous have the whole earth for their tomb: it is not only the inscriptions on their graves in their own country that marks them out; no, in foreign lands also, not in any visible form but in people's hearts, their mem-

50 ory abides and grows. It is for you to try to be like them. Make up your minds that happiness depends on being free, and freedom depends on being courageous. Let there be no relaxation in the face of the perils of war . . .

PASSAGE 2—Gettysburg, Pennsylvania

55 But, in a larger sense, we cannot dedicate— we cannot consecrate—we cannot hallow—this ground. The brave men, living and dead, who struggled here, have consecrated it far above our poor power to add or detract. The world

60 will little note nor long remember what we say here, but it can never forget what they did here. It is for us, the living, rather, to be dedicated here to the unfinished work which they who fought here have thus far so nobly advanced. It

65 is rather for us to be here dedicated to the great task remaining before us—that from these honored dead we take increased devotion to the cause for which they gave their last full measure of devotion; that we here highly resolve

70 that these dead shall not have died in vain; that

this nation under God, shall have a new birth of freedom; and that government of the people, by the people, for the people, shall not perish from the earth.

1. Why does Pericles "not agree" (line 6) that a speech such as the one he is giving can further honor fallen soldiers?

   (A) Public officials give too many boring speeches.
   (B) Fallen soldiers are seldom the subject of speeches.
   (C) Past speakers concentrated too much on winning personal fame.
   (D) The potential inadequacies of the speech could detract from the glory of the fallen soldiers.
   (E) The glory achieved in battle is best remembered by loved ones, not by public officials.

2. The word "state" in line 30 means

   (A) stage of development
   (B) political unit
   (C) declaration
   (D) luxury
   (E) furor

3. In the second paragraph of Passage 1, Pericles primarily stresses that

   (A) a democratic spirit will help Athens win the war.
   (B) Athens will always be remembered.
   (C) people in neighboring countries envy Athenians.
   (D) the customs of others seem strange to Athenians.
   (E) the Athenian form of government is an admirable one.

4. Which best summarizes the reason given in Passage 1 for the soldiers having earned "praises that never grow old" (line 40)?

   (A) People in foreign lands will praise the Greeks for ages.
   (B) Memorials dedicated to heroic events will always be honored.
   (C) The Athenians will honor their military heroes annually.
   (D) The memory of great feats will repeatedly inspire others.
   (E) Relatives and friends of the heroes will never forget them.

5. It can be inferred from the content and tone of Passage 1 that Pericles' primary feeling was one of

   (A) sadness because Athens had lost so many courageous soldiers.
   (B) dismay at his responsibility to guide the Athenians safely.
   (C) annoyance because the Athenians might not appreciate the sacrifices that had been made for them.
   (D) concern about whether the audience would agree with his views.
   (E) pride in Athens and determination that it would continue into the future.

6. In Passage 2, the word "consecrate" (line 56) means

   (A) absolve
   (B) adore
   (C) make sacred
   (D) begin praising
   (E) enjoy properly

7. The "unfinished work" referred to in line 9 is the

   (A) battle of Gettysburg
   (B) defense of freedom
   (C) establishment of a government
   (D) dedication of the battlefield
   (E) honoring of the fallen soldiers

8. Which statement from Passage 1 does NOT have a parallel idea conveyed in Passage 2?

   (A) "These men have shown themselves valiant in action" (lines 6–7)
   (B) "our system of government does not copy the institutions of our neighbors" (lines 14–15)
   (C) "They gave Athens their lives, to her and to all of us" (lines 38–39)
   (D) "It is for you to try to be like them" (lines 50–51)
   (E) "freedom depends on being courageous" (lines 52–53)

9. Which statement is best supported by a comparison of the two excerpts?

   (A) Both excerpts urge an end to existing hostilities.
   (B) Both excerpts are appeals to the audience for personal political support.
   (C) Both excerpts emphasize the cruelty of the opponents of the state.
   (D) The intent and the development of ideas of both excerpts are similar.
   (E) The purpose of both excerpts is to prepare the audience for the eventual outbreak of war.

Answers to Reading Quizzes

Quiz 1
1. A
2. D
3. E
4. A

Quiz 2
1. D
2. A
3. D
4. C

Quiz 3
1. B
2. D
3. A
4. C

Quiz 4
1. D
2. A
3. C

Quiz 5
1. B
2. C
3. A

Quiz 6
1. C
2. D
3. E
4. A
5. B
6. E

Quiz 7
1. E
2. D
3. A
4. B
5. D
6. A

Quiz 8
1. C
2. B
3. A

Quiz 9
1. C
2. D
3. B
4. A

Quiz 10
1. D
2. D
3. C

Quiz 11
1. D
2. A
3. E

Quiz 12
1. E
2. B
3. D

Quiz 13
1. B
2. A
3. D
4. C

Quiz 14
1. E
2. A
3. D
4. B
5. C

Quiz 15 (Double Reading Passage)
1. D
2. E
3. E
4. D
5. E
6. C
7. B
8. B
9. D

Part III
Vocabulary Building That Is Guaranteed to Raise Your SAT Score

Knowing Word Meanings
Is Essential for a Higher
SAT Score

Improving your vocabulary is essential if you want to get a high score on the Critical Reading section of the SAT. We shall explain why this is so.

The Critical Reading section of the SAT consists of two different question types: Sentence Completions and Reading Comprehension. Almost all SAT exam takers come across many "tough" words in this part, whose meanings they do not know. These students, thereby, lose many, many points because if they do not know the meanings of the words in the questions, they aren't able to answer the questions confidently—and so, they are likely to answer incorrectly.

Every correct answer on the SAT gives you approximately 10 points. The Nineteen Sentence Completion questions contain quite a number of "tough" words whose meanings you will have to know in order to answer these questions correctly.

We must also bring to your attention the fact that several "tough" words show up in the Reading Comprehension passages of every SAT exam. Knowing the meanings of these difficult words will, of course, help you to understand the passages better. It follows that knowing what the passages are all about will give you many more correct answers for the Reading Comprehension questions that appear in the SAT—*and each correct answer nets you approximately 10 points*.

Ten Steps to Word Power

1. Learn those Latin and Greek roots, prefixes, and suffixes that make up many English words. It has been estimated that more than half of all English words come from Latin and Greek. Word Building with Roots, Prefixes, and Suffixes begins on page 70; also learn the Hot Prefixes and Roots starting on page 84.

2. Learn the Vocabulary Strategies beginning on page 42.

3. Take the Vocabulary Tests beginning on page 158.

4. Look at the list of SAT words on page 90.

5. Try to learn as many of the words and their opposites on page 92.

6. Have a college-level dictionary at home. Carry a pocket dictionary with you. Refer to a dictionary whenever you are not sure of the meaning of a word.

7. Read—read—read. By reading a great deal, you will encounter new and valuable words. You will learn the meanings of many of these words by context—that is, you will perceive a clear connection between a new word and the words that surround that word. In this way, you will learn the meaning of that new word.

8. Listen to what is worthwhile listening to. Listen to good radio and TV programs. Listen to people who speak well. Go to selected movies and plays. Just as you will increase your vocabulary by reading widely, you will increase your vocabulary by listening to English that is spoken well.

9. Play word games like crossword puzzles, anagrams, and Scrabble.

10. If you have time, look through the Vocabulary Review List on p. 104. You might want to make flash cards of these words and their meanings.

No One Can Dispute This Fact!

You will pile up SAT points by taking advantage of the valuable vocabulary building study and practice materials that are offered to you in the following pages of this chapter.

A Gruber Prefix-Root-Suffix List that Gives You the Meaning of Over 200,000 Words

Word Building with Roots, Prefixes, and Suffixes

According to some linguistic studies, approximately 60 percent of our English words are derived from Latin and Greek. The following Latin and Greek roots, prefixes, and suffixes frequently show up in some of the words that appear in SAT reading skills passages. Learn these Latin and Greek word parts to increase your reading vocabulary immensely—and thus score well on your SAT reading skills test. These prefixes, roots, and suffixes can give you the meaning of over 200,000 words!

LATIN AND GREEK ROOTS

"The shortest and best way of learning a language is to know the roots of it; that is, those original primitive words of which other words are formed."

-Lord Chesterfield

ROOT	MEANING AND EXAMPLE	ROOT	MEANING AND EXAMPLE
ag, act = do, drive, act; as a*g*ent, counter*act*.		**cad, cas** = fall; as *cad*ence, *cas*ual, ac*cid*ent.	
alt = high; as *alt*itiude, *alt*ar.		**cant** = sing; as *cant*icle, *chant*.	
anim = mind; as un*anim*ous, *anim*osity.		**cap, capt** = take, hold; as *cap*able, *capt*ive.	
ann = year; as *ann*als, bi*enn*ial.		**capit** = head; as *capit*al.	
aper, apert = open; as a*per*ient, a*pert*ure.		**carn** = flesh; as *carn*ivorous (vor = devour).	
apt = fit, join; as ad*apt*.		**ced, cess** = go, yield; as ac*ced*e, ac*cess*.	
arch = rule, govern; as an*arch*y.		**celer** = swift; as *celer*ity.	
art = skill; as *art*.		**cent** = hundred; as *cent*ury.	
aud = hear, listen; as *aud*ible.		**cing, cinct** = bind; as sur*cing*le, *cinct*ure, suc*cinct*.	
aur - gold; as *aur*iferous (ferr = carry).		**clin** = lean, bend; as de*clin*e.	
bas = low; as de*bas*e.		**commod** = suitable; as *commod*ious.	
bat = beat; as *bat*tle.		**commun** = common; as *commun*ity.	
bit = bite; as *bit*e, *bit*ter.		**cor, cord** = heart; as ac*cord*.	
brev = short; as ab*brev*iate.		**coron** = crown; as *coron*ation.	

corpus, corpor = body; as *corpus*cle; *corpor*al.

cred = believe; as *cred*ible.

cur = care; as ac*cur*ate.

curr, curs = run; as *curr*ent, *curs*ory.

cycle = circle; as bi*cycle*.

dat = give; as *dat*e, e*dit*ion.

dent = tooth; as *dent*ist.

di = day, as *di*al.

dict = speak, say; as contra*dict*.

dign = worthy; as *dign*ity, dis*dain*.

domin = lord, master; as *domin*ate.

dorm = sleep, as *dorm*ant.

duc, duct = lead, bring; as in*duc*e, con*duct*.

equ = equal; as *equ*animity (anim = mind).

fa = speak; as af*fa*ble.

fac = face, form; as ef*fac*e.

fac, fact = make, form, do; as *fac*ile, *fact*ion.

felic = happy; as *felic*ity.

ferr = carry, bear, bring; as *fer*tile, con*fer*.

fess = acknowledge; as con*fess*.

fid = faith, trust; as con*fid*e.

fin = end, limit; as *fin*al.

form = shape; as con*form*.

fort = strong; as *fort*itude.

frang, fract = break; as *frag*ile, *fract*ion.

fund, fus = pour, melt; as *fus*ible, con*found*.

gen, gener = kind, race; as *gen*der, *gener*al.

gest = carry; bring; as con*gest*ion.

grad, gress = step, go; as *grad*ual, di*gress*.

gran = grain; as *gran*ary.

graph = write; as auto*graph*.

grat = pleasing; as *grat*eful.

gross = fat, thick; as *gross*.

hor = hour; *hor*ology.

hospit = host, guest; as *hospit*able.

integr = entire, whole; as *integr*al.

ject = throw; as in*ject*.

judic = judge; as *judic*iary.

junct = join; as con*junct*ion.

jur = swear; as ad*jur*e.

jur = law, right; as *jur*ist.

lat = carry, bring; as di*lat*e.

leg = send, bring; as *leg*acy, al*leg*e.

leg, lect = gather, choose; as *leg*ion, ec*lect*ic.

liber = free; as *liber*ty.

lin = flax; as *lin*en, *lin*ing.

lingu = tongue; as *lingu*ist.

liter = letter; as *liter*al, *liter*ary.

loc = place; as *loc*al, dis*loc*ate.

log = word, speech, reason; as cata*log*ue, *log*ic.

loqu, locut = speak, talk; as *loqu*acious, circum-*locut*ion

lus, lus = sport, play; as *lud*icrous, il*lus*ion.

magn = great; as *magn*itude.

major = greater; as *major*ity.

man = hand; as *man*ual, *main*tain.

man, mans = stay, dwell; as *man*or, *mans*ion.

mar = the sea; as *mar*ine.

mater, matr = mother; as *mater*nal, *matr*imony.

medi = middle, between; as *medi*ate.

medic = physician; as *medic*ine.

mens = measure; as *mens*uration.

ment = mind; as *ment*al.

merc = merchandise, trade; as com*merc*e.

merg = dip, sink; as sub*merg*e.

meter, metr = measure; as chrono*meter*, sym-*metr*y.

migr = wander; as *migr*ate.

mir = wonder, look; as ad*mir*e, *mir*ror.

mit, miss = send; as ad*mit*, com*miss*ion.

mon, monit = advise, remind; as *mon*ument, *monit*or.

mort = death; as *mort*al.

mot = move; as *mot*or.

mult = many; as *mult*itude

mun, munit = fortify; as *munit*ion

nat = born; as *nat*al.

nav = ship; as *nav*al.

not = known; as *not*ice.

numer = number; as *numer*ous.

nunci, nounce = tell; as e*nunci*ate, an*nounce*.

ocul = eye, as *ocul*ist.

pan = bread; as *pan*try.

par = equal; as dis*par*ity.

par = get ready; as com*par*e.

parl = speak; as *parl*ey.

pars, part = par; as *pars*e; a*part*.

pass = step; as com*pass*.

past = feed; as *past*ure.

pat, pass = suffer, feel; as *pat*ient, *pass*ive.

pater, patr = father; as *pater*nal, *patr*ician.

ped = foot; as bi*ped*.

pel, puls = drive; as com*pel*, ex*puls*ion.

pen = pain, punishment; as *pen*al.

pend, pens = hang, weigh, pay; as *pend*ant, *pens*ion

pet, petit = seek; as im*pet*us, *petit*ion.

petr = stone, rock; as *petr*ify.

phil, philo = loving; as *philo*sophy (soph = wisdom).

phon = sound; as *phon*ic.

physi = nature; as *physi*ology (log = word, reason).

pict = paint; as *pict*ure.

plac = please; as *plac*able.

ple, plet = fill; as com*ple*ment, com*plet*e.

plen = full; as *plen*ty.

plic = fold, bend; as com*plic*ate.

plum = feather; as *plum*age.

plumb = lead; as *plumb*er.

pon = to place, put; as com*pon*ent.

port = gate; as *port*al.

pos = to place, put; as com*pos*e.

pot = drink; as *pot*ion.

potent = powerful; as *potent*ate.

prehend, prehens = take, grasp; as ap*prehend*, *prehens*ile.

prim = first; as *prim*ary.

punct = prick, point; as *punct*ure.

quadr = square, fourfold; as *quadr*ant.

quant = how much; as *quant*ity.

quer, quisit = seek, ask; as *quer*y, in*quisit*ion.

quies = rest; as ac*quies*cent.

radi = ray; as *radi*ant.

rap, rapt = seize, grasp; as *rap*acious, *rapt*ure.

rat = think, calculate; as *rat*io.

rect = ruled, straight, right; as *rect*angle.

reg = rule, govern; as *reg*ent.

rid, ris = laugh; as *rid*iculous, *ris*ible.

riv = stream; as *riv*er, de*riv*e.

rog, rogat = ask; as inter*rogat*e.

rupt = break; as *rupt*ure.

sacr = holy; as *sacr*ed.

sal = salt; as *sal*ine.

sal = leap; as *sal*ient.

sanct = holy; as *sanct*ion.

sat, satis = enough; as *sat*e, *satis*fy.

sci = know; as *sci*ence.

scop = watch, view; as horo*scop*e.

scrib, script = write; as de*scrib*e, sub*script*ion.

sec, sect = cut; as *sec*ant, bi*sect*.

sen = old; as *sen*ior.

sent, sens = feel, think; as *sent*iment, *sens*ible.

sequ, secut = follow; as *sequ*el, con*secut*ive.

serv = keep; as con*serv*e.

sist = to place, stand; as as*sist*.

sol = alone; as *sol*itude.

son = sound; as con*son*ant.

sort = lot, kind; as as*sort*.

spec, spect = look, appear; as *spec*imen, pro*spect*.

speci = kind, as *speci*es.

spir = breathe; as a*spir*e.

stat = standing; as *stat*us.

stell = star; con*stell*ation.

string, strict = draw tight, bind; as *string*ent.

stru, struct = build; as con*stru*e, con*struct*.

su = follow; as per*su*e.

suad, suas = persuade; as dis*suad*e, per*suas*ion.

sum, sumpt = take; as as*sum*e, pre*sumpt*ion.

surg, surrect = rise; as in*surg*ent, in*surrect*ion.

tact = touch; as con*tact*.

tail = cut; as *tail*or.

tang = touch; as *tang*ent.

teg, tect = cover; as *teg*ument, de*tect*.

tempor = time; as *tempor*ary.

tend, tent = stretch, reach; as con*tend*, con*tent*.

test = witness; as at*test*.

tort = twist, wring; as con*tort*.

tract = draw; as at*tract*.

trit = rub; as at*trit*ion

trud, trus = thrust; as in*trud*e, abs*trus*e.

un = one; as *un*animous (anim = mind).

und = wave, flow; as in*und*ate.

ut, util = use, useful; as *ut*ensil, *util*ize.

vad, vas = go; as e*vad*e.

val = be strong; as *val*id.

ven, vent = come; as con*ven*e, con*vent*ion.

vert, vers = turn; as per*vert*, *vers*ion.

vi, via = way, road; as *via*duct (duct = lead, bring), de*vi*ous.

vic = a change, turn; as *vic*arious.

vid, vis = see, appear; as e*vid*ent, *vis*ible.

viv = live; as *viv*acity.

voc = call; as *voc*ation.

volv, volu, volut = roll; as circum*volv*e, *volu*ble, re*volut*ion.

vot = vow; as *vot*ive.

PREFIXES AND SUFFIXES

English Prefixes

Following is a list of the principal prefixes and suffixes of Anglo-Saxon (old form of English), Latin, and Greek origin, now in use in the English language:

Those used to form nouns:

fore = before; as, *fore-father*.

mis = wrong; as, *mis-deed, mis-chance*.

un = the opposite of; as, *un-truth, un-belief*.

Those used to form adjectives:

a = on; as, *a-live, a-board, a-sleep*.

for = quite, thoroughly; as, *for-lorn*.

un = not; as, *un-true, un-wise*.

mis = wrong; as, *mis-shapen*.

Those used to form verbs:

a = out, from, away, often used to intensify the meaning of the verb; as, *a-rise, a-wake, a-rouse*.

be = by, and is used in several ways:

1. To intensify the meaning of the verb; as, *be-daub, be-smear*.

2. To change intransitive verbs to transitive ones; as, *be-speak, be-think*.

3. To form transitive verbs out of adjectives and nouns; as, *be-friend, be-night, be-troth*.

for = through, thoroughly, used to intensify the meaning of the verb; as, *for-bid, for-give, for-get*.

fore = before; as *fore-bode, fore-tell*.

mis = wrongly; as, *mis-believe, mis-call*.

un = back; as, *un-bind, un-do*.

with = back, against; as, *with-draw, with-stand*.

Those used to form adverbs:

a = on; as, *a-foot, a-field*.

be = on; as, *be-fore, be-sides*.

Latin Prefixes

Latin prefixes frequently vary their forms in composition, the final letter being changed to harmonize in sound with the first syllable of the base. Thus, *ad* becomes *ac* in *accede*; *al* in *allude*; *at* in *attract*; and so on. This process is called assimilation of sound.

The following are the more commonly used prefixes of Latin origin.

a, ab, abs = from, away; as, *a-vert*, *ab-jure*, *abs-ent*.

ad = to; as, *ad-here*. By assimilation *ad* takes the forms *a*, *ac*, *af*, *al*, *an*, *ap*, *as*, and *at*, as *a-spire*, *ac-cord*, *af-fect*, *al-lude*, *an-nex*, *ap-peal*, *as-sume*, *at-tract*.

amb, am (from *ambi*) = about; as, *amb-ition*, *am-putate*.

ante or **anti** = before; as, *ante-date*, *anti-cipate*.

bis, bi = twice; as, *bi-sect*.

circum = around; as, *circum-navigate*.

com, con = together; as, *com-mand*, *con-vival*. This prefix assumes the forms *col* and *cor* before *l* and *r*, and *co* before a vowel; as, *col-lect*, *cor-rect*, *com-mit*, *co-eval*, *co-worker*.

contra, contro, or counter = against; as, *contra-dict*, *contro-vert*, *counter-act*.

de = down, from, about; as, *de-scend*, *de-part*, *de-scribe*.

demi = half; as, *demi-god*.

dis, di, dif = apart, in two, denoting difference or negation; as, *dis-sent*, *di-vision*, *dif-ficulty*.

ex, e, or **ef** = out of, from; as, *ex-alt*, *e-lect*, *ef-face*.

extra = out of, beyond; as, *extra-ordinary*.

in = in, into; as, *in-vade*. This prefix changes by assimilation into *il*, *im*, *ir*; as, *il-lustrate*, *im-merse*, *ir-ritate*. In its French form, *en*, it is found in *en-chant*, *en-dure*, etc.

in = not; by assimilation *il*, *im*, *ir*; as *in-distinct*, *il-legal*, *im-piety*, *ir-revocable*.

inter, intro = between, within, among; as *inter-pose*, *intro-duce*, *enter-prise*.

male = ill; as, *mal-treat*, *male-volent*.

non = not; as, *non-sense*.

ob = in front of, against; by assimilation *oc*, *of*, *op*; as, *ob-viate*, *oc-cupy*, *of-fend*, *op-pose*.

pene, pen = almost; as, *pen-insula*.

per = through; by assimilation, *pel* and *pil*; as, *per-ceive*, *pel-lucid*, *pil-grim*.

post = after; as, *post-pone*, *post-script*.

pre = before; as, *pre-dict*, *pre-cede*.

preter = past, beyond; as, *preter-ite*, *preter-natural*.

pro = forward, before; as, *pro-ceed*, *pro-gress*. *Pro* is found in the forms *pur* and *por* in *pur-chase*, *pur-sue*, *por-tray*.

pro = instead of; as, *pro-noun*.

re, red = back again; as, *re-cede*, *re-adopt*, *red-olent*.

retro = backwards; as, *retro-grade*, *retro-spect*.

se, sed = apart, away; as, *se-cede*, *sed-ition*.

semi = half; as, *semi-circle*.

sine = without; as, *sinecure*.

sub = under, up from below; by assimilation, *suc*, *suf*, *sug*, *sum*, *sup*, *sur*, *sus*; as, *sub-ject*, *suc-cor, suf-fer, sug-gest, sum-mon, sup-press, sur-prise, sus-tain.*

subter = under; as, *subter-fuge.*

super, sur = above, beyond; as, *super-pose, super-natural, sur-name.*

trans = across; as, *trans-form.*

ultra = beyond; as, *ultra-liberal.*

un, uni = one; as, *un-animous, uni-form.*

vice = instead of; as, *vice-chancellor, vice-roy.*

Greek Prefixes

The following are the Greek prefixes in most common use:

a, an = not; as, *an-archy, a-morphous.*

amphi = on both sides, round about; as, *amphi-bious, amphi-theater.*

ana = up, back; as, *ana-tomy, ana-lysis.*

anti, ant = against, opposite to; as, *anti-dote, ant-arctic.*

apo, ap = away from; as, *apo-state, apo-stle, ap-helion.*

archi, arche, arch = first, chief; as, *archi-tect, arche-type, arch-bishop.*

auto, auth = self; as, *auto-crat, auto-nomy, auth-entic.*

cata, cat = down, over; as, *cata-logue, cat-astrophe.*

dia = through, across; as, *dia-meter, dia-gonal.*

dis, di = twice; as, *dis-syllable, di-pthong.*

dys = ill; as, *dys-peptic.*

ec, ex = out of; as, *ec-centric, ex-odus.*

en, el, em = in, on, at; as, *en-comium, el-lipse, em-phasis.*

epi = upon; as, *epi-taph, epi-demic.*

eu, ev = well; as, *eu-logy, ev-angelist.*

hemi = half; as *hemi-sphere.*

hyper = over, above; as, *hyper-bole, hyper-critical.*

meta, met = after, changed for; as, *meta-phor, met-onymy.*

mono = alone; as, *mono-gram, mono-poly.*

pan = all; as, *pan-acea, pan-orama.*

para, par = beside, against; as, *para-dox, par-enthesis.*

peri = around; as, *peri-meter, peri-gee, peri-helion.*

poly = many; as, *poly-gamy, poly-gon, poly-technic.*

pro = before; as, *pro-phet, pro-logue.*

syn, syl, sym, sy = with; as, *syn-tax, syl-lable, sym-pathy, sy-stem.*

English Suffixes

The principal English suffixes are the following:

Those used to form abstract nouns:

dom, denoting judgment, authority, dominion; as, *wis-dom, free-dom, king-dom.*

hood, head, denoting state, rank, character; as, *man-hood, god-head.*

ing, denoting action, state; as, *read-ing, hear-ing.*

ness, denoting state, quality; as, *good-ness, great-ness.*

red, denoting mode, fashion; as, *hat-red, kind-red.*

ship, denoting shape, manner, form; as, *friend-ship, wor-ship.*

Those used to form diminutives:

en, as, *maid-en, kitt-en* (from *cat*), *kitch-en* (from *cook*).

ie, as, *bird-ie, dog-g-ie, Ann-ie.*

ing, as, *farth-ing* (from *fourth*), *tith-ing* (from *tenth*).

kin, as, *bump-kin, lamb-kin, nap-kin.*

ling, as, *dar-ling, duck-ling, gos-ling.*

ock, as, *bull-ock, hill-ock.*

Miscellaneous:

er, ar, or, ier, yer, denoting the agent or doer; as, *paint-er, begg-ar, sail-or, cloth-ier, law-yer.*

ster (formerly a feminine suffix), denoting a female agent; as, spin-ster; also an agent of either sex; as, *huck-ster, poll-ster.* It is also used as a term of depreciation; as, *game-ster, young-ster.*

ard, art, characterizing a person by a peculiarity; as, *cow-ard, drunk-ard, brag-g-art.*

le, el, denoting an instrument; as *gird-le, hand-le, shov-el.*

ther, marking the agent and used in terms of relationship; as, *fa-ther, daugh-ter, mo-ther.*

craft, denoting skill, a trade; as, *book-craft, wood-craft.*

fare, denoting way, course; as, *thorough-fare, wel-fare.*

ric, denoting power, dominion; as, *bishop-ric.*

wright, a workman; as, *wheel-wright; play-wright.*

monger, a dealer; as, *news-monger.*

Those used to form adjectives:

ed, d, the suffix of the past participle, is added to nouns to form adjectives; as, *wing-ed, talent-ed, bright-eye-d, golden-hair-ed.*

en = made of; as, *wood-en, gold-en.*

fast = fast, firm; as, *stead-fast, shame-faced = shame-fast,* which is the old form of the word.

fold, denoting multiplication; as, *two-fold, mani-fold.*

ful = full; as, *hate-ful*, *will-ful*.

ing, the suffix of the present pariticiple; as, *pleas-ing*, *annoy-ing*.

ish = like, when added to nouns; as, *boy-ish*, *girl-ish*; when added to adjectives, the suffix means "somewhat," "rather"; as, *black-ish*, *green-ish*.

less = loose from, without; as, *fear-less*, *shame-less*. This suffix has no connection with the comparative of little.

like = like; as, *child-like*, *war-like*.

ly = like; as, *man-ly*, *sick-ly*. This suffix is a softened form of the preceding.

some = like, partaking of a certain quality; as, *glad-some*, *loath-some*. This suffix is found in a corrupt form in *buxom*, *flotsam*, and *jetsam*.

teen, ty = ten; as in the numerals.

th, ordinal; as, *fif-th*, *six-th*.

ward = becoming, leading to; as, *south-ward*, *for-ward*.

wise = mode, way, manner; as, *like-wise*, *other-wise*.

y, ey = of the nature of; as, *ic-y*, *clay-ey*.

Those used to form verbs:

en, imparting the idea of cause, forms transitive verbs from nouns and adjectives; as, *strength-en*, *black-en*, *fat-t-en*.

er, r, is added to adjectives and verbs, and imparts to the base word a frequentative and intensive force; as, *hind-er*, *low-er*, *wand-er* (from *wend*), *glimm-er* (from *gleam*).

le, l, is added to nouns and verbs, and imparts to the base word the sense of frequency, or dimunition; as, *nest-le*, *thrott-le* (from *throat*), *start-le*, *stradd-le* (from *stride*).

k, frequentative; as, *tal-k* (from *tell*), *har-k* (from *hear*).

se, to make, forms transitive verbs from adjectives; as, *clean-se*.

Those used to form adverbs:

es or **s,** the old suffix of the possessive case; as in *need-s*, *beside-s*, *then-ce*, *unaware-s*.

ere, denoting place in; as, *h-ere* (related to *he*), *th-ere* (related to *that*), *wh-ere* (related to *who*).

ly, a softened form of *like*; as, *on-ly*, *utter-ly*, *wicked-ly*.

ling, long, denoting direction; as in *dark-ling*, *head-long*, *side-long*.

ther, denoting place to; as, *hi-ther*, *thi-ther*, *whi-ther*.

ward, wards, denoting direction; as, *home-ward*, *back-wards*.

wise, mode or manner; as, *like-wise*, *other-wise*.

way, ways. In Old English, the accusative (objective case) of nouns was sometimes used with the force of an adverb. Hence the adverbs *al-ways*, *straight-way*. The general use of the possessive suffix *-es* or *-s* o form adverbs is accountable for the forms *al-ways*, *straight-ways*, *side-ways*.

Latin Suffixes

The principal suffixes of Latin origin are the following:

Those used to form nouns:

1. Those used to form abstract nouns:

age = act, condition, collection of; as, *cour-age, hom-age, foli-age.*

ance, ancy, ence, or **ency** = state or quality of being; as *abund-ance, const-ancy, indulg-ence, consist-ency.*

ice = that which; as *just-ice.*

ment = state of being, that which; as, *excite-ment, command-ment.* It is also used to denote *instrument,* as in *docu-ment, orna-ment.*

mony = state of being, that which; as, *acri-mony, testi-mony.*

ion = the act of, state of being; as, *redempt-ion, evas-ion, act-ion.*

tude, denoting condition; as, *forti-tude, grati-tude.*

ty = state or quality of; as, *chari-ty, cruel-ty.*

ure or **eur** = state of, that which; as, *grand-eur, creat-ure.*

y, denoting condition of faculty; as, *miser-y, victor-y.*

2. Those used to denote simply a person, or one who performs the action signified by the base.

ain or **an** = connected with; as, *artis-an, chapl-ain.*

ant or **ent** = one who; as, *assist-ant, stud-ent.*

ary, ier, eer, or **er** = one who; as, *secret-ary, brigad-ier, engin-eer, marin-er.*

ate = one who; as, *advoc-ate, cur-ate.* In the French form, *ee* or *e,* this suffix denotes the object of an action; as, *legat-ee, nomin-ee, employ-e.*

ist = one who practises or is devoted to; as *evangel-ist, theor-ist.*

or or **er** = one who; as, *conspirat-or, success-or, doct-or, preach-er.*

trix, denoting a female agent; as, *execu-trix.*

3. Those used to form diminutives:

el or **le,** as, *lib-el* (from *liber,* a book), *cast-le* (from *castrum,* a fort).

cle or **cule,** as, *vesi-cle, animal-cule.*

ule, as, *glob-ule.*

ette or **let,** as, *ros-ette, stream-let.*

4. Those used to form collective nouns:

ry, as, *bandit-ry.*

Those used to form adjectives:

aceous or **acious** = made of, having the quality of; as, *farin-aceous, cap-acious.*

al = belonging to; as *leg-al, reg-al.*

an, ane, or **ain** = connected with; as *hum-an, hum-ane, cert-ain.*

ar or **er** = belonging to; as, *regul-ar, premi-er.*

are, arious = relating or belonging to; as, *station-ary, greg-arious.*

able or **ible** = that may be done; as, *port-able, sens-ible.*

ant or **ent**, equivalent to the force of the present participle inflection *ing*; as, *discord-ant*, *curr-ent*.

escent = becoming; as, *putr-escent*.

esque = partaking of; as, *pictur-esque*.

ic = belonging to; as, *civ-ic*, *rust-ic*.

id = having the quality of; as, *acr-id*, *frig-id*.

ile, il, eel, or **le** = capable of being; as, *doc-ile*, *civ-il*, *gent-eel*, *ab-le*.

ine = belonging to; as, *can-ine*, *sal-ine*.

ive = inclined to; as, *plaint-ive*, *abus-ive*.

ory = fitted or relating to; as, *admonit-ory*.

ose or **ous** = full of; as, *verb-ose*, *curi-ous*.

Those used to form verbs:

ate = to perform the act of, cause; as, *navig-ate*.

fy = to make; as, *beauti-fy*, *magni-fy*.

ish = to make; as, *fin-ish*.

Greek Suffixes

The principal suffixes of Greek origin are the following:

ic = belonging to; as, *aromat-ic, graph-ic.*

isk, a diminutive; as, *aster-isk, obel-isk.*

ize or **ise,** forming verbs; as, *anglic-ize, critic-ize.*

st = agent; as, *bapti-st, botani-st.*

y, making abstract nouns; as, *philosoph-y, monarch-y.*

Hot Prefixes and Roots

Here is a list of the most important prefixes and roots that impart a certain meaning or feeling. They can be instant clues to the meanings of more than 110,000 words.

PREFIXES THAT MEAN *TO*, *WITH*, *BETWEEN*, OR *AMONG*

PREFIX	MEANING	EXAMPLES
ad, ac, af, an, ap, ap, as, at	to, toward	adapt—to fit into adhere—to stick to attract—to draw near
com, con, co, col	with, together	combine—to bring together contact—to touch together collect—to bring together co-worker—one who works together with another worker
in, il, ir, im	into	inject—to put into impose—to force into illustrate—to put into example irritate—to put into discomfort
inter	between, among	international—among nations interact—to act among the people
pro	forward, going ahead	proceed—to go forward promote—to move forward

PREFIXES THAT MEAN *BAD*

PREFIX	MEANING	EXAMPLES
mal	wrong, bad	malady—illness malevolent—bad malfunction—bad functioning
mis	wrong, badly	mistreat—to treat badly mistake—to get wrong

PREFIXES THAT MEAN *AWAY FROM*, *NOT*, OR *AGAINST*

PREFIX	MEANING	EXAMPLES
ab	away from	absent—not to be present, away abscond—to run away
de, dis	away from, down, the opposite of, apart, not	depart—to go away from decline—to turn down dislike—not to like dishonest—not honest distant—apart
ex, e, ef	out, from	exit—to go out eject—to throw out efface—to rub out, erase
in, il, ir, im	not	inactive—not active impossible—not possible ill-mannered—not mannered irreversible—not reversible
non	not	nonsense—no sense nonstop—having no stops
un	not	unhelpful—not helpful uninterested—not interested
anti	against	anti-freeze—a substance used to prevent freezing anti-social—refers to someone who's not social
ob	against, in front of	obstacle—something that stands in the way of obstinate—inflexible

PREFIXES THAT DENOTE DISTANCE

PREFIX	MEANING	EXAMPLES
circum	around	circumscribe—to write or inscribe in a circle circumspect—to watch around or be very careful
equ, equi	equal, the same	equalize—to make equal equitable—fair, equal
post	after	postpone—to do after postmortem—after death
pre	before	preview—a viewing that goes before another viewing prehistorical—before written history
trans	across	transcontinental—across the continent transit—act of going across
re	back, again	retell—to tell again recall—to call back, to remember
sub	under	subordinate—under something else subconcious—under the conscious
super	over, above	superimpose—to put something over something else superstar—a star greater than other stars
un, uni	one	unity—oneness unanimous—sharing one view unidirectional—having one direction

ROOTS

ROOT	MEANING	EXAMPLES
cap, capt, cept, ceive	to take, to hold	captive—one who is held receive—to take capable—to be able to take hold of things concept—an idea or thought held in mind
cred	to believe	credible—believable credit—belief, trust
curr, curs, cours	to run	current—now in progress, running cursor—a moveable indicator recourse—to run for aid
dic, dict	to say	indicate—to say by demonstrating diction—verbal saying
duc, duct	to lead	induce—to lead to action aqueduct—a pipe or waterway that leads water somewhere
fac, fic, fect, fy	to make, to do	facile—easy to do fiction—something that has been made up satisfy—to make happy affect—to make a change in
jec, ject	to throw	project—to put forward trajectory—a path of an object that has been thrown
mit, mis	to send	admit—to send in missile—something that gets sent through the air
pon, pos	to place	transpose—to place across compose—to put into place many parts deposit—to place in something
scrib, script	to write	describe—to write or tell about scripture—a written tablet

spec, spic	to look	specimen—an example to look at inspect—to look over
ten, tain	to hold	maintain—to hold up or keep retentive—holding
ven, vent	to come	advent—a coming convene—to come together

A List of SAT Words Appearing More Than Once on Actual SAT Exams

We have made a computerized analysis of frequently occurring words on 47 complete SAT exams. (1,175 questions have been examined.) Following is a list of 167 SAT words appearing *more than once* on these 47 actual SAT exams.

The definitions of these words have not been included here because we want you to *refer to a dictionary* to learn the meanings of these words, which have been repeated in subsequent SAT question sections.

Note that after each word a numeral indicates the number of times that the word has appeared on the 47 actual SAT exams.

Also note that certain pairs of words have a left-side bracket. The bracket indicates that the words are very closely allied in meaning—so if you learn the meaning of one of the two words in the pair, you will easily arrive at the meaning of the other word of the pair.

Learn the meanings of these words, as they have a tendency to be repeated in questions of the SAT.

abolish 2	coalesce 2	distend 1	guile 2	parsimony 2
abridge 2	coalescence 1	distention 1	hackneyed 2	paucity 2
abstemious	cohere 1	drawback 2	hefty 2	penury 2
accent 1	coherent 1	efface 3	hideous 2	peripheral 2
accented 1	compress 1	effervesce 1	hilarity 2	periphery 2
accolade 2	compression 1	effervescent 1	humane 2	placate 2
acquiesce 2	confide 1	enhance 2	hypocrisy 1	precise 1
affirmation 2	confidential 1	enigmatic 2	hypocritical 1	precision 1
amass 2	confound 2	ephemeral 3	innocuous 2	premature 2
ambivalence 1	congeal 2	equilibrium 3	irascible 2	premeditated 2
ambivalent 1	contaminant 1	euphonious 1	jettison 2	prevalent 2
ambulatory 2	contaminate 2	euphony 1	kindle 2	proclivity 2
ameliorate 2	converge 2	evacuate 2	leniency 1	prodigal 1
amity 2	convivial 2	evanescent 2	lenient 1	prodigious 2
anchor 2	copious 2	expedite 1	levity 1	profuse 1
antediluvian 2	corroborate 2	expeditious 1	levitate 1	profusion 2
ascendancy 2	corrugated 2	expendable 1	listless 2	pulverize 1
atrophy 2	corrupt 1	expenditures 1	maladroit 2	pulverized 1
bane 1	corruption 1	exclude 2	mitigate 2	rant 2
baneful 1	cursory 2	facilitate 2	mobile 2	recalcitrant 2
bizarre 2	daunt 3	fallow 2	munificent 2	recant 2
blunder 2	dauntless 1	fertile 2	munificence 1	replete 2
bungle 2	debilitate 2	flourish 3	myriad 2	rescind 2
burgeon 2	deplete 2	flower 1	nefarious 2	reserve 2
capitulate 1	discrepancy 3	fraudulent 3	obscure 1	ruffle 2
capitulation 1	disentangle 2	fruitful 1	obscurity 1	rupture 2
capricious 4	disputatious 1	fruitless 1	opaque 1	saccharine 2
clemency 2	dispute 2	garner 2	opacity 1	salubrious 2

somber 4	subtle 2	tantamount 2	turbulence 3	vilification 2
⌈ specify 1	summary 2	⌈ tenacious 1	venturesome 3	⌈ virulence 1
⌊ specificity 1	summon 3	⌊ tenacity 1	viable 2	⌊ virulent 1
spurn 2	sumptuous 2	⌈ transience 1	⌈ vibrancy 1	whet 2
squander 2	⌈ surreptitious 1	⌊ transient 1	⌊ vibrant 1	zany 2
stymie 2	⌊ surreptitiously 1			

The Most Important/Frequently Used SAT Words and Their Opposites

Following is a list of popular SAT words and their opposites. *Note:* These words fit into specific categories, and it may be a little easier memorizing the meaning of these important words knowing what category they fit into.

POSITIVE	NEGATIVE	POSITIVE	NEGATIVE
TO PRAISE	TO BELITTLE	TO CALM OR MAKE BETTER	TO MAKE WORSE OR RUFFLE
acclaim	admonish	abate	alienate
applaud	assail	accede	antagonize
commend	berate	accommodate	contradict
eulogize	calumniate	allay	dispute
exalt	castigate	ameliorate	fend off
extol	censure	appease	embitter
flatter	chastise	assuage	estrange
hail	chide	comply	incense
laud	decry	concede	infuriate
panegyrize	denigrate	conciliate	nettle
resound	denounce	gratify	oppugn
tout	disparage	mitigate	oppose
	excoriate	mollify	rebuff
	execrate	pacify	repel
	flay	palliate	repulse
	lambaste	placate	snub
	malign	propitiate	
	reprimand	quell	
	reproach	satiate	
	scold		
	upbraid		
	vilify		

POSITIVE	**NEGATIVE**	**POSITIVE**	**NEGATIVE**
PLEASANT	UNPLEASANT	GENEROUS	CHEAP
affable	callous	altruistic	frugal
amiable	cantankerous	beneficent	miserly
agreeable	captious	benevolent	niggardly
captivating	churlish	charitable	paltry
congenial	contentious	effusive	parsimonious
cordial	gruff	hospitable	penurious
courteous	irascible	humanitarian	provident
decorous	ireful	magnanimous	skinflinty
engaging	obstinate	munificent	spartan
gracious	ornery	philanthropic	tight-fisted
obliging	peevish		thrifty
sportive	perverse		
unblemished	petulant		
undefiled	querulous		
	testy		
	vexing		
	wayward		

POSITIVE	NEGATIVE	POSITIVE	NEGATIVE
ABUNDANT OR RICH	SCARCE OR POOR	YIELDING	NOT YIELDING
affluent	dearth	accommodating	adamant
bounteous	deficit	amenable	determinate
copious	destitute	compliant	immutable
luxuriant	exiguous	deferential	indomitable
multifarious	impecunious	docile	inflexible
multitudinous	impoverished	flexible	intractable
myriad	indigent	hospitable	intransigent
opulent	insolvent	inclined	recalcitrant
pecunious	meager	malleable	relentless
plenteous	paltry	obliging	resolute
plentiful	paucity	pliant	steadfast
plethoric	penurious	submissive	tenacious
profuse	scanty	subservient	
prosperous	scarcity	tractable	
superabundant	sparse		
teeming			
wealthy			

POSITIVE	NEGATIVE	POSITIVE	NEGATIVE
COURAGEOUS	TIMID	LIVELY	BLEAK
audacious	diffident	brisk	dejected
dauntless	indisposed	dynamic	forlorn
gallant	laconic	ebullient	lackluster
intrepid	reserved	exhilaration	lugubrious
stalwart	reticent	exuberant	melancholy
undaunted	subdued	inspiring	muted
valiant	timorous	provocative	prostrate
valorous		scintillating	somber
		stimulating	tenebrous
		titillating	

POSITIVE	NEGATIVE	POSITIVE	NEGATIVE
CAREFUL	CARELESS	HAUGHTY	HUMBLE
chary	culpable	affected	demure
circumspect	felonious	aristocratic	diffident
conscientious	indifferent	arrogant	indisposed
discreet	insouciant	audacious	introverted
exacting	lackadaisical	authoritarian	laconic
fastidious	lax	autocratic	plebian
gingerly	negligent	condescending	reluctant
heedful	perfunctory	disdainful	restrained
judicious	rash	egotistical	reticent
meticulous	remiss	flagrant	subdued
provident	reprehensible	flippant	subservient
prudent	temerarious	imperious	taciturn
punctilious		impertinent	timid
scrupulous		impudent	timorous
scrutiny		insolent	unassuming
wary		ostentatious	unostentatious
		pompous	unpretentious
		proud	
		supercilious	
		vainglorious	

Note: In many cases you can put a prefix "im" or "un" in front of the word and change its meaning to an opposite.

Example: Pecunious. Opposite: Impecunious

Ostentatious. Opposite: Unostentatious

Practice Questions

1. Example: Find the opposite of EXTOL:

   (A) oppose

   (B) restrain

   (C) enter

   (D) deviate

   (E) denigrate

2. ALLAY (opposite):

   (A) incense

   (B) drive

   (C) berate

   (D) signify

   (E) determine

3. DECOROUS (opposite):

   (A) scanty

   (B) irascible

   (C) musty

   (D) pliant

   (E) rigid

4. AMENABLE (opposite):

   (A) tiresome

   (B) uncultured

   (C) intransigent

   (D) soothing

   (E) careless

5. MUNIFICENT (opposite):

   (A) simple

   (B) pallid

   (C) crafty

   (D) penurious

   (E) stable

6. PLETHORIC (opposite):

   (A) impecunious

   (B) slothful

   (C) indifferent

   (D) reticent

   (E) sly

7. METICULOUS (opposite):

   (A) timid

   (B) plenteous

   (C) peevish

   (D) intractible

   (E) perfunctory

8. IMPERIOUS (opposite):

   (A) unostentatious

   (B) lackadaisical

   (C) insolvent

   (D) churlish

   (E) immutable

9. TIMOROUS (opposite):

   (A) judicious

   (B) intrepid

   (C) multifarious

   (D) benevolent

   (E) tenebrous

10. LUGUBRIOUS (opposite):

    (A) flexible

    (B) unblemished

    (C) ebullient

    (D) concilatory

    (E) impertinent

Answers to Practice Questions

1. Choice E is correct. EXTOL fits into the category of TO PRAISE. Denigrate fits into the category TO BELITTLE—the opposite category.

2. Choice A is correct. ALLAY fits into the category of TO CALM. Incense fits into the opposite category—TO MAKE WORSE or TO RUFFLE.

3. Choice B is correct. DECOROUS fits into the category of PLEASANT. The opposite category is UNPLEASANT. Irascible fits into this category.

4. Choice C is correct. AMENABLE fits into the category of YIELDING. Intransigent fits into the opposite category—NOT YIELDING.

5. Choice D is correct. MUNIFICENT fits into the category of GENEROUS. Penurious fits into the category of CHEAP, the opposite category.

6. Choice A is correct. PLETHORIC fits into the category of ABUNDANT or RICH. Impecunious fits into the opposite category of SCARCE or POOR.

7. Choice E is correct. METICULOUS fits into the category of CAREFUL. Perfunctory fits into the category of CARELESS (or mechanical).

8. Choice A is correct. IMPERIOUS fits into the category of HAUGHTY (high-brow). Unostentatious fits into the category of HUMBLE, the opposite category.

9. Choice B is correct. TIMOROUS fits into the category of TIMID. Intrepid fits into the opposite category of COURAGEOUS.

10. Choice C is correct. LUGUBRIOUS fits into the category of BLEAK or dismal. Ebullient fits into the opposite category of LIVELY.

Words Commonly Mistaken
for Each Other

Review the following list of words quickly, and mark the pairs that you have trouble remembering. This way, you'll be able to focus your attention on these on subsequent reviews.

AGGRAVATE/IRRITATE
—to make worse
—to annoy

ALLUSION/ILLUSION
—reference
—error in vision

ARBITER/ARBITRARY
—a supposedly unprejudiced judge
—prejudiced

ASCENT/ASSENT
—upward movement
—agreement; to agree

ASCETIC/AESTHETIC
—self-denying
—pertaining to the beautiful

AVERSE/ADVERSE
—disciplined
—opposed

BAN/BANE
—prohibit
—woe

CANVAS/CANVASS
—coarse cloth
—examine; solicit

CAPITAL/CAPITOL
—excellent; chief town; money; punishable by death or life imprisonment
—state house

CENSURE/CENSOR
—find fault
—purge or remove offensive passages

COMPLACENT/COMPLAISANT
—self-satisfied; smug
—kindly; submissive

COMPLEMENT/COMPLIMENT
—that which completes
—praise

CONSUL/COUNCIL/COUNSEL
—diplomatic representative
—group of advisors
—advice

CONTEMPTIBLE/CONTEMPTUOUS
—despicable
—scornful

CONTINUAL/CONTINUOUS
—occurring in steady, but not unbroken, order
—occurring without interruption

COSMOPOLITAN/METROPOLITAN	—sophisticated —pertaining to the city
CREDIBLE/CREDITABLE	—believable —worthy of praise
DEMURE/DEMUR	—pretending modesty —hesitate; raise objection
DEPRECATE/DEPRECIATE	—disapprove regretfully —undervalue
DISCREET/DISCRETE	—judicious; prudent —separate
DISINTERESTED/UNINTERESTED	—unprejudiced —not interested
DIVERS/DIVERSE	—several —varied
ELICIT/ILLICIT	—extract —unlawful
EMEND/AMEND	—correct a text or manuscript —improve by making slight changes
EMINENT/IMMINENT	—high in rank —threatening; at hand
EQUABLE/EQUITABLE	—even-tempered —just
EXULT/EXALT	—rejoice —raise; praise highly
FORMALLY/FORMERLY	—in a formal manner —at a previous time
GOURMET/GOURMAND	—lover of good food —glutton
GORILLA/GUERRILLA	—large ape —mercenary
HAIL/HALE	—frozen pellets; to call; originate —strong, healthy
HEALTHY/HEALTHFUL	—possessing health —bringing about health
IMPLY/INFER	—indicate or suggest —draw a conclusion from
INCREDIBLE/INCREDULOUS	—unbelievable —unbelieving
INDIGENT/INDIGENOUS	—poor —native

INGENIUS/INGENUOUS	—skillful; clever; resourceful —frank; naïve
INTERNMENT/INTERMENT	—imprisonment —burial
MAIZE/MAZE	—corn —confusing network
MARTIAL/MARITAL	—warlike —pertaining to marriage
MENDACIOUS/MERITORIOUS	—lying —possessing merit; praiseworthy
PERSONAL/PERSONABLE	—private —attractive
PERSPICACIOUS/PERSPICUOUS	—shrewd; acute —clear; lucid
PRACTICAL/PRACTICABLE	—sensible; useful —timely; capable of being accomplished
PRODIGAL/PRODIGIOUS	—wastefully lavish —extraordinarily large
PROPHECY/PROPHESY	—prediction —to predict
PROVIDED/PROVIDING	—on condition that —furnishing; giving
REGAL/REGALE	—royal —entertain lavishly
RESPECTFULLY/RESPECTIVELY	—with respect —in the order already suggested
SANCTION/SANCTITY	—authorize —holiness
SOCIAL/SOCIABLE	—pertaining to human society —companionable; friendly
STATUE/STATURE	—piece of sculpture —height
URBAN/URBANE	—pertaining to the city —polished; suave
VENAL/VENIAL	—corrupt, mercenary —pardonable

Vocabulary Prefix-Root-Suffix Test

1. The meaning of TENACIOUS is:
   - (A) sticking to something
   - (B) hard to see
   - (C) terrible
   - (D) careful

2. The meaning of IRREVERSIBLE is:
   - (A) not being able to turn back
   - (B) not being able to understand
   - (C) careless
   - (D) being directionless

3. What is the meaning of PRECURSOR?
   - (A) something that goes before(
   - (B) something that gets someone angry
   - C) a careful observation
   - (D) a hard tool

4. What is the meaning of UNIDIRECTIONAL?
   - (A) no direction
   - (B) one direction
   - (C) many directions
   - (D) two directions

5. What is the meaning of PARITY?
   - (A) abundance
   - (B) simplicity
   - (C) equality
   - (D) sympathy

6. What is the meaning of TACTILE?
   - (A) something that is hard
   - (B) something that is easy to see
   - (C) something that can be written on
   - (D) something that can be touched

7. What is the best meaning of the underlined suffix?
   director
   - (A) one who
   - (B) place where
   - (C) quality of
   - (D) full of

8. What is the best meaning of the underlined suffix?
   anthropology
   - (A) being
   - (B) the quality of
   - (C) the study of
   - (D) place where

9. Which is the prefix of the following word? *inject*
   - (A) i
   - (B) in
   - (C) inj
   - (D) inject

10. Which is the suffix of *antagonism*?
    - (A) nism
    - (B) ism
    - (C) onism
    - (D) tagonism

Vocabulary Prefix-Root-Suffix Test Answers

1. A — TEN = hold fast
2. A — IR = not
3. A — PRE = before, CURS = to run
4. B — UNI = one
5. C — PAR = equal
6. D — TACT = touch
7. A — or = one who
8. C — ogy = the study of
9. B — prefix = in, root=ject=to throw
10. B — suffix = ism

Vocabulary Review List

A

abase—to degrade

abash—to embarrass

abate—to decrease

abattoir—a slaughterhouse

abdicate—to give up

aberration—a deviation

abet—to aid

abeyance—temporary suspension

abhor—to detest

abject—miserable

abjure—to give up on oath

ablution—washing the body

abnegate—to renounce

abominate—to loathe

aboriginal—first; existing someplace since the beginning

abort—to cut short

abrade—to rub off

abridge—to shorten

abrogate—to cancel by authority

abscond—to run away

absolve—to free of guilt

abstemious—moderate in eating and drinking

abstract—a summary

abstruse—hard to understand

abut—to border on

abysmal—bottomless; wretched

accede—to take on the duties (of); to attain (to)

acclivity—an upward slope

accolade—a demonstration of honor

accouterments—one's clothes

accretion—accumulation

accrue—to accumulate

acerbity—sharpness

acme—a peak

acquiesce—to yield

acquit—to clear of a charge

acrid—sharp

acrimony—bitterness

actuate—to put into motion

acumen—keenness

adage—an old saying

adamant—unyielding

adduce—to give as proof

adept—skilled; expert

adhere—to stay fast

adipose—fatty

adjudicate—to judge

adjunct—something added

adjure—to charge under oath

admonish—to warn

adroit—skillful

adulation—flattery

adulterate—to make impure

adumbration—a foreshadowing; an outlining

advent—an arrival

adventitious—accidental

adversity—misfortune

advocate—to support

aesthetic—pertaining to beauty

affable—friendly

affected—artificial

affidavit—a sworn statement in writing

affinity—a close relationship

affirmation—assertion

affluent—wealthy

affray—a noisy quarrel

affront—an insult

agenda—a program

agglomerate—to gather into a mass

aggrandize—to make greater

aggravate—to make worse

aggregate—a group of things together

aggrieved—wronged

aghast—horrified

agile—nimble

agnostic—one who doesn't know

agrarian—agricultural

akimbo—with hands on hips

alacrity—eagerness

albeit—although

alchemy—early chemistry

alienate—to make unfriendly

allay—to calm

allege—to declare

allegory—a symbolic story

alleviate—to relieve

allocate—to distribute

allude—to refer indirectly

alluvial—pertaining to soil deposits left by water

altercation—an angry argument

altruism—unselfish concern for others

amass—to accumulate

amatory—showing love

ambidextrous—skillful; able to use both hands equally well

ambrosia—the food of the gods

ambulant—moving about

ameliorate—to improve

amenable—easily led

amenity—a pleasant quality

amiable—friendly

amity—friendship

amnesty—pardon

amorphous—shapeless

amplify—to increase

amulet—a charm

anachronism—something misplaced in time

analgesic—a pain reliever

analogous—comparable

anarchy—absence of government

anathema—a curse

anchorite—a recluse

ancillary—serving as an aid

animadversion—a critical comment

animate—to bring to life

animosity—hatred

annals—yearly records

anneal—to heat and then cool; to strengthen

annuity—a yearly payment

annul—to invalidate

anomaly—an abnormality

antediluvian—before the biblical flood; very old

anterior—toward the front

anthropoid—resembling man

antipathy—a strong dislike

antipodes—exact opposites

antithesis—opposite

apathetic—indifferent

aperture—an opening

apex—a peak

aphorism—an adage

aplomb—self-possession; poise

apocryphal—of doubtful authenticity

apogee—the highest point

apoplexy—sudden paralysis

apostate—one who abandons his faith or cause

apothecary—druggist

apothegm—a saying

apotheosis—deification

appall—to shock or dismay

apparition—a ghost

appease—to pacify

appellation—a name or title

append—to attach

apposite—apt

apprise—to notify

appurtenance—an accessory or possession

aquiline—curved or hooked

arabesque—an elaborate architectural design

arable—plowable (land)

arbiter—a judge or umpire

arbitrary—left to one's judgment; despotic

arboreal—pertaining to trees

archaic—ancient or old-fashioned

archetype—an original model or perfect example

archipelago—a group of islands

archives—a place where records are kept; records

ardor—passion

arduous—laborious

argot—jargon

armada—a fleet of warships

arraign—to bring to court to answer charges

arrant—complete; out-and-out

arrears—unpaid debts

arrogate—to appropriate

articulate—to join; to speak clearly

artifact—a man-made object, particularly a primitive one

artifice—ingenuity; trickery

artisan—a skilled craftsman

ascendant—rising

ascetic—self-denying

ascribe—to assign or attribute

aseptic—free of bacteria

askance—with a sideways look; suspiciously

askew—crookedly

asperity—harshness

aspersion—a slanderous remark

assail—to assault

assay—to test or analyze; to try

asseverate—to assert

assiduous—diligent

assimilate—to incorporate

assuage—to lessen

astral—pertaining to the stars

astute—clever; shrewd

atavism—a throwback to an earlier state; a reappearance of a characteristic from an earlier generation

atheist—one who believes there is no God

athwart—across

atrophy—to waste away

attenuate—to weaken

attest—to confirm

attribute—a characteristic

attrition—wearing away

atypical—abnormal

audacious—bold

audible—loud enough to be heard

augment—to enlarge

augur—to foretell

august—inspiring reverence and respect

aural—pertaining to the ear or hearing

auspices—sponsorship

auspicious—favorable

austerity—severity; the condition of denying oneself

autocrat—a dictator

autonomy—self-government; independence

auxiliary—a thing or person that gives aid

avarice—greed

aver—to affirm

averse—opposed

avid—greedy

avocation—a hobby

avoirdupois—weight

avow—to acknowledge

avuncular—pertaining to an uncle; like an uncle

awry—not straight

B

bacchanal—a drunken party

badger—to tease or annoy

badinage—playful talk; banter

baffle—to perplex

baleful—harmful

balk—to obstruct; to refuse to move

balm—something that soothes or heals

banal—trite; commonplace

bandy—to toss back and forth; exchange

baneful—deadly

barbaric—uncivilized

baroque—very ornate

barrage—a prolonged attack of artillery fire or words

barrister—a man of the legal profession

bastion—a fortification or defense

bate—to lessen

bathos—sentimentality

batten—to thrive

bayou—a marshy body of water

beatific—blissful

beatitude—perfect happiness

bedizen—to dress in a showy way

bedlam—a madhouse; a place of chaos

beguile—to charm or deceive

behemoth—a large and powerful animal or thing

behoof—behalf; interest

belabor—to beat; to scold or criticize

beleaguer—to besiege

belie—to contradict

bellicose—warlike

belligerent—warlike

benediction—a blessing

benefactor—one who provides benefits

benevolent—kindly

benighted—surrounded by darkness; unenlightened

benign—kindly; harmless

benison—a blessing

berate—to scold

berserk—frenzied

beset—to attack

bestial—like a beast; brutish

bestow—to present (as a gift); to confer

bestride—to mount with one leg on each side

bete noire—something or someone hated or feared

bibliophile—one who loves books

bibulous—inclined to drink alcoholic beverages

biennial—every two years

bigot—an intolerant person

bilious—bad-tempered

billingsgate—vulgar, abusive talk

binate—paired

bivouac—a temporary encampment

bizarre—odd; eccentric

blanch—to make white; to bleach; (a person) to turn white

bland—mild

blandishment—flattery

blasphemy—profanity

blatant—unpleasantly loud

blazon—to make known; to adorn or decorate

bleak—unsheltered; bare

blight—anything that kills, withers, or stunts

blithe—gay

bloated—swollen

bludgeon—a club

bluster—to act in a noisy manner

bode—to foreshadow

boisterous—rowdy

bolster—to support

bombastic—using unnecessarily pompous language

bondage—slavery

boor—a rude person

bootless—useless

bounty—generosity

bourgeois—pertaining to the middle class

bovine—cowlike

bowdlerize—to remove offensive passages (from a book)

braggadocio—a braggart

brandish—to shake or wave (something) in a menacing way

brash—impudent

bravado—a show of bravery

brazen—shameless

breach—a violation

brevity—briefness

brigand—a bandit

broach—to open or introduce

bromidic—dull

bruit—to rumor

brusque—abrupt in manner

bucolic—rural; pastoral

buffoonery—clowning

bullion—gold or silver in bars

bulwark—a defense

bumptious—conceited or forward

burgeon—to grow

burlesque—to imitate in order to ridicule

burnish—to polish

buttress—a support

buxom—healthy; plump

C

cabal—a small group of conspirators

cache—a hiding place; hidden things

cacophony—harsh sound

cadaver—a corpse

cadence—rhythm

cadre—a basic structure; a nucleus or framework

caitiff—a mean person

cajole—to coax or wheedle

caliber—quality or value

calk, caulk—to fill cracks or seams

calligraphy—penmanship

callous—unfeeling

callow—immature

calumny—slander

camaraderie—fellowship

canaille—rabble; mob

canard—a false, often mali-cious report

candor—frankness

canny—shrewd

cant—slang or argot

canvass—to go through for opinions, votes, etc.

capacious—roomy

capitulate—to surrender

capricious—erratic, changeable

captious—quick to find fault

captivate—to fascinate

careen—to lean to the side or from side to side

caricature—an imitation or drawing that exagger-ates certain features of the subject

carmine—red

carnage—slaughter

carnal—bodily

carousal—a rowdy drinking party

carp—to make petty com-plaints

carrion—decaying flesh

carte blanche—a free hand; unlimited authority

castigate—to punish

casualty—a mishap

casuistry—false reasoning

cataclysm—an upheaval

catalyst—an agent of change

catapult—to shoot or launch; to leap

catastrophe—a calamity

categorical—absolute

catholic—universal

causerie—a chat

caustic—corrosive

cauterize—to burn

cavalcade—a procession

caveat—a warning

cavil—to quibble

cede—to give up one's rights to (something); to transfer ownership of

celerity—speed

celestial—heavenly

celibate—unmarried

censure—to blame or criticize

cerebration—thought; thinking

cessation—stopping

cession—the giving up (of something) to another

chafe—to rub for warmth; to irritate

chaff—husks of grain; any-thing worthless

chagrin—embarrassment

chaotic—totally disorderly

charlatan—imposter; quack

charnel—a place where corpses or bones are put

chary—watchful

chaste—pure

chastise—to punish

chattel—personal property

chauvinism—fanatical patriotism or partisanship

checkered—characterized by diverse experiences

chicanery—trickery or deception

chide—to rebuke

chimerical—imaginary

choleric—quick-tempered

chronic—long-lasting or perpetual

chronicle—a historical record arranged in order of time

churlish—rude

circuitous—roundabout

circumlocution—an indirect or lengthy way of saying something

circumscribe—to encircle

circumspect—cautious

circumvent—to surround; to prevent (something) by cleverness

citadel—a fortress

cite—to quote

civility—politeness

clandestine—secret

clarion—clear (sound) like a trumpet

cleave—to split

cleft—a split

clemency—leniency

cliché—an overworked expression

climacteric—a crucial period or event

climactic—pertaining to the climax, or high point

clique—an exclusive group of people

cloister—a monastery or convent

cloy—to satiate

coadjutor—an assistant

coalesce—to unite or merge

codicil—an addition or supplement

coerce—to force

coffer—a strongbox

cogent—forceful

cogitate—to think over

cognate—related

cognizant—aware

cognomen—a name

cohesion—tendency to stick together

cohort—a group or band; an associate

coincident—happening at the same time

collaborate—to work together

collateral—side by side; parallel

collocation—an arrangement

colloquial—conversational; informal (speech)

colloquy—a formal discussion or conference

collusion—conspiracy

colossal—huge

comatose—pertaining to a coma

comely—attractive

comestible—edible

comity—politeness

commensurate—equal in size or measure

comminuted—powdered

commiseration—sympathy or sorrow

commodious—spacious

commutation—an exchange or substitution

compassion—deep sympathy

compatible—able to get along well together

compendious—brief but comprehensive

compile—to gather in an orderly form

complacent—self-satisfied

complaisant—obliging; agreeable

complement—that which completes something

compliant—submissive

component—a part of the whole

comport—to behave or conduct (oneself)

compunction—guilt; remorse

concatenate—linked together; connected

concede—to acknowledge or admit as true

conciliate—to make up with

concise—brief and clear

conclave—a private or secret meeting

conclusive—decisive

concoct—to devise

concomitant—accompanying

concordat—an agreement

concourse—a crowd; a space for crowds to gather

concupiscent—having strong sexual desire or lust

concurrent—running together or at the same time

condescend—to deal with someone beneath oneself on his own level, sometimes patronizingly

condign—deserved or suitable

condolence—expression of sympathy

condone—to pardon or overlook

conducive—tending or leading

conduit—a pipe or channel for liquids

configuration—an arrangement

confiscate—to seize by authority

conflagration—a large fire

confute—to prove wrong

congeal—to solidify

congenital—existing from birth

conglomerate—a mass or cluster

congruent—corresponding

congruous—suitable, fitting

conjecture—a guess

conjoin—to unite

conjugal—pertaining to marriage

conjure—to produce by magic

connive—to pretend not to see another's wrongdoing; to cooperate or conspire in wrongdoing

connoisseur—one with expert knowledge and taste in an area

connotation—an idea suggested by a word or phrase that is different from the literal meaning of the word or phrase

consanguinity—blood relationship; close relationship

conscript—to draft (as for military service)

consecrate—to dedicate

consensus—general agreement

consign—to hand over; to put in the care of another

consonance—agreement

consort—a spouse, particularly of a king or queen; a traveling companion

consternation—great emotion that leaves one helpless and confused

constituency—the people served by an elected official

constrain—to confine or hold back

constrict—to make smaller by applying pressure; to restrict

construe—to interpret

consummate—to bring to completion; to finish

contaminate—to pollute

contemn—to scorn

contentious—quarrelsome; controversial

context—the words around a particular portion of a speech or passage; sur-roundings and background

contiguous—touching along one side; adjacent

continence— self-restraint; moderation

contingent—possible; accidental; depending on something else

contortion—a twisting

contraband—smuggled merchandise

contravene—to oppose; to dispute

contrition—remorse or repentance

contrivance—something that is thought up or devised; an invention

controvert—to contradict; to debate

contumacious—insubordinate; disobedient

contumely—humiliating rudeness

contusion—bruise

conundrum—a puzzling question or problem

convene—to assemble

conversant—familiar (with)

conveyance—a vehicle or other means of carrying

convivial—pertaining to festivity; sociable

convoke—to call together

convolution—a twisting together; a twist or coil

copious—plentiful

corollary—a proposition that follows from another that has been proved

corporeal—bodily

corpulent—very fat

correlation—a mutual relationship; a correspondence

corroborate—to confirm

corrosive—capable of eating or wearing away; sarcastic; biting

corsair—a pirate or pirate ship

cortege—a procession

coterie—a clique

countermand—to revoke (an order)

coup d'etat—an overthrow of a government

covenant—an agreement

covert—hidden

covetous—envious

cower—to shrink in fear

coy—bashful; reserved; coquettish

cozen—to cheat or deceive

crabbed—ill-tempered

crass—grossly stupid or dull

craven—cowardly

credence—belief

credulous—easily or too easily convinced

creed—a statement of belief, religious or otherwise

crepitate—to crackle

criterion—a standard for judging

crone—a hag

crony—a close companion

crux—a problem; the deciding point

cryptic—hidden

cudgel—a stick or club

culinary—pertaining to the kitchen or cooking

cull—to pick or select

culminate—the highest point

culpable—blameworthy

cumbersome—burdensome; clumsy

cuneate—wedge-shaped

cupidity—greed

curmudgeon—a bad-tempered person

curry—to try to obtain favor by flattery

cursory—superficial

curtail—to cut short

cynic—a person who believes all actions are motivated by selfishness

D

dais—a platform in a hall or room

dally—to play or trifle; to waste time

dank—damp

dastard—a mean coward

daunt—to intimidate

dauntless—bold

dearth—scarcity

debacle—an overwhelming defeat or failure

debase—to lower in dignity, quality, or value

debauch—to corrupt

debilitate—to weaken

debonair—courteous; gay

decadence—decay

decamp—to break camp; to run away

deciduous—falling off at a certain time or yearly (as leaves from trees)

decimate—to kill a large part of

declivity—a downgrade; a slope

decorous—proper

decoy—a lure or bait

decrepit—weak from age

decry—to speak against publicly

deduce—to reason out logically; to conclude from known facts

de facto—actual

defalcate—to misuse money left in one's care; to embezzle

defamation—slander

default—neglect; failure to do what is required

defection—desertion

deference—regard for another's wishes

defile—to make dirty or pollute; to dishonor

definitive—conclusive; distinguishing

deflect—to turn aside; to deviate

defunct—dead; no longer operating

deign—to condescend

delete—to strike out or erase

deleterious—harmful

delineate—to sketch or design; to portray

delude—to mislead

delusion—a false belief

demagogue—one who stirs people up by emotional appeal in order to gain power

demarcate—to mark the limits of

demean—to degrade

demeanor—bearing or behavior

demise—death

demolition—destruction

demonic—pertaining to a demon or demons

demur—to delay; to object

demure—serious; prim

denizen—an inhabitant

denouement—the outcome or solution of a plot

depict—to portray

depilate—to rid of hair

deplete—to reduce or exhaust

deplore—to lament or feel sorry about

deploy—to station forces or troops in a planned way

depravity—corruption

deprecate—to express disapproval of

depreciate—to lessen in value

depredate—to plunder or despoil

deranged—insane

derelict—abandoned

deride—to mock; to laugh at

derogatory—expressing a low opinion

descant—to discuss at length

descry—to detect (something distant or obscure)

desecrate—to make profane

desiccate—to dry up

desist—to stop

despicable—contemptible

despoil—to strip; to pillage

despotism—tyranny

destitute—lacking; in extreme need of things

desuetude—state of disuse

desultory—aimless; random

deterrent—something that discourages (someone) from an action

detonate—to explode

detraction—belittling the worth of something or someone

detriment—injury; hurt

deviate—to turn aside

devious—winding; going astray

devoid—lacking

devolve—to transfer to another person

devout—pious

dexterous—skillful

diabolical—devilish

diadem—a crown

diapason—the entire range of musical sounds

diaphanous—transparent or translucent

diatribe—a bitter denunciation

dichotomy—a division into two parts

dictum—an authoritative statement

didactic—instructive

diffident—unconfident; timid

diffusion—the act of spreading (something) out in all directions

digress—to turn aside or deviate, especially in writing or speaking

dilapidation—a state of disrepair

dilate—to expand

dilatory—tending to delay; tardy

dilemma—a choice of two unsatisfactory alternatives

dilettante—one who involves himself in the arts as a pastime

diligent—hard-working

diminution—a lessening

dint—means

dire—terrible; fatal; extreme

dirge—funereal music

disavowal—a denial

discernible—able to be seen or distinguished

discerning—having good judgment; astute

disclaim—to disown

discomfit—to frustrate the plans of

disconcert—to upset or confuse

disconsolate—sad; dejected

discordant—not harmonious

discountenance—to make ashamed; to discourage

discreet—showing good judgment in conduct; prudent

discrete—separate; not connected

discretion—individual judgment; quality of being discreet

discursive—passing from one subject to another

disdain—to think (someone or something) unworthy

disheveled—messy

disingenuous—insincere

disinterested—not influenced by personal advantage

disjointed—disconnected

disparage—to belittle

disparity—inequality

disperse—to scatter or distribute

disport—to amuse or divert

disputatious—inclined to dispute

disquisition—a formal inquiry; an elaborate essay

dissemble—to disguise or pretend

disseminate—to scatter

dissident—not agreeing

dissimulate—to dissemble; to pretend

dissipate—to scatter or disperse

dissolute—loose in morals

dissonance—discord

dissuade—to advise against; to divert by persuasion

distend—to expand

distrait—absent-minded; preoccupied

distraught—troubled; confused; harassed

diurnal—daily

diverge—to extend from one point in separate directions

diverse—differing; various

divest—to strip or deprive

divination—the act of foreseeing or foretelling

divulge—to reveal

docile—easy to teach or discipline

doff—to take off

doggerel—poorly written verse

dogma—a belief or doctrine; a positive statement of opinion

dogmatic—positive in manner or in what one says

doldrums—low spirits

dolorous—sorrowful

dolt—a stupid fellow

domicile—a home

dormant—sleeping; inactive

dorsal—pertaining to the back

dossier—collected docments on a person

dotage—senility

doughty—valiant

dour—stern; sullen

dregs—sediment; the most worthless part of some-thing

drivel—silly talk

droll—amusing and strange

dross—waste or refuse

drudgery—tiresome work

dubious—doubtful

ductile—able to be drawn or hammered thin without breaking

dulcet—sweet-sounding

duplicity—deception; double-dealing

durance—imprisonment

duress—imprisonment; compulsion

E

ebullient—enthusiastic

eccentricity—oddity

éclat—brilliant success; acclaim

eclectic—made up of material collected from many sources

ecumenical—universal; intended to bring together the Christian churches

edict—a decree

edifice—a (usually large) building

edify—to instruct and improve

educe—to elicit or draw forth

efface—to rub out

effectual—efficient

effervesce—to bubble; to be lively or boisterous

effete—exhausted; worn out

efficacy—power to have effect

elligy—an image or figure that represents a disliked person

effluence—a flowing forth

effrontery—shameless boldness

effulgent—radiant

effusive—pouring out; gushing

egotism—constant reference to oneself

egregious—flagrant

egress—emergence; exit

elation—high spirits

eleemosynary—pertaining to charity

elegy—a poem, particularly a lament for the dead

elicit—to draw out

elucidate—to explain; to throw light on

elusive—hard to grasp

emaciated—very thin

emanate—to flow forth

embellish—to ornament or beautify

embody—to give bodily form to; to make concrete

embroil—to confuse by discord; to involve in confusion

embryonic—undeveloped

emend—to correct

eminent—lofty; distinguished

emollient—something that soothes or softens (the body)

emolument—one's fees or salary

empirical—based on observation or experience

empyreal—heavenly

emulate—to imitate with the hope of equaling or surpassing

enclave—an area enclosed inside a foreign territory

encomium—high praise

encompass—to encircle; to contain

encroach—to trespass

encumber—to impede or burden

endemic—native to a particular area

endue—to invest or endow

enervate—to weaken

engender—to cause or produce

engrossed—absorbed; fully occupied

engulf—to swallow up or overwhelm

enhance—to make greater; to heighten

enigma—a puzzle

enjoin—to order; to prohibit

ennui—boredom

enormity—great wickedness

ensconce—to shelter; to settle comfortably

ensue—to follow right after

enthrall—to captivate

entity—a being or thing

entourage—a group of associates or attendants

entreaty—a serious request

entrepreneur—a man of business

envenom—to make poisonous; to embitter

environs—surroundings; vicinity

ephemeral—short-lived

epicure—a connoisseur of food and drink

epigram—a short, pointed poem or saying

epistle—a long, formal letter

epithet—a descriptive phrase; an uncomplimentary name

epitome—an abstract; a part that represents the whole

epoch—a period of time

equable—uniform; tranquil

equanimity—even temper

equestrian—pertaining to horses

equilibrium—a state of balance between various forces or factors

equity—fairness

equivocal—ambiguous; doubtful

equivocate—to deceive; to lie

erode—to eat away

errant—wandering

erudite—scholarly

escarpment—a steep slope

eschew—to avoid

esculent—edible

esoteric—for a limited, specially initiated group

espouse—to marry; to advocate (a cause)

esprit de corps—group spirit

estimable—worthy of respect or esteem

estival—pertaining to summer

estranged—separated

ethereal—celestial; spiritual

ethnic—pertaining to races or cultures

eugenic—pertaining to the bearing of genetically healthy offspring

eulogy—high praise

euphemism—an inoffensive expression substituted for an unpleasant one

euphoria—a feeling of well-being

euthanasia—painless death

evanescent—fleeting

evasive—not frank or straightforward

evince—to make evident; to display

eviscerate—to disembowel

evoke—to call forth

evolve—to develop gradually; to unfold

exacerbate—to make more intense; to aggravate

exact—to call for; to require

exasperate—to vex

excise—to cut away

excoriate—to strip of skin; to denounce harshly

exculpate—to free from blame

execrable—detestable

exemplary—serving as a good example

exhort—to urge

exigency—an emergency

exiguous—meager

exonerate—to acquit

exorbitant—excessive; extravagant

exorcise—to drive out (an evil spirit)

expatiate—to talk freely and at length

expedient—advantageous

expedite—to speed up or make easy

expeditious—efficient and quick

expiate—to atone for

expound—to set forth

expunge—to blot out; to erase

expurgate—to rid (a book) of offensive material

extant—in existence

extemporaneous—not planned

extenuate—to make thin; to diminish

extirpate—to pluck out

extol—to praise

extort—to take from a person by force

extradition—the surrender by one state to another of an alleged criminal

extraneous—not essential

extricate—to free

extrinsic—unessential; extraneous

extrovert—one whose interest is directed outside himself

extrude—to force or push out

exuberant—profuse; effusive

exude—to discharge or ooze; to radiate; to diffuse

F

fabricate—to build; to lie

façade—the front of a building

facet—a small plane of a gem; an aspect

facetious—humorous; joking

facile—easy; expert

facilitate—to make easier

faction—a clique or party

factious—producing or tending to dissension

factitious—artificial

factotum—an employee with many duties

faculty—an ability; a sense

fain—gladly

fallacious—misleading; containing a fallacy

fallible—capable of error

fallow—(land) left unplanted during a growing season

falter—to move unsteadily; to stumble or stammer

fanaticism—excessive enthusiasm

fastidious—hard to please; easy to offend

fatalism—the belief that all events are ruled by fate

fatuous—foolish

fauna—animal life

faux pas—an error in social behavior

fawn—to seek favor by demeaning oneself

fealty—loyalty

feasible—practical

feckless—weak; careless

feculent—filthy; foul

fecundity—fertility; productiveness

feign—to pretend

feint—a move intended to throw one's opponent off guard

felicitous—apt; happy in expression

fell—cruel; fierce

felonious—wicked

ferment—a state of unrest

ferret—to search out

fervent, fervid—hot; ardent

fete—a lavish entertainment, often in someone's honor

fetid—stinking

fetish—an object supposed to have magical power; any object of special devotion

fetter—to shackle or restrain

fettle—state of the body and mind

fiasco—a complete failure

fiat—a command

fickle—changeable

fidelity—faithfulness

fiduciary—pertaining to one who holds something in trust for another

figment—an invention; a fiction

filch—to steal

filial—pertaining to a son or daughter

finale—a conclusion

finesse—skill; cunning

finite—limited

fissure—a narrow opening or cleft

flaccid—flabby

flag—to droop or lose vigor

flagellate—to whip or flog

flagitious—wicked and vile

flagrant—glaring (as an error)

flail—to beat

flamboyant—ornate; showy

flatulent—gas-producing; windy in speech

flaunt—to show off; to display

flay—to skin; to pillage; to censure harshly

fledgling—a young bird that has his feathers; an immature person

flippant—pert

florid—flowery; ornate

flotsam—ship wreckage floating on the sea; drifting persons or things

flout—to reject

fluctuate—to waver

fluent—fluid; easy with words

flux—a moving; a flowing

foible—a failing or weakness

foist—to pass off fraudulently

foment—to stir up

foppish—like a dandy

foray—a raid

forbearance—patience

foreboding—a feeling of coming evil

formidable—threatening

forswear—to renounce

forte—strong point

fortitude—strength; courage

fortuitous—accidental

foster—to rear; to promote

fractious—unruly

fraught—filled

fray—a commotion or fight

freebooter—a plunderer; a pirate

frenetic—frantic; frenzied

frenzy—violent emotional excitement

fresco—a painting done on fresh plaster

freshet—a stream or rush of water

frigid—very cold

fritter—to waste

frivolous—of little importance or value; trivial

froward—obstinate

fructify—to bear fruit

frugal—thrifty

fruition—use or realization; enjoyment

frustrate—to counteract; to prevent from achieving something

fulminate—to explode suddenly; to thunder forth verbally

fulsome—offensive particularly because of insincerity

funereal—appropriate to funerals

furor—a fury or frenzy

furtive—stealthy

fusion—union

futile—useless

G

gadfly—a fly that attacks livestock; a person who annoys people or moves them to action

gainsay—to deny

gambol—to skip and frolic

gamut—the whole range

gape—to open wide

Gargantuan—gigantic

garish—gaudy

garner—to gather or store

garnish—to decorate

garrulous—talkative

gasconade—boastful talk

gelid—icy; frozen

generality—a broad, vague statement

generic—pertaining to a whole class, kind, or group

genial—favorable to growth; kindly

genre—a kind or category

gentility—of the upper classes; having taste and refinement

gentry—people of education and good birth

germane—relevant and pertinent to the case at hand

germinal—in the first stage of growth

gesticulation—gesture

ghastly—horrihle

gibbet—gallows

gibe—to scoff at; to deride

gist—the main point in a debate or question

glaucous—bluish- or yellowish-green

glean—to gather what has been left in a field after reaping; to pick up, little by little

glib—fluent

gloaming—dusk

gloat—to look at with evil satisfaction or greed

glut—to overfill

glutinous—gluey

gluttony—excess in eating

gnarled—twisted

gnomic—wise and pithy

goad—to urge; to drive

gorge—to stuff

gouge—to scoop out; to tear out

gradation—arrangement by grades or steps

gradient—a slope; the degree of a slope

graphic—vivid; pertaining to writing

granary—a storehouse for grain

grandiloquent—using pompous language

grandiose—imposing; splendid

gratis—free

gratuitous—given freely; unwarranted

gregarious—tending to flock together

grimace—an expression that twists the face

grotesque—distorted; bizarre; absurd

grotto—a cave

grovel—to lie prone; to act humble or abject

grueling—punishing

gudgeon—a person who is easy to trick

guerdon—a reward

guile—deceit

guileless—innocent

gullible—easily tricked

gustatory—pertaining to
tasting

gusto—liking; great
appre-ciation or relish

guttural—pertaining to the
throat

H

habiliments—clothing; equipment

habitable—able or fit to be lived in

hackneyed—trite

haggard—unruly; looking worn and wasted from exertion or emotion

haggle—to bargain

halcyon—peaceful

hale—healthy and sound

hallucination—a perception of something imaginary

hamper—to obstruct or hinder

haphazard—random

hapless—unlucky

harangue—a long speech; a tirade

harass—to worry or torment

harbinger—a forerunner

harp—to persist in talking or writing (about something)

harridan—a shrewish old woman

harrow—to rob or plunder

harry—to raid; to torment or worry

haughty—showing scorn for others; proud

hauteur—haughtiness

hawser—a large rope or cable for mooring or anchoring a ship

hector—to bully

hedonism—the pursuit of pleasure as the primary goal of life

heedless—careless; unmindful

hegemony—leadership; dominance

heinous—abominable

herbaceous—pertaining to herbs or leaves

herculean—of great size, strength, or courage

heresy—a religious belief opposed hy the church

heterodox—unorthodox; inclining toward heresy

heterogeneous—dissimilar; varied

hiatus—a gap or break

hibernal—pertaining to winter

hierarchy—an arrangement in order of rank

hieratic—priestly

hieroglyphic—written in symbols; hard to read or understand

hilarity—mirth

hinder—to restrain or hold back

hirsute—hairy

histrionic—theatrical

hoary—white; white-haired

holocaust—destruction by fire

homage—allegiance or honor

homicide—the killing of one person by another

homily—a long, dull sermon

homogeneous—similar; uniform

hone—to sharpen

hortatory—encouraging; giving advice

horticulture—the growing of plants

hybrid—of mixed or unlike parts

hydrous—containing water

hyperbole—exaggeration

hypercritical—too critical

hypochondriac—one who constantly believes he is ill

hypocritical—pretending to be what one is not

hypothetical—assumed; supposed

I

iconoclast—one who attacks traditional ideas

ideology—a body of ideas

idiom—a language or dialect; a particular phrasing that is accepted in use, although its meaning may be different from the literal meaning of the words

idiosyncrasy—a personal peculiarity

idolatry—worship

idyll—a poem based on a simple scene

igneous—pertaining to or produced by fire

ignoble—dishonorable; base

ignominious—shameful; degrading

illicit—unlawful; prohibited

illusory—unreal; deceptive

imbibe—to drink, drink in, or absorb

imbroglio—a confusion; a misunderstanding

imbue—to color; to inspire (with ideas)

immaculate—spotless; clean

immanent—existing within

imminent—about to happen

immolate—to sacrifice

immutable—unchangeable

impair—to make worse or weaker; to reduce

impale—to fix on a pointed object

impalpable—not capable of being felt; not capable of being grasped by the mind

impasse—a situation with no escape or solution

impassive—not feeling pain; calm

impeccable—faultless

impecunious—poor; penniless

impede—to obstruct or delay

impending—about to happen

impenitent—without regret

imperious—domineering

impermeable—unable to be penetrated

impertinent—irrelevant; impudent

imperturbable—unable to be disturbed; impassive

impervious—impenetrable; not affected (by something)

impetuous—rushing; rash or impulsive

impetus—a force; a driving force

impiety—lack of reverence (for God or parents)

implacable—incapable of being pacified

implicate—to involve; to imply

implicit—implied; absolute

impolitic—unwise

import—meaning; significance

importune—to urge persistently

impotent—weak; powerless

imprecate—to pray for (evil)

impregnable—unable to be conquered or entered

impresario—a manager in the performing arts

impromptu—offhand

impropriety—being improper

improvident—not providing for the future

impugn—to oppose or challenge

impunity—freedom from punishment or harm

impute—to charge another (with a negative trait)

inadvertent—heedless; unintentional

inane—empty; foolish

inarticulate—unable to speak understandably or at all

incantation—a chant supposed to work magic

incapacitate—to disable

incarcerate—to imprison

incendiary—pertaining to destruction by fire

inception—beginning

incessant—never-ending

inchoate—just begun; incipient

incipient—in the first stage of existence

incisive—keen, sharp

inclement—stormy; harsh

incognito—disguised

incongruous—incompatible; inappropriate

inconsequential—unimportant

incontrovertible—undeniable

incorrigible—unreformable

increment—increase; the amount of increase

incriminate—to accuse of a crime; to involve in a crime

incubus—a nightmare; an oppressive burden

inculcate—to instill

inculpate—to incriminate

incursion—an inroad; a brief raid

indefatigable—untiring

indemnify—to insure; to reimburse

indict—to charge formally with

indigenous—growing or living in a particular area

indite—to compose and write

indolent—lazy; idle

indomitable—hard to discourage or defeat

indubitable—unquestionable

indulgent—giving in to one's own desires; kind or lenient

indurate—hardened

ineffable—inexpressible

ineluctable—unavoidable

inept—unfit; clumsy

inert—powerless to move; slow

inexorable—unrelenting; unalterable

infallible—incapable of error

infamous—notorious

inference—something that is drawn as a conclusion

infernal—pertaining to hell; diabolical

infidel—one who doesn't believe in a particular doctrine or religion

infinite—limitless; vast

infirmity—weakness

influx—a flowing in

infringe—to violate

ingenious—having genius; clever; original

ingenuous—candid; frank

ingrate—an ungrateful person

ingratiate—to win another's favor by efforts

inherent—innate; characteristic

inhibit—to hold back or repress

inimical—hostile; in opposition

iniquitous—wicked

injunction—a command; an order enjoining or prohibiting (someone) from doing something

innate—existing in someone from birth or in something by its nature

innocuous—harmless; noncontroversial

innuendo—an indirect remark or reference

inordinate—unregulated; immoderate

inscrutable—obscure; not easily understood

insensate—not feeling; inanimate; insensitive

insidious—crafty

insinuate—to work gradually into a state; to hint

insipid—tasteless; dull

insolent—impudent; disrespectful

insolvent—bankrupt; unable to pay debts

insouciant—carefree; indifferent

instigate—to urge on to some action; to incite

insular—like an island; isolated; narrowminded

insuperable—unable to be overcome

insurgent—a person who rises up against (political) authority

intangible—unable to be touched; impalpable

integrity—wholeness; soundness; honesty

intelligentsia—intellectuals as a group

inter—to bury

interdict—to prohibit; to restrain or impede

interim—meantime

interjection—something thrown in or interrupted with; an exclamation

intermittent—periodic; starting and stopping

internecine—mutually harmful or destructive

interpolate—to insert

interregnum—a break, as between governments or regimes

intestate—without a (legal) will to distribute one's property after death

intimate—to hint

intractable—unruly or stubborn

intransigent—refusing to agree or compromise

intrepid—fearless

intrinsic—inherent; of the nature of a thing

introvert—a person who looks inside himself more than outside

intuition—immediate understanding

inundate—to flood

inured—habituated (to something unpleasant)

invective—a violent verbal attack

inveigh—to talk or write strongly (against)

inveigle—to trick or entice

inverse—opposite

investiture—the giving of office to someone

inveterate—of long standing

invidious—offensive

inviolable—not to be violated; unable to be violated

invulnerable—unable to be injured or wounded

iota—a tiny amount

irascible—quick-tempered

irksome—tiresome; annoying

irony—humor in which one says the opposite of what he means; an occurrence that is the opposite of what is expected

irremediable—incurahle or irreparable

irrevocable—unable to be called back or undone

iterate—to repeat

itinerant—traveling

J

jaded—tired; satiated

jargon—incoherent speech; a mixed language; the particular vocabulary of one group

jaundiced—yellow; prejudiced

jeopardy—peril

jettison—to throw overboard

jetty—a wall built out into the water

jocose—humorous

jocular—joking

jocund—cheerful

journeyman—a worker who has learned a trade

judicious—wise

juggernaut—any extremely strong and irresistible force

juncture—a point of joining; a critical point in the development of events

junket—a feast or picnic; a pleasure excursion

junta—men engaged in political intrigue

juxtapose—to place side by side

K

ken—understanding

kinetic—pertaining to motion

kith—friends

knavery—dishonesty; deceit

knell—to ring solemnly

knoll—a small hill

L

labyrinth—a maze

lacerate—to tear or mangle

lachrymose—tearful

lackadaisical—spiritless; listless

laconic—brief; using few words

lacuna—a gap where something is missing

laggard—one who is slow

laity—all the people who are not clergy

lambent—flickering; glowing

lampoon—to attack or ridicule

languid—weak; listless

languish—to lose vigor; to droop

larceny—theft

largess—generosity

lascivious—lewd: lustful

lassitude—weariness

latent—hidden or undeveloped

lateral—pertaining to the side or sides

latitude—freedom to act

laudatory—praising

leaven—to spread something throughout something else to bring about a gradual change

lecherous—lustful

legerdemain—trickery

lesion—an injury

lethal—deadly

lethargic—dull; sluggish

levity—gaiety

liaison—a linking up

libel—false printed material intended to harm a per-son's reputation

libertine—one who lives a morally unrestrained life

libidinous—lustful; lewd

licentious—morally unrestrained

liege—a name for a feudal lord or his subject

lieu—place (in lieu of)

limn—to paint or draw; to describe in words

limpid—clear

literal—word-for-word; actual

lithe—flexible; limber

litigation—carrying out a lawsuit

littoral—pertaining to the shore or coast

livid—black-and-blue; lead-colored

loath—reluctant

loathe—to detest

locution—a word or phrase; a style of speech

logistics—the part of military science having to do with obtaining and moving men and material

longevity—long life

loquacious—talkative

lout—a stupid person

lubricity—smoothness; trickiness

lucent—shining; giving off light

lucid—transparent; clear

lucrative—profitable

lucre—money

ludicrous—absurd

lugubrious—mournful

luminary—a body that sheds light; a person who enlightens; any famous person

lurid—sensational

lustrous—shining

luxuriant—lush; rich

M

macabre—gruesome; horrible

macerate—to soften by soaking; to break or tear into small pieces

Machiavellian—crafty and deceitful

machination—a secret plot or scheme

magnanimous—generous; not petty

magnate—an important person, often in a business

magniloquent—lofty or pompous

maim—to disable or mutilate (a person)

maladroit—clumsy

malaise—a vague feeling of illness

malcontent—discontented

malediction—a curse

malefactor—one who does evil

malevolent—wishing ill to others

malfeasance—a wrongdoing

malicious—spiteful

malign—to slander

malignant—evil; harmful

malinger—to pretend to be ill to avoid doing something

malleable—able to be hammered; pliable

mammoth—enormous

mandate—an official order or command

mandatory—required

maniacal—insane; raving

manifest—apparent or evident

manipulate—to work with the hands; to control by unfair means

manumission—liberation from slavery

marauder—a raider

maritime—pertaining to the sea

martial—pertaining to war or the military; warlike

martinet—a strict disciplinarian

masochist—one who enjoys suffering

masticate—to chew up

maternal—pertaining to a mother or motherhood

matrix—a die or mold

maudlin—foolishly sentimental

maunder—to act dreamily or vaguely

mauve—purple

maverick—one who refuses to go along with his group

mawkish—sickeningly sweet

maxim—a principle or truth precisely stated; a saying

mayhem—maiming another person; violence or destruction

meander—to wind or wander

mecca—a place where many people visit

mediate—to help two opposing sides come to agreement

mediocre—ordinary; average

mélange—a mixture

melee—a noisy fight among a lot of people

meliorate—to improve

mellifluous—sweet and smooth

mendacious—lying

mendicant—a beggar

menial—pertaining to servants; servile

mentor—a wise advisor or teacher

mercantile—pertaining to merchants or trade

mercenary—motivated by money; greedy

mercurial—like mercury; quick; changeable

meretricious—superficially alluring

mesa—a high, flat land with steep sides

metamorphosis—a change or transformation

metaphysical—pertaining to the nature of being or reality

mete—to distribute

meticulous—very careful about details

mettle—quality of character, especially good character

miasma—a vapor rising from a swamp; an unwholesome atmosphere

mien—manner or bearing

migrant—a person or an animal that moves from place to place

militate—to work (against)

mimetic—imitative

mimic—to imitate

minatory—threatening

mincing—acting overly dainty or elegant

minion—a favorite (follower); a subordinate

ministration—the carrying out of a minister's duties; service

minutiae—minor details

misadventure—a bit of bad luck

misanthrope—one who dislikes other people

misapprehension—misunderstanding

miscegenation—marriage between a man and a woman of different races

miscellany—a collection of varied things

misconstrue—to misinterpret

miscreant—an evil person

misdemeanor—a minor offense

misgiving—a doubt or fear

mishap—an unfortunate accident

misnomer—the wrong name applied to something

misogynist—one who hates women

mitigate—to make less painful

mnemonic—helping the memory

mobile—capable of moving or being moved

mode—a manner or style

modicum—a bit

modish—in style

modulate—to adjust or regulate

moiety—a share

mollify—to pacify

molt—to shed skin or other outer parts

molten—melted

momentous—very important

monetary—pertaining to money

monolith—a large piece of stone

moot—debatable

morbid—pertaining to disease; gruesome

mordant—biting; sarcastic

mores—ways or customs that are quite important to a culture

moribund—dying

morose—gloomy

mortify—to punish (oneself) by self-denial; to make (someone) feel ashamed

mote—a speck

motif—a main feature or theme

motility—ability to move by itself

motley—of many colors; made up of many unlike parts

mountebank—a quack

mufti—civilian clothes

mulet—to fine; to get money from someone by deceit

multiplicity—a great number (of various things)

mundane—worldly; commonplace

munificent—generous; lavish

muse—to ponder

mutable—changeable

mute—silent

mutilate—to damage by cutting off or injuring vital parts

mutinous—inclined to rebel or revolt

myopia—nearsightedness

myriad—a great number

N

nadir—the lowest point

naiad—a water nymph; a female swimmer

naiveté—simplicity; lack of sophistication

narcissism—love for and interest in the self

nascent—being born; starting to develop

natal—pertaining to one's birth

nauseous—sickening

nebulous—vague; indefinite

necromancy—black magic

nefarious—wicked

negation—denial; the absence of a positive quality

negligible—so unimportant that it can be neglected

nemesis—fair punishment; something that seems to defeat a person constantly

neolithic—pertaining to the Stone Age

neophyte—a beginner

nepotism—special consideration to relatives, particularly in assignment to offices or positions

nettle—to sting; to irritate or annoy

neurosis—a mental disorder

nexus—a connection

nicety—exactness and delicacy

niggardly—stingy

nihilist—one who believes there is no basis for knowledge; one who rejects common religious beliefs

nocturnal—pertaining to night

noisome—harmful; offensive

nomadic—moving from place to place

nomenclature—a system for naming

nominal—pertaining to names; slight

nonchalant—cool; indifferent

noncommittal—not aligning oneself with any side or point of view

nondescript—having few distinguishing qualities; hard to classify

nonentity—something that exists only in the mind; something or someone of little importance

nonpareil—without equal

nonplus—to perplex

non sequitur—something that does not follow logically from what went before

nostalgia—homesickness

notorious—well-known (often unfavorably)

novice—a beginner

noxious—harmful; unwhole-some

nuance—a slight variation of color, tone, etc.

nugatory—worthless

nullify—to make invalid or useless

nurture—to feed and/or raise (a child)

nutrient—a food

O

oaf—a clumsy, stupid person

obdurate—hardhearted; hardened; inflexible

obeisance—a motion of reverence

obese—very fat

obfuscate—to make unclear; to confuse

objurgate—to rebuke

oblation—an offering

oblique—slanting; indirect

obliquity—the state of being oblique

obliterate—to wipe out

oblivion—forgetfulness

obloquy—verbal abuse or the disgrace that results from it

obnoxious—offensive

obscure—dim; unclear

obsequious—too servile or submissive

obsession—an idea that persists in the mind

obsolete—out-of-date; no longer used

obstreperous—unruly

obtrude—to push out

obtrusive—pushy in calling attention to oneself

obtuse—blunt; dull

obviate—to make unnecessary

occlude—to close; to shut in or out

occult—hidden; secret; mysterious

odious—offensive

odoriferous—having a (pleasant) odor

odyssey—a long journey

officious—providing help that is not wanted

ogle—to look at openly and with desire

oleaginous—oily

olfactory—pertaining to the sense of smell

oligarchy—a slate ruled by a few persons

ominous—threatening

omnipotent—all-powerful

omniscient—all-knowing

omnivorous—eating both animals and vegetables

onerous—burdensome

onslaught—an attack

opaque—letting no light through

opiate—a medicine or anything else that quiets and deadens

opportune—at the right time

opprobrium—disgrace

optimum—best

opulence—wealth; abundance

oracular—wise; prophetic

ordure—filth

orifice—a mouth or opening

ornate—heavily decorated; showy

ornithologist—one who studies birds

orthodox—holding the accepted beliefs of a particular group

oscillate—to move back and forth

osculate—to kiss

ossify—to harden into bone; to settle into a habit

ostensible—apparent

ostentatious—showy; pretentious

ostracize—to banish or exclude

overt—open; observable

overweening—extremely proud

P

pacifist—one who opposes war

paean—a song of joy or praise

palatable—suitable for eating

palatial—like a palace

palaver—idle talk

pall—to become boring or otherwise bothersome

palliate—to lessen or ease (pain); to excuse

pallid—pale

palpable—able to be felt or to be grasped by the senses

paltry—insignificant

panacea—a cure-all

pander—to cater to another's unworthy desires, especially sexual

panegyric—a formal tribute

panoply—a suit of armor; a protective or showy covering

paradigm—an example or model

paradox—a statement that appears false but may be true; a statement that contradicts itself and is false

paragon—a model of perfection

paramount—chief; dominant

paranoia—a state in which one believes that others are against him or that he is a great or famous person

paraphernalia—personal possessions; equipment or gear

parasite—one who lives off another without giving anything in return

paregoric—a medicine

pariah—an outcast

parity—equality

parlance—a manner of speaking or writing

paroxysm—an attack or convulsion

parricide—the killing of a parent

parry—to ward off (a blow); to evade

parsimony—stinginess

partiality—bias; prejudice

parvenu—one who has risen in wealth or power quickly

passive—yielding; nonresisting

pastoral—pertaining to shepherds or rural life in general

patent—obvious

pathetic—pitiful

pathos—a feeling of pity or sorrow

patriarch—a father and ruler

patricide—the killing of one's father

patrimony—an inheritance

paucity—scarcity

pecadillo—a minor fault

peculate—to embezzle

pecuniary—pertaining to money

pedagogue—a teacher, often a narrow-minded one

pedantic—narrow-minded in teaching

pedestrian—ordinary and uninteresting

pejorative—derogatory

pellucid—clear; easy to understand

penance—voluntary self-punishment

penchant—a taste or liking

pendant—something that hangs

pendent—hanging

penitent—sorry or ashamed

pensive—thoughtful

penurious—stingy; poverty-stricken

penury—poverty

percussion—the impact of one thing against another

perdition—damnation; hell

peregrinations—travels

peremptory—final; undeniable or unopposable; dictatorial

perennial—lasting all through the year; lasting a long time

perfidious—treacherous

perforce—necessarily

perfunctory—without care; superficial

perigee—the point nearest the earth in an orbit

peripatetic—moving or walking about

periphery—the boundary of something; the perimeter

perjury—telling a lie under oath

permeable—able to be passed through

permeate—to pass through; to spread through

permutation—a complete change

pernicious—deadly

perpetrate—to do (something bad)

perpetual—eternal

perquisite—a benefit in addition to one's regular pay; prerogative

persiflage—a light style of talking; banter

perspective—the appearance of things caused by their positions and distances; a way of seeing things in their true relation to each other

perspicacious—keen; acute in judgment

pertinacious—persistent

pertinent—relevant

perturb—to upset or alarm

peruse—to study; to read casually

pervade—to spread throughout

perverse—wrong or corrupt; perverted; stubborn

perversion—an abnormal-form; a twisting or distortion

pervious—able to be passed

through or penetrated; open-minded

pessimist—one who looks on the dark side and expects the worst

pestilence—an epidemic; anything harmful

petrify—to turn to stone; to harden; to stun with fear

petulant—pert; irritable

phalanx—military ranks in close formation; a group of individuals

philander—to carry on light love affairs

philanthropist—one who gives money to help others

philistine—a narrow and conventional person who ignores the arts and culture

phlegmatic—sluggish; calm

phobia—an irrational, unwarranted fear (of something)

physiognomy—one's face and facial expressions

pied—spotted

piety—truthfulness to religious duties; devotion to family

pillage—to loot or plunder

pinion—to cut or tie a bird's wings to keep it from flying; to bind a man's arms; to shackle

pious—devout

piquant—sharp or biting to the taste; stimulating

pique—to offend or provoke

pithy—meaningful; concise

pittance—a meager amount

placate—to pacify

placid—calm; quiet

plaintive—mournful

plait—to pleat or braid

platitude—a dull or commonplace remark

platonic—intellectual or spiritual but not sexual (relationship)

plaudit—applause; an expression of approval

plausible—apparently true

plebeian—a common man

plebiscite—a vote by the people on a political issue

plenary—full; complete

plenipotentiary—a man who has full power as a governmental representative

plethora—excess

plutocracy—government by the wealthy

poach—to trespass; to steal

pogrom—a systematic persecution or killing of a group

poignant—sharply affecting the senses or feelings

politic—prudent; crafty

poltroon—a coward

polygamy—having more than one husband or wife

polyglot—speaking or writing several languages

pommel—the knob on the end of a sword or on a saddle

pompous—stately; self-important

ponder—to consider carefully

portend—to foreshadow

portent—an omen

portly—stout

posit—to place in position; to set forth as fact

posterity—all future generations

posthumous—born after one's father is dead; published after the writer's death; happening after death

postprandial—after dinner

potable—drinkable

potentate—a ruler

potential—possible; latent

potpourri—a collection of varied things

poultice—a hot, soft mass, sometimes put on sore parts of the body

practicable—feasible; usable

pragmatic—practical; dealing with daily matters

prate—to chatter

precarious—uncertain; risky

precedent—a legal occurrence that is an example for future ones

precept—a rule of conduct

precipitate—to throw downward, to bring on

precipitous—like a precipice; abrupt

preclude—to make impossible; to prevent

precocious—developing earlier than usual

precursor—a forerunner

predatory—living by robbing or exploiting others; feeding on other animals

predicate—to state as a quality of someone or something; to affirm

predilection—a preference

predispose—to make receptive

preeminent—better than others in a particular quality

prefatory—introductory

prelude—opening

premeditate—to think out ahead of time

premise—a statement on which an argument is based

premonition—a forewarning; a foreboding

preponderate—to sink downward; to predominate

preposterous—absurd

prerogative—a right or privilege

presage—to warn; to predict

prescience—foreknowledge

presentiment—a premonition or foreboding

presumption—taking something upon oneself without permission; forwardness

pretentious—claiming greatness; showing off

preternatural—abnormal; supernatural

prevaricate—to avoid the truth; to lie

primordial—existing from the beginning; original

pristine—in original condition; pure and unspoiled

privy (to)—told about (something) in secret

probity—honesty

proboscis—a long snout; a nose

proclivity—a slope; a tendency

procrastinate—to delay or postpone

prodigal—wasteful; generous

prodigious—wonderful; huge

profane—nonreligious; irreverent

proffer—to offer

proficient—skilled

profligate—immoral; wasteful

profound—very deep

profusion—a great abundance

progenitor—a forefather

progeny—children or descendants

prognosis—a forecast

proletarian—a worker

prolific—producing a lot (of children, fruit, or ideas)

prolix—wordy; longwinded

promiscuous—containing many various elements; engaging in indiscriminate sexual affairs

promontory—a headland

promulgate—to make known

prone—lying face downward; disposed (to do something)

propagate—to breed or reproduce

propensity—a natural tendency

propinquity—nearness; kinship

propitiate—to appease

propitious—gracious; boding well; advantageous

proponent—one who puts forth an idea

propound—to propose

propriety—suitability

prosaic—commonplace

proscribe—to outlaw or forbid

prosody—the study or the art of verse or versification

prostrate—lying face downward; overcome

protege—one who is helped in his career by another

protocol—a document outlining points of agreement; a system of proper conduct in diplomatic encounters

prototype—a model

protract—to prolong

protrude—to stick out

protuberant—sticking out

provident—providing for future needs

proviso—a condition (that one must meet)

provoke—to excite; to anger

prowess—boldness; skill

proximity—nearness

proxy—a person who acts for another

prudent—careful; wise

puerile—childish

pugnacious—quarrelsome

puissant—powerful

pulchritude—beauty

pulmonary—pertaining to the lungs

punctilious—careful about detail; exact

pungent—sharp: biting

punitive—pertaining to punishment

purloin—to steal

purport—to claim

purveyor—one who supplies

purview—scope; range

pusillanimous—timid; uncourageous

putative—reputed

putrid—rotten; stinking

Q

quack—one who practices medicine without training; a charlatan

quaff—to drink

quagmire—a bog; a difficult situation

quail—to lose courage

qualm—a sudden ill feeling; a sudden misgiving

quandary—a dilemma

queasy—nauseous; uneasy

quell—to subdue; to quiet

querulous—complaining

query—a question

quibble—to object to something for petty reasons

quiescent—inactive

quietude—quiet; rest

quintessence—the most perfect example

quip—a witty remark

quirk—a twist (as of luck); an evasion; a peculiarity

quixotic—like Don Quixote; romantic and idealistic

quizzical—comical; teasing; questioning

R

rabble—a mob; the masses

rabid—violent; fanatical

raillery—satire; leasing

raiment—clothing

ramification—a branching; a consequence or result of something

rampant—growing or spreading richly; wild and uncontrollable in behavior

rancid—spoiled, as stale fat

rancor—hate

rankle—to provoke anger or rancor

rant—to rave

rapacious—greedy; predatory

rapine—taking away people's property by force; plunder

rapprochement—a bringing together

rarefied—thin; refined

ratiocination—reasoning

rationalize—to explain rationally; to find motives for one's behavior that are not the true ones

raucous—loud and rowdy

ravage—to ruin

ravening—look greedily for prey

ravenous—extremely hungry

rebate—to return (part of money paid); to deduct (from a bill)

rebuke—to scold sharply

recalcitrant—stubborn; hard to handle

recant—to take back (a belief or statement)

recapitulate—to summarize

recidivist—one who falls back into crime or other bad behavior

reciprocal—done in return; occurring on both sides

recision—the act of rescinding

recluse—one who lives apart from others

reconcile—to bring together again; to make consistent

recondite—not understandable by most people; obscure

reconnaissance—looking over a situation to get-information

recourse—turning to (someone or something) for help

recreant—cowardly; disloyal

recrimination—answering an attack by attacking in return

rectify—to make right

rectitude—moral uprightness

recumbent—lying down; resting

recurrent—happening again one or more times

redeem—to get back; to save from sin; to make (oneself) worthy again by making amends

redolent—sweet-smelling

redoubtable—fearful

redress—to rectify

redundant—more than enough; wordy

refection—refreshment

refraction—the bending of a light ray or sound wave

refractory—stubborn

refulgent—shining

refutation—disproof

regale—to entertain with a feast

regeneration—renewal; rebirth

regime—a system or period of government

regimen—a system of diet and other physical care designed to aid the health

regressive—going backward

reimburse—to pay back

reiterate—to repeat over and over

rejuvenate—to make seem young again

relegate—to send away (to someplace)

relevant—pertaining to the matter in question

relinquish—to give (something) up

relish—to enjoy

remediable—curable; correctable

reminisce—to remember

remiss—careless in one's duty

remission—forgiveness; a letting up

remnant—remainder

remonstrate—to protest

remunerative—profitable

render—to give over; to give up; to cause to become

renegade—one who gives up his religion or cause and joins the opposition

renounce—to give up (a right, for example)

renovate—to renew

reparable—able to be repaired

reparation—a repairing; making up for a wrong

repartee—a clever reply; clever conversation back and forth

repast—a meal

repercussion—an effect of an event

repertoire—the selection of works a performer or group is prepared to perform

replenish—to refill

replete—full; stuffed

repository—a place where things are kept

reprehensible—deserving criticism

reprieve—a postponement of punishment

reprimand—a formal rebuke

reprisal—force used in retaliation for an act by another country

reproach—to make (someone) feel ashamed

reprobate—a person of no principles

reprove—to rebuke or disapprove

repudiate—to disown; to deny

repugnant—contradictory; offensive

requiem—a Mass or music for the dead

requisite—required

requite—to return or repay

rescind—to repeal (an order)

resilient—elastic; buoyant

respite—a delay; a letup

resplendent—splendid

restitution—restoration; reimbursement

restive—balky; unruly; restless

resurgent—rising again

resuscitate—to revive

retaliate—to return injury or evil in kind

retentive—holding; able to remember

reticent—speaking very little

retinue—a group of followers or attendants

retort—to answer in kind; to reply sharply or cleverly

retract—to take back

retribution—just punishment or reward

retrieve—to recover (something); to save

retroactive—applying to the past

retrograde—going backward

retrospective—looking backward

revelry—merrymaking

reverberate—to echo

reverie—a daydream

revert—to go back to a former state

revile—to abuse; to scold

revoke—to withdraw; to rescind

revulsion—a sudden change in feeling; disgust

rheumy—watery

ribald—vulgar; coarse

rife—occurring everywhere; plentiful

rigor—strictness; exactness

risible—laughable

risqué—daring

robust—healthy and strong

rococo—an elaborate architectural style

roseate—rosy; cheerful

rote—routine

rotund—rounded; stout

rubicund—reddish

rudiment—a basic principle; a first stage

rueful—pitiable; mournful

ruminate—to ponder

rummage—to search through

ruse—a trick

ruthless—cruel

S

sable—black

saccharine—pertaining to sugar; too sweet

sacerdotal—priestly

sacrilegious—in violation of something sacred

sacrosanct—holy; not to be violated

sadist—one who gets pleasure from hurting others

sagacious—perceptive; shrewd

sage—wise

salacious—lecherous; pornographic

salient—leaping; standing out; prominent

saline—salty

sallow—having a sickly, yellowish coloring

salubrious—healthful

salutary—conducive to good health

sanctity—holiness

sang-froid—coolness; calmness

sanguine—blood-colored; cheerful and optimistic

sapient—wise

sardonic—sarcastic

sartorial—pertaining to tailors or clothing

sate—to safisfy completely

satiate—to glut

saturate—to soak

saturnine—gloomy

savant—a scholar

savoir faire—tact

savor—to season; to taste or smell appreciatively

scabrous—scaly; improper

scapegoat—one who is blamed for the wrongs of another

scathing—harsh; biting

schism—a split

scintilla—a tiny bit

scintillate—to sparkle; to show verbal brilliance

scion—an offspring

scoff—to jeer (at)

scourge—a whip; a punishment

scruple—a qualm or doubt

scrupulous—very careful in doing what is correct

scrutiny—close inspection

scurrilous—coarse; vulgar

scuttle—to scurry; to sink (a ship); to abandon (a plan)

sebaceous—pertaining to fat

secede—to withdraw

secular—worldly

sedate—calm; serious

sedentary—sitting much of the time

seditious—pertaining to revolt against the government

sedulous—diligent

seethe—to boil; to foam

seine—a fishing net

seismic—pertaining to earthquakes

semantic—pertaining to meaning

semblance—appearance

senile—showing mental deterioration due to old age

sensual—pertaining to the body or the senses

sententious—pointed; full of trite wordings

sentient—feeling; conscious

sepulcher—a tomb

sequester—to set apart; to withdraw

serene—calm

serrated—having notches along the edge

servile—slavelike

sever—to separate; to cut in two

shackle—to hold back; to restrain

shambles—a slaughter-house; a place of disorder

shard—a broken piece (of pottery)

sheathe—to put (a knife or sword) into its covering

shibboleth—a phrase or a practice that is observed by a particular group

shoddy—cheap; poorly made

shunt—to turn aside

sidereal—pertaining to the stars or constellations

simian—pertaining to monkeys

simile—a figure of speech that compares things by using *like* or *as*

simper—to smile in a silly way

simulate—to pretend or fake

sinecure—a job that requires little work

sinister—threatening; evil

sinuous—winding; devious

skeptical—doubting

skittish—playful; jumpy

skulk—to slink

slake—to satisfy

slatternly—dirty; untidy

sleazy—flimsy (as a fabric); cheap or shoddy

slothful—lazy

slough—to shed; a swamp

slovenly—careless or untidy

sluggard—a lazy person

sobriety—soberness

sojourn—a temporary stay

solecism—a misuse of grammar; a breach of-manners

solicitous—expressing care; eager

soliloquy—a talking to oneself

solstice—the point at which the sun is farthest north or south of the equator

solvent—able to pay one's debts

somatic—pertaining to the body

somnambulism—sleep-walking

somnolent—sleepy; making one sleepy

sonorous—rich and full (sound)

soothsayer—one who predicts the future

sophisticated—urbane; not naive

sordid—dirty; ignoble

soupçon—a trace or hint

spasmodic—intermittent

specious—appearing correct but not really so

specter—a ghost

spectral—ghostly

splenetic—bad-tempered

spontaneous—arising naturally or by its own force

sporadic—occasional

sportive—playful

spurious—false; not real

squalid—filthy; sordid

squander—to waste

staid—sober

stalwart—sturdy; brave; firm

stamina—endurance

stark—prominent; barren; blunt

status—position or slate

staunch, stanch—to stop (blood) flowing from a wound; to stop or check

stellar—pertaining to the stars

stentorian—very loud

stigma—a sign of disgrace

stilted—elevated; pompous

stint—to hold hack in distributing or using

stipend—a salary or allowance

stoical—showing no reaction to various emotions or events

stolid—unexcitable

strait—a narrow waterway; a difficult situation

strategem—a scheme or trick

striated—striped or furrowed

stricture—censure; a limitation

strident—having a harsh or shrill sound

stringent—strict

stultify—to make stupid, dull, or worthless

suave—urbane; polished

subaltern—a subordinate

subjugate—to conquer

sublimate—to purify

sublime—exalted; grand

suborn—to get someone to do something illegal

sub rosa—in private

subsequent—coming later

subservient—servile

subsidiary—supplementary; secondary

subsidy—a grant of money

subsistence—a means of providing one's basic needs

substantiate—to confirm

subterfuge—any means by which one conceals his intentions

subtle—thin; characterized by slight differences and qualities; not obvious

subversive—inclined to overthrow or harm the government

succinct—clear and brief

succor—to aid

succulent—juicy

suffuse—to spread throughout

sully—to soil

sultry—hot and close

summation—adding up

sumptuous—lavish

sunder—to split apart

sundry—miscellaneous

superannuated—too old to be of use; outdated

supercilious—haughty

superficial—pertaining to the surface aspects of something

supernuous—more than the amount needed

superlative—of the best kind; supreme

supersede—to take the place of

supine—lying on the back

supple—flexible

supplicant—one who prays for or asks for (something)

surcease—an end

surfeit—to provide too much of something; to satiate

surly—rude and ill-tempered

surmise—a guess made on the basis of little evidence

surreptitious—secret

surrogate—a substitute

surveillance—a watch over someone

sustenance—maintenance

sybaritic—loving luxury

sycophant—one who flatters to gain favor of important people

sylvan—pertaining to the woods

symmetry—balance

symposium—a meeting for the exchange of ideas

synchronize—to regulate several things so they will correspond in time

synopsis—a summary

synthesis—a putting together

synthetic—not natural; artificial

T

tacit—unspoken; understood rather than declared

taciturn—reluctant to speak

tactful—saying and doing the appropriate thing when people's feelings are involved

tactile—pertaining to the sense of touch

taint—to infect or spoil

talisman—a charm supposed to have magic power

tangible—touchable; objective

tantamount—equal (to)

tantalize—to tempt (someone) with something he cannot have

tautological—employing needless repetition of an idea

tawdry—cheap and gaudy

tawny—tan in color

tedious—tiresome

temerity—foolish boldness

temperate—moderate

template—a pattern

temporal—temporary; worldly

tenacious—holding fast

tenet—a principle

tentative—proposed but not final; hesitant

tenuous—thin; slight

tenure—the period of time for which something is held; a permanent status in a job based on length of service

tepid—lukewarm

termagant—a shrewish old woman

terminal—pertaining to the end

terrestrial—earthly; pertain-ing to land

terse—concise

tertiary—third

testy—irritable

theocracy—rule of a state by God or by God's authority

therapeutic—curing

thermal—pertaining to heat

thespian—pertaining to drama; an actor

thralldom—slavery

throes—pangs

thwart—to obstruct or prevent

tirade—a lengthy, violent speech

titanic—huge

tithe—a tenth of something

titular—pertaining to a title; in name only

toady—one who tries to gain another's favor; sycophant

tome—a hook, especially a large one

torpid—dormant; slowmoving

tortuous—twisting; devious

toxic—poisonous

tract—a stretch of land

tractable—easy to manage or control

traduce—to slander

trammel—to confine or entangle

tranquil—calm; peaceful

transcend—to go beyond

transcribe—to write out in one form from another

transgression—a breaking of a rule; a violation of a limit

transient—not permanent

transition—a change from one thing to another

transitory—fleeting

translucent—allowing light through

transmute—to change from one form to another

transpire—to become known

transverse—lying across

trappings—one's clothes and equipment

trauma—a severe injury or shock

travail—hard work; pain

traverse—to go across

travesty—a burlesque; a distortion (of something)

treatise—a formal, written presentation of a subject

trek—to travel slowly

tremor—a trembling; a vibration

tremulous—trembling; afraid

trenchant—keen; forceful

trepidation—uncertainty and anxiety

tribulation—great unhappiness; a trying circumstance

tribunal—a law court

trite—overworked; no longer novel

troth—truth; one's word, as a promise

truckle—to submit and be servile

truculent—cruel; rude

truism—a statement that is known to be true

trumpery—something pretentious but not worth anything

truncate—to cut off part of

truncheon—a club

tryst—a meeting

tumid—swollen; inflated

turbid—muddy; dense

turbulence—a state of commotion or agitation

turgid—swollen; pompous

turncoat—a renegade; a traitor

turnkey—a jailer

turpitude—vileness

tutelage—care; guardianship

tyro—a beginner

U

ubiquitous—omnipresent

ulterior—on the far side; later; beyond what is said

ultimate—the farthest, final, or highest

ultimatum—a nonnegotiable demand

umbrage—offense

unadulterated—pure

unanimity—agreement

unassuming—modest

unbridled—uncontrolled; free

uncanny—strange; weird

unconscionable—done without applying one's conscience

uncouth—clumsy; not having culture or polish

unction—ointment; an intense manner of behavior; unctuousness

unctuous—oily; displaying fake religious feeling

undulate—to move in waves

unearth—to dig up

unequivocal—clear

unfaltering—unhesitating

unfathomable—not understandable

ungainly—awkward

unguent—an ointment

unimpeachable—undoubtable; above reproach

unique—unlike any other

unkempt—untidy

unmitigated—unrelieved

unprecedented—never having occurred before

unremitting—not letting up

unruly—unmanageable

unseemly—not proper

untenable—unable to be held

unwitting—unconscious; unaware

unwonted—rare

upbraid—to rebuke

urbane—polished and refined

usurp—to take by force

usury—lending money at outrageously high interest rates

utilitarian—useful

utopian—idealistic; perfect

uxorious—overly fond of one's wife

V

vacillate—to move one way and then the other; to waver

vacuous—empty; stupid

vagary—a peculiarity

vainglorious—vain and boastful

valiant—brave

validate—to confirm legally

vanguard—the group in front

vapid—dull

variegated—having a variety of colors in splotches; diverse

vaunt—a boast

veer—to change direction

vegetate—to have a dull, inactive existence

vehement—having great force or passion

venal—bribable

vendetta—a feud

vendor—a seller

vengeance—punishment; revenge

vencer—a thin covering of fine wood over cheaper wood; a thin and superficial display of a noble quality

venerable—old and honorable

venerate—to respect deeply

venial—forgivable

vent—to allow (steam or feelings) to escape

veracious—truthful

verbatim—word-fo-word

verbiage—wordiness

verbose—wordy

verdant—green

verily—truly

verisimilar—appearing to be true

verity—truth

vernacular—the common speech of an area or its people

versatile—changeable; adaptable

vertigo—dizziness

vestige—a trace

viable—able or likely to live

viand—something to eat

vicarious—substitute; done or experienced by one person through another

vicissitudes—changes

victuals—food

vie—to compete

vigilant—watchful

vilify—to slander

vindicate—to free of blame

vindictive—seeking revenge

virile—manly; masculine

virtuoso—a skilled performer

virulent—deadly

visage—one's face

viscid—sticky; viscous

viscous—sticky; viscid

visionary—like a vision; unrealistic

vitiate—to spoil or debase

vitriolic—bitter

vituperation—harsh language

vivacious—lively

vivid—lively; intense

vociferous—loud

volatile—turning to vapor quickly; changeable

volition—employing one's will

voluble—talkative

voluptuous—sensual; inclined toward luxury

voracious—greedy

votary—one who has taken a vow; a follower or supporter of a cause

vouchsafe—to grant

vulnerable—in a position to be attacked or injured

W

waggish—playful

waive—to give up (a right, etc.)

wan—pale

wane—to decrease

wanton—morally loose; unwarranted

warranty—a guarantee

wary—cautious

wastrel—one who wastes (money)

weal—welfare

wheedle—to coax

whet—to sharpen

whimsical—fanciful

whit—(the) least bit

wily—sly

windfall—a surprising bit of good luck

winnow—to pick out the good elements or parts of something

winsome—charming

witless—foolish

witticism—a clever remark

wizened—withered; dried up

wont—accustomed

wraith—a ghost

wreak—to allow to be expressed; to inflict

wrest—to take away by force

wry—twisted; stubborn

Y

yeoman—a man who has a
small amount of land

Z

zany—clownish; crazy

zealot—one who is extremely devoted to his cause

zenith—the highest point

zephyr—a breeze

zest—spirited enjoyment

Four Vocabulary Practice Tests

Vocabulary Test 1

1. OBNOXIOUS
   - (A) dreamy
   - (B) visible
   - (C) angry
   - (D) daring
   - (E) objectionable

2. VERBATIM
   - (A) word for word
   - (B) at will
   - (C) without fail
   - (D) in secret
   - (E) in summary

3. ENTICE
   - (A) inform
   - (B) observe
   - (C) permit
   - (D) attract
   - (E) disobey

4. ACCLAIM
   - (A) discharge
   - (B) excel
   - (C) applaud
   - (D) divide
   - (E) speed

5. TURBULENCE
   - (A) treachery
   - (B) commotion
   - (C) fear
   - (D) triumph
   - (E) overflow

6. DEFER
   - (A) discourage
   - (B) postpone
   - (C) empty
   - (D) minimize
   - (E) estimate

7. ADAGE
   - (A) proverb
   - (B) supplement
   - (C) tool
   - (D) youth
   - (E) hardness

8. ENSUE
   - (A) compel
   - (B) remain
   - (C) absorb
   - (D) plead
   - (E) follow

9. ZENITH
   - (A) lowest point
   - (B) compass
   - (C) summit
   - (D) middle
   - (E) wind direction

10. HYPOTHETICAL
    - (A) magical
    - (B) visual
    - (C) two-faced
    - (D) theoretical
    - (E) excitable

11. SUPERFICIAL
    - (A) shallow
    - (B) unusually fine
    - (C) proud
    - (D) aged
    - (E) spiritual

12. DISPARAGE
    - (A) separate
    - (B) compare
    - (C) refuse
    - (D) belittle
    - (E) imitate

13. PROTAGONIST
    - (A) prophet
    - (B) explorer
    - (C) talented child
    - (D) convert
    - (E) leading character

14. LUDICROUS
    - (A) profitable
    - (B) excessive
    - (C) disordered
    - (D) ridiculous
    - (E) undesirable

15. INTREPID

   (A) moist
   (B) tolerant
   (C) fearless
   (D) rude
   (E) gay

16. FILCH

   (A) hide
   (B) swindle
   (C) drop
   (D) steal
   (E) covet

17. URBANE

   (A) well-dressed
   (B) polished
   (C) rural
   (D) friendly
   (E) prominent

18. DECANT

   (A) bisect
   (B) speak wildly
   (C) bequeath
   (D) pour off
   (E) abuse verbally

19. ANTITHESIS

   (A) contrast
   (B) conclusion
   (C) resemblance
   (D) examination
   (E) dislike

20. HERETICAL

   (A) heathenish
   (B) impractical
   (C) quaint
   (D) rash
   (E) unorthodox

Vocabulary Test 2

1. IMPROMPTU
    - (A) offhand
    - (B) laughable
    - (C) fascinating
    - (D) rehearsed
    - (E) deceptive

2. CHIVALROUS
    - (A) crude
    - (B) military
    - (C) handsome
    - (D) foreign
    - (E) courteous

3. HAVOC
    - (A) festival
    - (B) disease
    - (C) ruin
    - (D) sea battle
    - (E) satchel

4. REJUVENATE
    - (A) reply
    - (B) renew
    - (C) age
    - (D) judge
    - (E) reconsider

5. STILTED
    - (A) stiffly formal
    - (B) talking much
    - (C) secretive
    - (D) fashionable
    - (E) senseless

6. SOLILOQUY
    - (A) figure of speech
    - (B) historical incident
    - (C) monologue
    - (D) isolated position
    - (E) contradiction

7. AFFABLE
    - (A) monotonous
    - (B) affected
    - (C) wealthy
    - (D) sociable
    - (E) selfish

8. NEBULOUS
    - (A) subdued
    - (B) eternal
    - (C) dewy
    - (D) cloudy
    - (E) careless

9. STEREOTYPED
    - (A) lacking originality
    - (B) illuminating
    - (C) pictorial
    - (D) free from disease
    - (E) sparkling

10. STUPEFY
    - (A) lie
    - (B) talk nonsense
    - (C) bend
    - (D) make dull
    - (E) overeat

11. SAGE
    - (A) wise man
    - (B) tropical tree
    - (C) tale
    - (D) era
    - (E) fool

12. ADMONISH
    - (A) polish
    - (B) escape
    - (C) worship
    - (D) distribute
    - (E) caution

13. BESET

(A) plead
(B) perplex
(C) pertain to
(D) deny
(E) deprive

14. FIGMENT

(A) ornamental openwork
(B) perfume
(C) undeveloped
(D) statuette
(E) invention

15. GLIB

(A) dull
(B) thin
(C) weak
(D) fluent
(E) sharp

16. COALESCE

(A) associate
(B) combine
(C) contact
(D) conspire
(E) cover

17. QUACK

(A) clown
(B) philanthropist
(C) jester
(D) dressmaker
(E) charlatan

18. GAUCHE

(A) clumsy
(B) stupid
(C) feeble-minded
(D) impudent
(E) foreign

19. REDUNDANT

(A) necessary
(B) plentiful
(C) sufficient
(D) diminishing
(E) superfluous

20. ATROPHY

(A) lose leaves
(B) soften
(C) waste away
(D) grow
(E) spread

Vocabulary Test 3

1. COMPREHEND
   (A) agree
   (B) settle
   (C) decide
   (D) reprieve
   (E) understand

2. ARDENT
   (A) eager
   (B) silvery
   (C) difficult
   (D) youthful
   (E) argumentative

3. EPITAPH
   (A) witty saying
   (B) satirical poem
   (C) concluding speech
   (D) seat beside a wall
   (E) inscription on a tomb

4. BEFIT
   (A) assist
   (B) suit
   (C) slander
   (D) stretch
   (E) effect

5. HABITAT
   (A) routine
   (B) carriage
   (C) long-term resident
   (D) dwelling place
   (E) article of clothing

6. REVERBERATE
   (A) uncover
   (B) blame
   (C) resound
   (D) regain
   (E) restore to life

7. PRECEDENCE
   (A) procession
   (B) impulsiveness
   (C) formality
   (D) priority
   (E) hesitation

8. SUFFICE
   (A) endure
   (B) annex
   (C) be foolish
   (D) be adequate
   (E) eat up

9. PERTINENT
   (A) convincing
   (B) applicable
   (C) habitual
   (D) foolproof
   (E) careful

10. TEMPESTUOUS
    (A) violent
    (B) short-lived
    (C) hard-hearted
    (D) heated
    (E) outrageous

11. VEHEMENT
    (A) thorough
    (B) unexpected
    (C) forceful
    (D) smooth-running
    (E) airy

12. REMUNERATION
    (A) understanding
    (B) finality
    (C) indebtedness
    (D) protest
    (E) compensation

13. FRIVOLITY

(A) lightness
(B) irritability
(C) falseness
(D) ornamentation
(E) impurity

14. AURA

(A) bitterness
(B) delight
(C) part of the ear
(D) prophet
(E) distinctive atmosphere

15. PERSONABLE

(A) self-centered
(B) attractive
(C) insulting
(D) intimate
(E) sensitive

16. RESILIENCE

(A) submission
(B) elasticity
(C) vigor
(D) determination
(E) recovery

17. ANALOGY

(A) similarity
(B) transposition
(C) variety
(D) distinction
(E) appropriateness

18. FACETIOUS

(A) obscene
(B) shrewd
(C) impolite
(D) complimentary
(E) witty

19. DIATRIBE

(A) debate
(B) monologue
(C) oration
(D) tirade
(E) conversation

20. MALEDICTION

(A) curse
(B) mispronunciation
(C) grammatical error
(D) talctless remark
(E) epitaph

Vocabulary Test 4

1. INTRIGUE
   - (A) request
   - (B) plot
   - (C) veto
   - (D) poison
   - (E) trespass

2. EXPLICIT
   - (A) violent
   - (B) incomplete
   - (C) forgotten
   - (D) lengthy
   - (E) definite

3. CEDE
   - (A) force
   - (B) stop
   - (C) yield
   - (D) keep
   - (E) warn

4. STEALTHY
   - (A) disobedient
   - (B) slender
   - (C) discontented
   - (D) sly
   - (E) vulgar

5. DAUNTLESS
   - (A) lazy
   - (B) poor
   - (C) bold
   - (D) modest
   - (E) uncivilized

6. DEBONAIR
   - (A) gay
   - (B) corrupt
   - (C) fragile
   - (D) extravagant
   - (E) healthful

7. JARGON
   - (A) unintelligible speech
   - (B) kind of gait
   - (C) word game
   - (D) exaggeration
   - (E) misinformation

8. PONDEROUS
   - (A) conceited
   - (B) shameless
   - (C) fearful
   - (D) heavy
   - (E) abundant

9. AMNESTY
   - (A) loss of memory
   - (B) ill will
   - (C) general pardon
   - (D) indistinctness
   - (E) improvement

10. DELETE
    - (A) injure
    - (B) delay
    - (C) please
    - (D) erase
    - (E) reveal

11. PILFER
    - (A) drain
    - (B) pray
    - (C) steal
    - (D) laugh
    - (E) toy with

12. CHAGRIN
    - (A) delight
    - (B) deceit
    - (C) wit
    - (D) caution
    - (E) vexation

13. DEFAMATION
    - (A) slander
    - (B) debt
    - (C) infection
    - (D) embezzlement
    - (E) deterioration

14. SUNDRY
    - (A) quiet
    - (B) various
    - (C) luxurious
    - (D) cheerless
    - (E) brittle

15. PALATIAL
   (A) tasty
   (B) magnificent
   (C) disordered
   (D) extreme
   (E) secure

16. AGGREGATE
   (A) result
   (B) difference
   (C) quotient
   (D) product
   (E) sum

17. APLOMB
   (A) caution
   (B) timidity
   (C) self-assurance
   (D) shortsightedness
   (E) self-restraint

18. THERAPEUTIC
   (A) curative
   (B) restful
   (C) warm
   (D) stimulating
   (E) professional

19. TRANSMUTE
   (A) remove
   (B) change
   (C) duplicate
   (D) carry
   (E) explain

20. ATTRITION
   (A) annihilation
   (B) encirclement
   (C) counter attack
   (D) appeasement
   (E) wearing down

Answers to Vocabulary Tests

Test 1		Test 2		Test 3		Test 4	
(1)	E	(1)	A	(1)	E	(1)	B
(2)	A	(2)	E	(2)	A	(2)	E
(3)	D	(3)	C	(3)	E	(3)	C
(4)	C	(4)	B	(4)	B	(4)	D
(5)	B	(5)	A	(5)	D	(5)	C
(6)	B	(6)	C	(6)	C	(6)	A
(7)	A	(7)	D	(7)	D	(7)	A
(8)	E	(8)	D	(8)	D	(8)	D
(9)	C	(9)	A	(9)	B	(9)	C
(10)	D	(10)	D	(10)	A	(10)	D
(11)	A	(11)	A	(11)	C	(11)	C
(12)	D	(12)	E	(12)	E	(12)	E
(13)	E	(13)	B	(13)	A	(13)	A
(14)	D	(14)	C	(14)	E	(14)	B
(15)	C	(15)	D	(15)	B	(15)	B
(16)	D	(16)	B	(16)	B	(16)	E
(17)	B	(17)	E	(17)	A	(17)	C
(18)	D	(18)	A	(18)	E	(18)	A
(19)	A	(19)	E	(19)	D	(19)	B
(20)	E	(20)	C	(20)	A	(20)	E

Part IV
Two SAT Critical Reading Practice Tests

Three Important Reasons for Taking These Practice Tests

Each of the two Practice SATs in the final part of this book is modeled very closely after the actual SAT. You will find that each of these Practice Tests has

a) the same level of difficulty as the actual SAT

and

b) the same question formats as the actual SAT questions.

Accordingly, *taking each of the following tests is like taking the actual SAT*. There are three important reasons for taking each of these Practice SATs:

1. To find out in which areas of the SAT you are still weak.

2. To know just where to concentrate your efforts to eliminate these weaknesses.

3. To reinforce the Critical Thinking Skills—Sixteen Verbal Strategies—that you learned in Part 1 of this book, Sixteen Verbal (Critical Reading) Strategies. As we advised at the beginning of Part 1, diligent study of these strategies will result in a sharp rise in your SAT Verbal scores.

These three reasons for taking the two Practice Tests in this section of the book tie up closely with a very important educational principle:

WE LEARN BY DOING!

Ten Tips for Taking the Practice Tests

1. Observe the time limits exactly as given.

2. Allow no interruptions.

3. Permit no talking by anyone in the "test area."

4. Use the Answer Sheets provided at the beginning of each Practice Test. Don't make extra marks. Two answers for one question constitute an omitted question.

5. Use scratch paper to figure things out. (On your actual SAT, you are permitted to use the testbook for scratchwork.)

6. Omit a question when you start "struggling" with it. Go back to that question later if you have time to do so.

7. Don't get upset if you can't answer several of the questions. You can still get a high score on the test. Even if only 40 to 60 percent of the questions you answer are correct, you will get an average or above-average score.

8. You get the same credit for answering an easy question correctly as you do for answering a tough question correctly.

9. It is advisable to guess if you are sure that at least one of the answer choices is wrong. If you are not sure whether one or more of the answer choices are wrong, statistically it will not make a difference to your total score if you guess or leave the answer blank.

10. *Your SAT score increases by approximately 10 points for every answer you get correct.*

SAT Critical Reading
Practice Test 1

Learn How You'd Do on an SAT and What You Should Do to Improve

This Critical Reading SAT Test is very much like the actual Critical Reading SAT. It follows the genuine SAT very closely. Taking this test is like taking the actual SAT. The purpose of taking this test is:

1. to find out what you are *weak* in and what you are *strong* in;
2. to know where to concentrate your efforts in order to be fully prepared for the actual test.

Taking this test will prove to be a very valuable TIME SAVER for you. Why waste time studying what you already know? Spend your time profitably by studying what you *don't* know. That is what this test will tell you.

In this book, we do not waste precious pages. We get right down to the business of helping you to increase your SAT scores.

Other SAT preparation books place their emphasis on drill, drill, drill. We do not believe that drill work is of primary importance in preparing for the SAT exam. Drill has its place. In fact, this book contains a great variety of drill material questions, practically all of which have explanatory answers. But drill work must be coordinated with learning Critical Thinking Skills. These skills will help you to think clearly and critically so that you will be able to answer many more SAT questions correctly.

Ready? Start taking the test. It's just like the real thing.

Start with number 1 for each new section. If a section has fewer questions than answer spaces, leave the extra answer spaces blank. Be sure to erase any errors or stray marks completely.

SECTION 1

1 Ⓐ Ⓑ Ⓒ Ⓓ Ⓔ	11 Ⓐ Ⓑ Ⓒ Ⓓ Ⓔ	21 Ⓐ Ⓑ Ⓒ Ⓓ Ⓔ	31 Ⓐ Ⓑ Ⓒ Ⓓ Ⓔ
2 Ⓐ Ⓑ Ⓒ Ⓓ Ⓔ	12 Ⓐ Ⓑ Ⓒ Ⓓ Ⓔ	22 Ⓐ Ⓑ Ⓒ Ⓓ Ⓔ	32 Ⓐ Ⓑ Ⓒ Ⓓ Ⓔ
3 Ⓐ Ⓑ Ⓒ Ⓓ Ⓔ	13 Ⓐ Ⓑ ○ Ⓓ Ⓔ	23 Ⓐ Ⓑ Ⓒ Ⓓ Ⓔ	33 Ⓐ Ⓑ Ⓒ Ⓓ Ⓔ
4 Ⓐ Ⓑ Ⓒ Ⓓ Ⓔ	14 Ⓐ Ⓑ Ⓒ Ⓓ Ⓔ	24 Ⓐ Ⓑ Ⓒ Ⓓ Ⓔ	34 Ⓐ Ⓑ Ⓒ Ⓓ Ⓔ
5 Ⓐ Ⓑ ○ Ⓓ Ⓔ	15 Ⓐ Ⓑ Ⓒ Ⓓ Ⓔ	25 Ⓐ Ⓑ Ⓒ Ⓓ Ⓔ	35 Ⓐ Ⓑ Ⓒ Ⓓ Ⓔ
6 Ⓐ Ⓑ Ⓒ Ⓓ Ⓔ	16 Ⓐ Ⓑ Ⓒ Ⓓ Ⓔ	26 Ⓐ Ⓑ Ⓒ Ⓓ Ⓔ	36 Ⓐ Ⓑ Ⓒ Ⓓ Ⓔ
7 Ⓐ Ⓑ Ⓒ Ⓓ Ⓔ	17 Ⓐ Ⓑ Ⓒ Ⓓ Ⓔ	27 Ⓐ Ⓑ Ⓒ Ⓓ Ⓔ	37 Ⓐ Ⓑ Ⓒ Ⓓ Ⓔ
8 Ⓐ Ⓑ Ⓒ Ⓓ Ⓔ	18 Ⓐ Ⓑ Ⓒ Ⓓ Ⓔ	28 Ⓐ Ⓑ Ⓒ Ⓓ Ⓔ	38 Ⓐ Ⓑ Ⓒ Ⓓ Ⓔ
9 Ⓐ Ⓑ Ⓒ Ⓓ Ⓔ	19 Ⓐ Ⓑ Ⓒ Ⓓ Ⓔ	29 Ⓐ Ⓑ Ⓒ Ⓓ Ⓔ	39 Ⓐ Ⓑ Ⓒ Ⓓ Ⓔ
10 Ⓐ Ⓑ Ⓒ Ⓓ Ⓔ	20 Ⓐ Ⓑ Ⓒ Ⓓ Ⓔ	30 Ⓐ Ⓑ Ⓒ Ⓓ Ⓔ	40 Ⓐ Ⓑ Ⓒ Ⓓ Ⓔ

SECTION 2

1 Ⓐ Ⓑ Ⓒ Ⓓ Ⓔ	11 Ⓐ Ⓑ Ⓒ Ⓓ Ⓔ	21 Ⓐ Ⓑ Ⓒ Ⓓ Ⓔ	31 Ⓐ Ⓑ Ⓒ Ⓓ Ⓔ
2 Ⓐ Ⓑ Ⓒ Ⓓ Ⓔ	12 Ⓐ Ⓑ Ⓒ Ⓓ Ⓔ	22 Ⓐ Ⓑ Ⓒ Ⓓ Ⓔ	32 Ⓐ Ⓑ Ⓒ Ⓓ Ⓔ
3 Ⓐ Ⓑ Ⓒ Ⓓ Ⓔ	13 Ⓐ Ⓑ Ⓒ Ⓓ Ⓔ	23 Ⓐ Ⓑ Ⓒ Ⓓ Ⓔ	33 Ⓐ Ⓑ Ⓒ Ⓓ Ⓔ
4 Ⓐ Ⓑ Ⓒ Ⓓ Ⓔ	14 Ⓐ Ⓑ Ⓒ Ⓓ Ⓔ	24 Ⓐ Ⓑ Ⓒ Ⓓ Ⓔ	34 Ⓐ Ⓑ Ⓒ Ⓓ Ⓔ
5 Ⓐ Ⓑ Ⓒ Ⓓ Ⓔ	15 Ⓐ Ⓑ Ⓒ Ⓓ Ⓔ	25 Ⓐ Ⓑ Ⓒ Ⓓ Ⓔ	35 Ⓐ Ⓑ Ⓓ Ⓒ ○ Ⓔ
6 Ⓐ Ⓑ Ⓒ Ⓓ Ⓔ	16 Ⓐ Ⓑ Ⓒ Ⓓ Ⓔ	26 Ⓐ Ⓑ Ⓒ Ⓓ Ⓔ	36 Ⓐ Ⓑ Ⓒ Ⓓ Ⓔ
7 Ⓐ Ⓑ Ⓒ Ⓓ Ⓔ	17 Ⓐ Ⓑ Ⓒ Ⓓ Ⓔ	27 Ⓐ Ⓑ Ⓒ Ⓓ Ⓔ	37 Ⓐ Ⓑ Ⓒ Ⓓ Ⓔ
8 Ⓐ Ⓑ Ⓒ Ⓓ Ⓔ	18 Ⓐ Ⓑ Ⓒ Ⓓ Ⓔ	28 Ⓐ Ⓑ Ⓒ Ⓓ Ⓔ	38 Ⓐ Ⓑ Ⓒ Ⓓ Ⓔ
9 Ⓐ Ⓑ Ⓒ Ⓓ Ⓔ	19 Ⓐ Ⓑ Ⓒ Ⓓ Ⓔ	29 Ⓐ Ⓑ Ⓒ Ⓓ Ⓔ	39 Ⓐ Ⓑ Ⓒ Ⓓ Ⓔ
10 Ⓐ Ⓑ Ⓒ Ⓓ Ⓔ	20 Ⓐ Ⓑ Ⓒ Ⓓ Ⓔ	30 Ⓐ Ⓑ Ⓒ Ⓓ Ⓔ	40 Ⓐ Ⓑ Ⓒ Ⓓ Ⓔ

SECTION 3

1 Ⓐ Ⓑ Ⓒ Ⓓ Ⓔ	11 Ⓐ Ⓑ Ⓒ Ⓓ Ⓔ	21 Ⓐ Ⓑ Ⓒ Ⓓ Ⓔ	31 Ⓐ Ⓑ Ⓒ Ⓓ Ⓔ
2 Ⓐ Ⓑ Ⓒ Ⓓ Ⓔ	12 Ⓐ Ⓑ Ⓒ Ⓓ Ⓔ	22 Ⓐ Ⓑ Ⓒ Ⓓ Ⓔ	32 Ⓐ Ⓑ Ⓒ Ⓓ Ⓔ
3 Ⓐ Ⓑ Ⓒ Ⓓ Ⓔ	13 Ⓐ Ⓑ Ⓒ Ⓓ Ⓔ	23 Ⓐ Ⓑ Ⓒ Ⓓ Ⓔ	33 Ⓐ Ⓑ Ⓒ Ⓓ Ⓔ
4 Ⓐ Ⓑ Ⓒ Ⓓ Ⓔ	14 Ⓐ Ⓑ Ⓒ Ⓓ Ⓔ	24 Ⓐ Ⓑ Ⓒ Ⓓ Ⓔ	34 Ⓐ Ⓑ Ⓒ Ⓓ Ⓔ
5 Ⓐ Ⓑ Ⓒ Ⓓ Ⓔ	15 Ⓐ Ⓑ Ⓒ Ⓓ Ⓔ	25 Ⓐ Ⓑ Ⓒ Ⓓ Ⓔ	35 Ⓐ Ⓑ Ⓓ Ⓒ ○ Ⓔ
6 Ⓐ Ⓑ Ⓒ Ⓓ Ⓔ	16 Ⓐ Ⓑ Ⓒ Ⓓ Ⓔ	26 Ⓐ Ⓑ Ⓒ Ⓓ Ⓔ	36 Ⓐ Ⓑ Ⓒ Ⓓ Ⓔ
7 Ⓐ Ⓑ Ⓒ Ⓓ Ⓔ	17 Ⓐ Ⓑ Ⓒ Ⓓ Ⓔ	27 Ⓐ Ⓑ Ⓒ Ⓓ Ⓔ	37 Ⓐ Ⓑ Ⓒ Ⓓ Ⓔ
8 Ⓐ Ⓑ Ⓒ Ⓓ Ⓔ	18 Ⓐ Ⓑ Ⓒ Ⓓ Ⓔ	28 Ⓐ Ⓑ Ⓒ Ⓓ Ⓔ	38 Ⓐ Ⓑ Ⓒ Ⓓ Ⓔ
9 Ⓐ Ⓑ Ⓒ Ⓓ Ⓔ	19 Ⓐ Ⓑ Ⓒ Ⓓ Ⓔ	29 Ⓐ Ⓑ Ⓒ Ⓓ Ⓔ	39 Ⓐ Ⓑ Ⓒ Ⓓ Ⓔ
10 Ⓐ Ⓑ Ⓒ Ⓓ Ⓔ	20 Ⓐ Ⓑ Ⓒ Ⓓ Ⓔ	30 Ⓐ Ⓑ Ⓒ Ⓓ Ⓔ	40 Ⓐ Ⓑ Ⓒ Ⓓ Ⓔ

SECTION 1

Time: 25 Minutes—Turn to Section 1 (page 173) of your answer sheet to answer the questions in this section.
24 Questions

Directions: For each question in this section, select the best answer from among the choices given and fill in the corresponding circle on the answer sheet.

Each sentence below has one or two blanks, each blank indicating that something has been omitted. Beneath the sentence are five words or sets of words labeled A through E. Choose the word or set of words that, when inserted in the sentence, best fits the meaning of the sentence as a whole.

Example:

Hoping to _____ the dispute, negotiators proposed a compromise that they felt would be _____ to both labor and management.

(A) enforce . . useful
(B) end . . divisive
(C) overcome . . unattractive
(D) extend . . satisfactory
(E) resolve . . acceptable

Ⓐ Ⓑ Ⓒ Ⓓ ●

1. In a rising tide of _____ in public education, Miss Anderson was an example of an informed and _____ teacher—a blessing to children and an asset to the nation.
(A) compromise . . inept
(B) pacifism . . inspiring
(C) ambiguity . . average
(D) mediocrity . . dedicated
(E) oblivion . . typical

2. It is _____ that primitive man considered eclipses to be _____ .
(A) foretold . . spectacular
(B) impossible . . ominous
(C) understandable . . magical
(D) true . . rational
(E) glaring . . desirable

3. By _____ the conversation, the girl had once again proved that she had overcome her shyness.
(A) appreciating
(B) recognizing
(C) hearing
(D) initiating
(E) considering

4. Only an authority in that area would be able to _____ such highly _____ subject matter included in the book.
(A) understand . . general
(B) confuse . . simple
(C) read . . useless
(D) comprehend . . complex
(E) misconstrue . . sophisticated

5. The professor displayed extreme stubbornness; not only did he _____ the logic of the student's argument, but he _____ to acknowledge that the textbook conclusion was correct.
(A) amplify . . hesitated
(B) reject . . refused
(C) clarify . . consented
(D) justify . . expected
(E) ridicule . . proposed

6. The _____ of the explorers was reflected in their refusal to give up.
(A) tenacity
(B) degradation
(C) greed
(D) harassment
(E) sociability

7. Ironically, the protest held in order to strengthen the labor movement served to _____ it.
(A) justify
(B) coddle
(C) weaken
(D) invigorate
(E) appease

8. In spite of David's tremendous intelligence, he was frequently _____ when confronted with practical matters.
(A) coherent
(B) baffled
(C) cautious
(D) philosophical
(E) pensive

Each passage below is followed by questions based on its content. Answer the questions on the basis of what is stated or implied in each passage and in any introductory material that may be provided.

Questions 9–10 are based on the following passage.

In the South American rain forest abide the greatest acrobats on earth. The monkeys of the Old World, agile as they are, cannot hang by their tails. It is only the monkeys of America that possess this skill.
5 They are called ceboids and their unique group includes marmosets, owl monkeys, sakis, spider monkeys, squirrel monkeys and howlers. Among these the star gymnast is the skinny, intelligent spider monkey. Hanging head down like a trapeze art-
10 ist from the loop of a liana, he may suddenly give a short swing, launch himself into space and, soaring outward and downward across a 50-foot void of air, lightly catch a bough on which he spied a shining berry. No owl monkey can match his leap, for their
15 arms are shorter, their tails untalented. The marmosets, smallest of the tribe, tough noisy hoodlums that travel in gangs, are also capable of leaps into space, but their landings are rough: smack against a tree trunk with arms and legs spread wide.

9. The title below that best expresses the ideas of this selection is:

(A) The star gymnast
(B) Monkeys and trees
(C) Travelers in space
(D) The uniqueness of monkeys
(E) Ceboid acrobats

10. Compared to monkeys of the Old World, American monkeys are

(A) smaller
(B) more quiet
(C) more dexterous
(D) more protective of their young
(E) less at home in their surroundings

Questions 11–12 are based on the following passage.

A critic of politics finds himself driven to deprecate the power of words, while using them copiously in warning against their influence. It is indeed in politics that their influence is most dangerous, so
5 that one is almost tempted to wish that they did not exist, and that society might be managed silently, by instinct, habit and ocular perception, without this supervening Babel of reports, arguments and slogans.

11. The author implies that critics of misused language

(A) become fanatical on this subject
(B) are guilty of what they criticize in others
(C) are clever in contriving slogans
(D) tell the story of the Tower of Babel
(E) rely too strongly on instincts

12. Which statement is true according to the passage?

(A) Critics of politics are often driven to take desperate measures.
(B) Words, when used by politicians, have the greatest capacity for harm.
(C) Politicians talk more than other people.
(D) Society would be better managed if mutes were in charge.
(E) Reports and slogans are not to be trusted.

Questions 13–24 are based on the following passage.

The following passage deals with the importance of castles in medieval Europe and how they affected the society at that time.

Medieval Europe abounded in castles. Germany alone had ten thousand and more, most of them now vanished; all that a summer journey in the Rhineland and the southwest now can show are
5 a handful of ruins and a few nineteenth century restorations. Nevertheless, anyone journeying from Spain to the Dvina, from Calabria to Wales, will find castles rearing up again and again to dominate the open landscape. There they still stand, in desolate
10 and uninhabited districts where the only visible forms of life are herdsmen and their flocks, with hawks circling the battlements, far from the traffic and comfortably distant even from the nearest small town: these were the strongholds of the European
15 aristocracy.

The weight of aristocratic dominance was felt in Europe until well after the French Revolution; political and social structure, the Church, the general tenor of thought and feeling were all influenced
20 by it. Over the centuries, consciously or unconsciously, the other classes of this older European society—the clergy, the bourgeoisie and the "common people"—adopted many of the outward characteristics of the aristocracy, who became their model,
25 their standard, their ideal. Aristocratic values and ambitions were adopted alongside aristocratic manners and fashions of dress. Yet the aristocracy were the object of much contentious criticism and complaint; from the thirteenth century onwards
30 their military value and their political importance were both called in question. Nevertheless, their opponents continued to be their principal imitators. In the eleventh and twelfth centuries, the reforming Papacy and its clerical supporters, although
35 opposed to the excessively aristocratic control of the Church (as is shown by the Investiture Contest) nevertheless themselves first adopted and then strengthened the forms of this control. Noblemen who became bishops or who founded new Orders
40 helped to implant aristocratic principles and forms of government deep within the structure and spiritual life of the Church. Again, in the twelfth and thirteenth centuries the urban bourgeoisie, made prosperous and even rich by trade and industry, were rising to
45 political power as the servants and legal proteges of monarchy. These "patricians" were critical of the aristocracy and hostile towards it. Yet they also imitated the aristocracy, and tried to gain admittance to the closed circle and to achieve equality of
50 status. Even the unarmed peasantry, who usually had to suffer more from the unrelieved weight of aristocratic dominance, long remained tenaciously loyal to their lords, held to their allegiance by that combination of love and fear, *amor et timor*, which
55 was so characteristic of the medieval relationship between lord and servant, between God and man.

The castles and strongholds of the aristocracy remind us of the reality of their power and superiority. Through the long warring centuries when
60 men went defenceless and insecure, the "house," the lord's fortified dwelling, promised protection, security and peace to all whom it sheltered.

From the ninth to the eleventh centuries, if not later, Europe was in many ways all too open. Attack
65 came from the sea, in the Mediterranean from Saracens and Vikings, the latter usually in their swift, dragon-prowed, easily manoeuvered longboats, manned by some sixteen pairs of oarsmen and with a full complement of perhaps sixty men. There
70 were periods when the British Isles and the French coasts were being raided every year by Vikings and in the heart of the continent marauding Magyar armies met invading bands of Saracens. The name of Pontresina, near St. Moritz in Switzerland, is a
75 memento of the stormy tenth century; it means *pons Saracenorum*, the "fortified Saracen bridge," the place where plundering expeditions halted on their way up from the Mediterranean.

It was recognized in theory that the Church
80 and the monarchy were the principal powers and that they were bound by the nature of their office to ensure peace and security and to do justice; but at this period they were too weak, too torn by internal conflicts to fulfill their obligations. Thus
85 more and more power passed into the hands of warriors invested by the monarchy and the Church with lands and rights of jurisdiction, who in return undertook to support their overlords and to protect the unarmed peasantry.
90 Their first concern, however, was self-protection. It is almost impossible for us to realize how primitive the great majority of these early medieval "castles" really were. Until about 1150 the fortified houses of the Anglo-Norman nobility were simple
95 dwellings surrounded by a mound of earth and a wooden stockade. These were the motte and bailey castles: the motte was the mound and its stockade, the bailey an open court lying below and also stockaded. Both were protected, where possible, by yet
100 another ditch filled with water, the moat. In the middle of the motte there was a wooden tower, the keep or *donjon*, which only became a genuine stronghold at a later date and in places where stone was readily available. The stone castles of the French and
105 German nobility usually had only a single communal room in which all activities took place.

In such straitened surroundings, where warmth, light and comfort were lacking, there

was no way of creating an air of privacy. It is easy
110 enough to understand why the life of the landed
nobility was often so unrestrained, so filled with
harshness, cruelty and brutality, even in later, more
"chivalrous" periods. The barons' daily life was
bare and uneventful, punctuated by war, hunting (a
115 rehearsal for war), and feasting. Boys were trained
to fight from the age of seven or eight, and their
education in arms continued until they were twenty-
one, although in some cases they started to fight as
early as fifteen. The peasants of the surrounding
120 countryside, bound to their lords by a great variety
of ties, produced the sparse fare which was all that
the undeveloped agriculture of the early medieval
period could sustain. Hunting was a constant neces-
sity, to make up for the lack of butcher's meat, and
125 in England and Germany in the eleventh and twelfth
centuries even the kings had to progress from one
crown estate to another, from one bishop's palace to
the next, to maintain themselves and their retinue.

13. According to the passage, class conflict in the
Middle Ages was kept in check by

(A) the fact that most people belonged to the same
class
(B) tyrannical suppressions of rebellions by powerful monarchs
(C) the religious teachings of the church
(D) the fact that all other classes admired and
attempted to emulate the aristocracy
(E) the fear that a relatively minor conflict would
lead to a general revolution

14. According to the author, the urban bourgeoisie
was hostile to the aristocracy because

(A) the bourgeoisie was prevented by the aristocracy from seeking an alliance with the kings
(B) aristocrats often confiscated the wealth of the
bourgeoisie
(C) the bourgeoisie saw the aristocracy as their
rivals
(D) the aristocrats often deliberately antagonized
the bourgeoisie
(E) the bourgeoisie felt that the aristocracy was
immoral

15. According to the passage, castles were originally
built

(A) as status symbols
(B) as strongholds against invaders
(C) as simple places to live in
(D) as luxurious chateaux
(E) as recreation centers for the townspeople

16. One of the groups that invaded central Europe
during the Middle Ages from the ninth century

on was the

(A) Magyars
(B) Franks
(C) Angles
(D) Celts
(E) Welsh

17. It can be seen from the passage that the aristocracy
was originally

(A) the great landowners
(B) members of the clergy
(C) the king's warriors
(D) merchants who became wealthy
(E) slaves who had rebelled

18. The reform popes eventually produced an aristocratic church because

(A) they depended on the aristocracy for money
(B) they themselves were more interested in money
than in religion
(C) they were defeated by aristocrats
(D) many aristocrats entered the structure of the
church and impressed their values on it
(E) the aristocrats were far more religious than
other segments of the population

19. The word "contentious" in line 28 is best interpreted to mean

(A) careful
(B) solid
(C) controversial
(D) grandiose
(E) annoying

20. According to the passage, hunting served the dual
purpose of

(A) preparing for war and engaging in sport
(B) preparing for war and getting meat
(C) learning how to ride and learning how to
shoot
(D) testing horses and men
(E) getting furs and ridding the land of excess
animals

21. The phrase *amor et timor* in line 54 is used to
describe

(A) the rivalry between the bourgeoisie and the
aristocracy
(B) the Church's view of man and his relationship
to God
(C) the peasant's loyalty to the aristocracy
(D) the adaptation of aristocratic manners and
dress
(E) the payment of food in exchange for protection

22. The passage indicates that protection of the peasantry was implemented by

    (A) the king's warriors
    (B) the Magyar mercenaries
    (C) the replacement of wood towers by stone donjons
    (D) the princes of the Church
    (E) the ruling monarchy

23. According to the passage, the effectiveness of the Church and king was diminished by

    (A) the ambition of the military
    (B) conflicts and weaknesses within the Church and Royal house
    (C) peasant dissatisfaction
    (D) the inherent flaws of feudalism
    (E) economic instability

24. "Retinue," the last word in the passage, refers to

    (A) food
    (B) all material goods
    (C) money
    (D) attendants
    (E) family

STOP
If you finish before time is called, you may check your work on this section only.
Do not turn to any other section in the test.

Take a 1-minute break
before starting section 2

SECTION 2

Time: 25 Minutes—Turn to Section 2 (page 173) of your answer sheet to answer the questions in this section.
   24 Questions

Directions: For each question in this section, select the best answer from among the choices given and fill in the corresponding circle on the answer sheet.

Each sentence below has one or two blanks, each blank indicating that something has been omitted. Beneath the sentence are five words or sets of words labeled A through E. Choose the word or set of words that, when inserted in the sentence, best fits the meaning of the sentence as a whole.

Example:

Hoping to _____ the dispute, negotiators proposed a compromise that they felt would be _____ to both labor and management.

(A) enforce . . useful
(B) end . . divisive
(C) overcome . . unattractive
(D) extend . . satisfactory
(E) resolve . . acceptable

Ⓐ Ⓑ Ⓒ Ⓓ ●

---

1. Governor Edwards combined _____ politics with administrative skills to dominate the state; in addition to these assets, he was also _____.
   (A) corrupt . . glum
   (B) inept . . civil
   (C) incriminating . . sincere
   (D) astute . . dapper
   (E) trivial . . lavish

2. After four years of _____ curbs designed to protect the American auto industry, the president cleared the way for Japan to _____ more cars to the United States.
   (A) profitable . . drive
   (B) flexible . . produce
   (C) motor . . direct
   (D) import . . ship
   (E) reciprocal . . sell

3. The photographs of Ethiopia's starving children demonstrate the _____ of drought, poor land use, and overpopulation.
   (A) consequences
   (B) prejudices
   (C) inequities
   (D) indications
   (E) mortalities

4. There had been a yearning for an end to _____ with the Soviet Union, but little evidence had existed that nuclear-arms agreements had contributed to our _____.
   (A) treaties . . silence
   (B) advantages . . relations
   (C) differences . . amity
   (D) tensions . . security
   (E) commerce . . decision

5. The union struck shortly after midnight after its negotiating committee _____ a company offer of a 20% raise.
   (A) applauded
   (B) rejected
   (C) considered
   (D) postponed
   (E) accepted

The passages below are followed by questions based on their content; questions following a pair of related passages may also be based on the relationship between the paired passages. Answer the questions on the basis of what is stated or implied in the passages and in any introductory material that may be provided.

Questions 6–9 are based on the following passages.

Passage 1

Home schooling is becoming more and more desirable because children do not have the burden of traveling to school and becoming exposed to other children's sickness and everything else that goes
5   with being in a crowded room. There is also the individual attention that the parent or tutor can give the student creating a better and more efficient learning environment. As standards become more and more flexible, home schooling may in fact be
10   the norm of the future.

Passage 2

In many studies, it was shown that students benefit in a classroom setting since the interaction and dialogue with other students creates a stimulating learning environment. The more students that are
15   in a class, the more diversity of the group and the more varied the feedback. With a good teacher and facilitator, a classroom can be very beneficial for the student's cognitive development.

6. In Passage 1, the author's condition for an effective learning condition is based on
    (A) flexible standards
    (B) the closeness of a parent and a child
    (C) the reduction of travel time
    (D) a one-on-one learning experience
    (E) the sanitary conditions in the learning environment

7. Which of the following is *not* addressed in Passage 2?
    (A) The advantage of classroom learning with the student interacting and sharing ideas with other students.
    (B) The student exposed to multi-cultural ways in approaching the learning experience.
    (C) The teacher playing an active role in the learning experience.
    (D) The more students in the classroom leading to the more feedback each student can receive.
    (E) The positive relationship between the different types of students and learning.

8. Which criterion is the same in home schooling and regular classroom schooling?
    (A) the health condition
    (B) the burden of travelling
    (C) the feedback with other students
    (D) the diversity of the students
    (E) the learning experience

9. How would one create a much more ideal environment for learning in either situation according to what is addressed in both passages?
    (A) In home schooling, the student could travel on weekends to cultural areas.
    (B) In school, the teacher could occasionally work with the student on an individual basis.
    (C) In home schooling, the student could be exposed to and interact with other students on a regular basis.
    (D) The student can spend one-half of his educational time in school and one-half of his educational time at home.
    (E) The student could learn at home and go to school to socialize.

Questions 10–15 are based on the following passage.

The following passage is about the literature of the African-American culture and its impact on society.

The literature of an oppressed people is the conscience of man, and nowhere is this seen with more intense clarity than in the literature of African-Americans. An essential element of African-
5 American literature is that the literature as a whole—not the work of occasional authors—is a movement against concrete wickedness. In African-American literature, accordingly, there is a grief rarely to be found elsewhere in American literature,
10 and frequently a rage rarely to be found in American letters: a rage different in quality, pro-founder, more towering, more intense—the rage of the oppressed. Whenever an African-American artist picks up pen or horn, his target is likely to be American racism,
15 his subject the suffering of his people, and the core element his own grief and the grief of his people. Almost all of African-American literature carries the burden of this protest.

The cry for freedom and the protest against
20 injustice indicate a desire for the birth of the New Man, a testament to the New Unknown World to be discovered, to be created by man. African-American literature is, as a body, a declaration that despite the perversion and cruelty that cling like
25 swamproots to the flesh of man's feet, man has options for freedom, for cleanliness, for wholeness, for human harmony, for goodness: for a human world. Like the spirituals that are a part of it, African-American literature is a passionate
30 assertion that man will win freedom. Thus, African American literature rejects despair and cynicism; it is a literature of realistic hope and life-affirmation. This is not to say that no African-American literary work reflects cynicism or despair, but rather that
35 the basic theme of African-American literature is that man's goodness will prevail. African-American literature is a statement against death, a statement as to what life should be: life should be vivacious, exuberant, wholesomely uninhibited, sensual, sen-
40 suous, constructively antirespectable, life should abound and flourish and laugh, life should be passionately lived and man should be loving: life should be not a sedate waltz or foxtrot but a vigorous breakdance; thus, when the African-American
45 writer criticizes America for its cruelty, the criticism implies that America is drawn to death and repelled by what should be the human style of life, the human way of living. Black literature in America is, then, a setting-forth of man's identity
50 and destiny; an investigation of man's iniquity and a statement of belief in his potential godliness;

a prodding of man toward exploring and finding deep joy in his humanity.

10. The author states or implies that
    (A) a separate-but-equal doctrine is the answer to American racism
    (B) African-American literature is superior to American literature
    (C) hopelessness and lack of trust are the keynotes of African-American literature
    (D) standing up for one's rights and protesting about unfairness are vital
    (E) traditional forms of American-type dancing should be engaged in

11. When the author, in referring to African-American literature, states that "life should be . . . constructively antirespectable" (lines 38–40), it can be inferred that people ought to
    (A) do their own thing provided what they do is worthwhile
    (B) show disrespect for others when they have the desire to do so
    (C) be passionate in public whenever the urge is there
    (D) shun a person because he is of another race or color
    (E) be enraged if their ancestors have been unjustly treated

12. With reference to the passage, which of the following statements is true about African-American literature?
    I. It expresses the need for nonviolent opposition to antiracism.
    II. It urges a person to have respect for himself and for others.
    III. It voices the need for an active, productive, and satisfying life.

    (A) I only
    (B) II only
    (C) I and III only
    (D) II and III only
    (E) I, II, and III

13. The tone of the passage is one of
    (A) anger and vindictiveness
    (B) hope and affirmation
    (C) forgiveness and charity
    (D) doubt and despair
    (E) grief and cruelty

14. Which of the following constitute(s) the author's view of a "human world?"

   I. harmony
  II. cleanliness
 III. wholeness

  (A) I only
  (B) I and II only
  (C) II and III only
  (D) I and III only
  (E) I, II, and III

15. The word "iniquity" (line 50) means

  (A) potential
  (B) creation
  (C) wickedness
  (D) cleverness
  (E) greatness

Questions 16–24 are based on the following passage.

The following passage is based on B. F. Skinner's book About Behaviorism *and discusses the pros and cons of Skinner's work on behaviorism and the various points made by Skinner.*

In his compact and modestly titled book *About Behaviorism*, Dr. B. F. Skinner, the noted behavioral psychologist, lists the 20 most salient objections to "behaviorism or the science of behavior," and he
5 has gone on to answer them both implicitly and explicitly. He has answers and explanations for everyone.

For instance, to those who object "that behaviorists deny the existence of feelings, sensations,
10 ideas, and other features of mental life," Dr. Skinner concedes that "a good deal of clarification" is in order. What such people are really decrying is "methodological behaviorism," an earlier stage of the science whose goal was precisely to close off
15 mentalistic explanations of behavior, if only to counteract the 2,500-year-old influence of mentalism. But Dr. Skinner is a "radical behaviorist." "Radical behaviorism . . . takes a different line. It does not deny the possibility of self-observation or self
20 knowledge or its possible usefulness. . . . It restores introspection. . . ."

For instance, to those who object that behaviorism "neglects innate endowment and argues that all behavior is acquired during the lifetime of the
25 individual," Dr. Skinner expresses puzzlement. Granted, "A few behaviorists . . . have minimized if not denied a genetic contribution, and in their enthusiasm for what may be done through the environment, others have no doubt acted as if a genetic
30 endowment were unimportant, but few would contend that behavior is 'endlessly malleable.' " And Dr. Skinner himself, sounding as often as not like some latter-day Social Darwinist, gives as much weight to the "contingencies of survival" in the evolution
35 of the human species as to the "contingencies of reinforcement" in the lifetime of the individual.

For instance, to those who claim that behaviorism "cannot explain creative achievements—in art, for example, or in music, literature, science,
40 or mathematics"—Dr. Skinner provides an intriguing ellipsis. "Contingencies of reinforcement also resemble contingencies of survival in the production of novelty. . . . In both natural selection and operant conditioning the appearance of 'mutations'
45 is crucial. Until recently, species evolved because of random changes in genes or chromosomes, but the geneticist may arrange conditions under which mutations are particularly likely to occur. We can also discover some of the sources of new forms
50 of behavior which undergo selection by prevailing contingencies or reinforcement, and fortunately the creative artist or thinker has other ways of introducing novelties." And so go Dr. Skinner's answers to the 20 questions he poses—questions that range
55 all the way from asking if behaviorism fails "to account for cognitive processes" to wondering if behaviorism "is indifferent to the warmth and richness of human life, and . . . is incompatible with the . . . enjoyment of art, music, and literature and with
60 love for one's fellow men."

But will it wash? Will it serve to silence those critics who have characterized B. F. Skinner variously as a mad, manipulative doctor, as a naive 19th-century positivist, as an unscientific technician, and
65 as an arrogant social engineer? There is no gainsaying that *About Behaviorism* is an unusually compact summary of both the history and "the philosophy of the science of human behavior" (as Dr. Skinner insists on defining behaviorism). It is a veritable
70 artwork of organization. And anyone who reads it will never again be able to think of behaviorism as a simplistic philosophy that reduces human beings to black boxes responding robotlike to external stimuli. Still, there are certain quandaries that *About*
75 *Behaviorism* does not quite dispel. For one thing, though Dr. Skinner makes countless references to the advances in experiments with human beings that behaviorism has made since it first began running rats through mazes many decades ago, he fails
80 to provide a single illustration of these advances. And though it may be true, as Dr. Skinner argues, that one can extrapolate from pigeons to people, it would be reassuring to be shown precisely how.

More important, he has not satisfactorily
85 rebutted the basic criticism that behaviorism "is scientistic rather than scientific. It merely emulates the sciences." A true science doesn't predict what it will accomplish when it is firmly established as a science, not even when it is posing as "the
90 philosophy of that science." A true science simply advances rules for testing hypotheses.

But Dr. Skinner predicts that behaviorism will produce the means to save human society from impending disaster. Two key concepts that keep
95 accreting to that prediction are "manipulation" and "control." And so, while he reassures us quite persuasively that his science would practice those concepts benignly, one can't shake off the suspicion that he was advancing a science just in order to save
100 society by means of "manipulation" and "control." And that is not so reassuring.

16. According to the passage, Skinner would be most likely to agree that

(A) studies of animal behavior are applicable to human behavior
(B) introspection should be used widely to analyze conscious experience
(C) behaviorism is basically scientistic
(D) behavioristic principles and techniques will be of no use in preventing widespread disaster
(E) an individual can form an infinite number of sentences that he has never heard spoken

17. The reader may infer that

(A) Skinner's philosophy is completely democratic in its methodology
(B) behaviorism, in its early form, and mentalism were essentially the same
(C) the book *About Behaviorism* is difficult to understand because it is not well structured
(D) methodological behaviorism preceded both mentalism and radical behaviorism
(E) the author of the article has found glaring weaknesses in Skinner's defense of behaviorism

18. When Skinner speaks of "contingencies of survival" (line 34) and "contingencies of reinforcement" (lines 35–36), the word "contingency" most accurately means

(A) frequency of occurrence
(B) something incidental
(C) a quota
(D) dependence on chance
(E) one of an assemblage

19. The author of the article says that Skinner sounds "like some latter-day Social Darwinist" (lines 32–33) most probably because Skinner

(A) is a radical behaviorist who has differed from methodological behaviorists
(B) has predicted that human society faces disaster
(C) has been characterized as a 19th-century positivist
(D) has studied animal behavior as applicable to human behavior
(E) believes that the geneticist may arrange conditions for mutations to occur

20. It can be inferred from the passage that "extrapolate" (line 82) means

(A) to gather unknown information by extending known information
(B) to determine how one organism may be used to advantage by another organism
(C) to insert or introduce between other things or parts

(D) to change the form or the behavior of one thing to match the form or behavior of another thing
(E) to transfer an organ of a living thing into another living thing

21. One *cannot* conclude from the passage that

(A) Skinner is a radical behaviorist but not a methodological behaviorist
(B) *About Behavior* does not show how behaviorists have improved in experimentation with human beings
(C) only human beings are used in experiments conducted by behaviorists
(D) methodological behaviorism rejects the introspective approach
(E) the book being discussed is to the point and well organized

22. In Skinner's statement that "few would contend that behavior is 'endlessly malleable' " (lines 30–31), he means that

(A) genetic influences are of primary importance in shaping human behavior
(B) environmental influences may be frequently supplemented by genetic influences
(C) self-examination is the most effective way of improving a behavior pattern
(D) the learning process continues throughout life
(E) psychologists will never come to a common conclusion about the best procedure for studying and improving human behavior

23. According to the author, which of the following is true concerning *scientistic* and *scientific* disciplines?

I. The scientific one develops the rules for testing the theory; the scientistic one does not.
II. There is no element of prediction in scientistic disciplines.
III. Science never assumes a philosophical nature.

(A) I only
(B) I and III only
(C) I and II only
(D) II and III only
(E) I, II, and III

24. The word "veritable" (line 69) means

(A) abundant
(B) careful
(C) political
(D) true
(E) believable

STOP

If you finish before time is called, you may check your work on this section only.
Do not turn to any other section in the test.

SECTION 3

Time: 20 Minutes—Turn to Section 3 (page 173) of your answer sheet to answer the questions in this section.
19 Questions

Directions: For each question in this section, select the best answer from among the choices given and fill in the corresponding circle on the answer sheet.

Each sentence below has one or two blanks, each blank indicating that something has been omitted. Beneath the sentence are five words or sets of words labeled A through E. Choose the word or set of words that, when inserted in the sentence, *best* fits the meaning of the sentence as a whole.

Example:

Hoping to _____ the dispute, negotiators proposed a compromise that they felt would be _____ to both labor and management.

(A) enforce . . useful
(B) end . . divisive
(C) overcome . . unattractive
(D) extend . . satisfactory
(E) resolve . . acceptable

Ⓐ Ⓑ Ⓒ Ⓓ ⬤

1. Illegally parked vehicles block hydrants and crosswalks, _____ the flow of traffic when double-parked, and _____ the law.

   (A) stem . . enforce
   (B) expedite . . violate
   (C) reduce . . resist
   (D) drench . . challenge
   (E) impede . . flout

2. With the film rental business _____ , the DVD player is changing the way millions of Americans use their _____ time.

   (A) advertising . . canceled
   (B) suffering . . valuable
   (C) stabilizing . . extra
   (D) recording . . unused
   (E) booming . . leisure

3. The fact that the _____ of confrontation is no longer as popular as it once was _____ progress in race relations.

   (A) practice . . inculcates
   (B) reticence . . indicates
   (C) glimmer . . foreshadows
   (D) insidiousness . . reiterates
   (E) technique . . presages

4. The _____ of scarcity amidst plenty characterizes even a rich country in a time of inflation.

   (A) coherence
   (B) tedium
   (C) facet
   (D) sequence
   (E) paradox

5. The scientist averred that a nuclear war could _____ enough smoke and dust to blot out the sun and freeze the earth.

   (A) pervert
   (B) extinguish
   (C) generate
   (D) evaluate
   (E) perpetrate

6. Until his death he remained _____ in the belief that the world was conspiring against him.

   (A) ignominious
   (B) taciturn
   (C) tantamount
   (D) obdurate
   (E) spurious

The two passages below are followed by questions based on their content and on the relationship between the two passages. Answer the questions on the basis of what is stated or implied in the passages and in any introductory material that may be provided.

Questions 7–19 are based on the following passages.

The following two passages are about violence. The first discusses televised violence; the second attempts to address the history of violence in general.

Passage 1

Violence is alive and well on television. Yet there appears to be a difference in the quality, variety and pervasiveness of today's televised violence. Some observers believe that, as a result of more than
5　three decades of television, viewers have developed a kind of immunity to the horror of violence. By the age of 16, for example, the average young person will have seen some 18,000 murders on television. One extension of this phenomenon may be an
10　appetite for more varied kinds of violence. On the basis of the amount of exposure, certain things that initially would have been beyond the pale have become more readily accepted.

Violence on TV has been more prevalent than
15　in recent years, in large measure because there are fewer situation comedies and more action series. But also because some 25 million of the nation's 85 million homes with television now receive one of the pay cable services which routinely show uncut
20　feature films containing graphic violence as early as 8 in the evening.

The evidence is becoming overwhelming that just as witnessing violence in the home may contribute to children learning and acting out violent
25　behavior, violence on TV and in the movies may lead to the same result. Studies have shown that a steady diet of watching graphic violence or sexually violent films such as those shown on cable TV has caused some men to be more willing to accept
30　violence against women such as rape and wife-beating. Not only actual violence, but the kind of violence coming through the television screen is causing concern. One of the principal developments is the increasing sophistication of the
35　weaponry. The simple gunfight of the past has been augmented by high-tech crimes like terrorist bombings. A gunfighter shooting down a sheriff is one thing. When you have terrorist bombs, the potential is there for hundreds to die. Programs
40　in the past used the occasional machine gun, but such weapons as the M-60 machine gun and Uzi semi-automatic have become commonplace today on network shows.

Many people are no longer concerned about
45　televised violence because they feel it is the way of the world. It is high time that broadcasters provide public messages on TV screens that would warn viewers about the potentially harmful effects of viewing televised violence.

Passage 2

50　We have always been a lawless and a violent people. Thus, our almost unbroken record of violence against the Indians and all others who got in our way—the Spaniards in the Floridas, the Mexicans in Texas; the violence of the vigilantes
55　on a hundred frontiers; the pervasive violence of slavery (a "perpetual exercise," Jefferson called it, "of the most boisterous passions"); the lawlessness of the Ku Klux Klan during Reconstruction and after; and of scores of race riots from those of New
60　Orleans in the 1960s to those of Chicago in 1919. Yet, all this violence, shocking as it doubtless was, no more threatened the fabric of our society or the integrity of the Union than did the lawlessness of Prohibition back in the Twenties. The explanation
65　for this is to be found in the embarrassing fact that most of it was official, quasi-official, or countenanced by public opinion: exterminating the Indian; flogging the slave; lynching the outlaw; exploiting women and children in textile mills and sweat-
70　shops; hiring Pinkertons to shoot down strikers; condemning immigrants to fetid ghettos; punishing [Blacks] who tried to exercise their civil or political rights. Most of this was socially acceptable—or at least not wholly unacceptable—just as so much
75　of our current violence is socially acceptable: the many thousands of automobile deaths every year; the mortality rate for black babies twice that for white; the deaths from cancer induced by cigarettes or by air pollution; the sadism of our penal system
80　and the horrors of our prisons; the violence of some police against the so-called "dangerous classes of society."

What we have now is the emergence of violence that is not acceptable either to the Establishment,
85　which is frightened and alarmed, or to the victims of the Establishment, who are no longer submissive and who are numerous and powerful. This is now familiar "crime in the streets," or it is the revolt of the young against the economy, the
90　politics, and the wars of the established order, or it is the convulsive reaction of the blacks to a century of injustice. But now, too, official violence

is no longer acceptable to its victims—or to their ever more numerous sympathizers: the violence
95 of great corporations and of government itself against the natural resources of the nation; the long drawn-out violence of the white majority against Blacks and other minorities; the violence of the police and the National Guard against the
100 young; the massive violence of the military against the peoples of other countries. These acts can no longer be absorbed by large segments of our society. It is this new polarization that threatens the body politic and the social fabric much as
105 religious dissent threatened them in the Europe of the sixteenth and seventeenth centuries.

7. The title that best summarizes the content of Passage 1 is

(A) TV's Role in the Rising Crime Rate
(B) Violence on TV—Past and Present
(C) TV Won't Let Up on Violence
(D) Violence Raises the TV Ratings
(E) Violence Galore on Cable TV

8. Which of the following types of TV programs would the author of Passage 1 be *least* likely to approve of?

(A) A cowboy Western called "Have Gun, Will Travel"
(B) A talk show dealing with teenage pregnancy caused by a rape
(C) A documentary dealing with Vietnam veterans suffering from the after-effects of herbicide spraying during the war
(D) A movie showing a bomb exploding in a bus carrying civilians on their way to work
(E) A soap opera in which a jealous husband is shown murdering his wife's lover, then his own wife

9. According to Passage 1,

(A) television programs are much different today from what they were a generation ago
(B) a very large percentage of the viewers are presently worried about the showing of violence on television
(C) situation comedy programs are more popular on TV now than ever before
(D) broadcasting stations are considering notifying viewers about possible dangers of watching programs that include violence
(E) violence on the television screen is more extreme than it was about 20 years ago

10. As an illustration of current "socially acceptable" violence the author of Passage 2 would probably include

(A) National Guard violence at Kent, Ohio, during the Vietnam War
(B) the Vietnam War

(C) the cruelties of our prison system
(D) the police behavior in Chicago at the 1968 Democratic Convention
(E) "crime in the streets"

11. It can be inferred that the author's definition of violence (Passage 2)

(A) includes the social infliction of harm
(B) is limited to nongovernmental acts of force
(C) is confined to governmental acts of illegal force
(D) is synonymous with illegal conduct by either government or citizen
(E) is shared by the FBI

12. The author of Passage 2 describes current violence as

I. acceptable neither to the authorities nor to the victims
II. carried out primarily by corporations
III. increasingly of a vigilante nature

(A) I only
(B) II only
(C) III only
(D) I and II only
(E) II and III only

13. The author of Passage 2 mentions all of the following forms of violence in the nineteenth century *except*

(A) the activities of the Klan during Reconstruction
(B) wiping out the Indians
(C) the New York City draft riots of the 1860s
(D) the Annexation of Texas and Florida
(E) the practice of slavery

14. Which action or activity would the author of Passage 2 be most likely to disapprove of?

(A) trying to prevent a mugging
(B) reading a science fiction story
(C) watching a rock music TV performance
(D) attending a Super Bowl football game
(E) participating in a country square dance

15. The word "pervasiveness" in line 3 of Passage 1 (also note "pervasive" in line 55 of Passage 2) means

(A) variety
(B) televised
(C) seeping through
(D) quality
(E) terribleness

16. Which of the following according to the author of Passage 1 is a contributing factor to the marked increase of violent deaths?

   I. cable television
  II. present feature films
 III. technology

  (A) I only
  (B) II only
  (C) II and III only
  (D) I and II only
  (E) I, II, and III

17. The author of Passage 2 would probably argue with the author of Passage 1 in the resolution of violence (lines 46–49) that

  (A) if violence were curtailed on television, it would pop up elsewhere.
  (B) television does not show a significant amount of violence to warrant warnings against such programs.
  (C) television can also influence the public toward non-violence.
  (D) there are more dangers to television than the portrayal of violence.
  (E) violence is inbred in television.

18. From the passages, which can we assume to be *false*?

  (A) Unlike the author of Passage 1, the author of Passage 2 believes that society is disgusted with violence.
  (B) The author of Passage 1 believes that sophisticated weaponry causes increased violence, whereas the author of Passage 2 believes that violence is inherent in society.
  (C) The type of violence discussed by the author of Passage 2 is much more encompassing than the type of violence discussed by the author of Passage 1.
  (D) Both authors propose a direct resolution for at least a start to the end of violence.
  (E) Both authors believe either that violence is a part of daily living or at least that many feel that violence is a part of daily living.

19. The word "polarization" in line 103 means

  (A) electrical tendencies
  (B) governments in different parts of the world
  (C) completely opposing viewpoints
  (D) extreme religious differences
  (E) cold climatic conditions

STOP

If you finish before time is called, you may check your work on this section only.
Do not turn to any other section in the test.

Answer Key for the SAT Practice Test 1 (Critical Reading and Writing)

Critical Reading

Section 1		Section 2		Section 3	
	Correct Answer		Correct Answer		Correct Answer
1	D	1	D	1	E
2	C	2	D	2	E
3	D	3	A	3	E
4	D	4	D	4	E
5	B	5	B	5	C
6	A	6	D	6	D
7	C	7	B	7	C
8	B	8	E	8	D
9	E	9	C	9	E
10	C	10	D	10	C
11	B	11	A	11	A
12	B	12	D	12	A
13	D	13	B	13	C
14	C	14	E	14	D
15	B	15	C	15	C
16	A	16	A	16	E
17	C	17	A	17	A
18	D	18	D	18	D
19	C	19	D	19	C
20	B	20	A		
21	C	21	A		
22	A	22	A	Number correct	
23	B	23	A		
24	D	24	D		
				Number incorrect	
Number correct		Number correct			
Number incorrect		Number incorrect			

Scoring the SAT Practice Test 1

Check your responses with the correct answers on the previous page. Fill in the blanks below and do the calculations to get your critical reading raw scores. Use the table to find your critical reading scaled scores.

Get Your Critical Reading Sore

How many critical reading questions did you get **right?**

Section 1: Questions 1–24   _____

Section 2: Questions 1–24   +   _____

Section 3: Questions 1–19   +   _____

Total   =   _____ **(A)**

How many critical reading questions did you get **wrong?**

Section 1: Questions 1–24   _____

Section 2: Questions 1–24   +   _____

Section 3: Questions 1–19   +   _____

Total   =   _____ **(B)**

$\times$ 0.25   =   _____

A–B   =   _____

Critical Reading Raw Score

Round critical reading raw score to the nearest whole number.

_____

Use the Score Conversion Table to find your critical reading scaled score.

_____

SAT Score Conversion Table

Raw Score	Critical Reading Scaled Score	Raw Score	Critical Reading Scaled Score
67	800	31	510
66	800	30	510
65	790	30	510
64	770	30	510
63	750	27	490
62	740	26	480
61	730	25	480
60	720	24	470
59	700	23	460
58	690	22	460
57	690	21	450
56	680	20	440
55	670	19	440
54	660	18	430
53	650	17	420
52	650	16	420
51	640	15	410
50	630	14	400
49	620	13	400
48	620	12	390
47	610	11	380
46	600	10	370
45	600	9	360
44	590	8	350
43	590	7	340
42	580	6	330
41	570	5	320
40	570	4	310
39	560	3	300
38	550	2	280
37	550	1	270
36	540	0	250
35	540	−1	230
34	530	−2	210
33	520	−3	200
32	520	−4	200
		and below	

This table is for use only with the test in this book.

CHART FOR SELF-APPRAISAL BASED ON THE PRACTICE TEST YOU HAVE JUST TAKEN

The Self-Appraisal Chart below tells you quickly where your SAT strengths and weaknesses lie. Check or circle the appropriate box in accordance with the number of your correct answers for each area of the Practice Test you have just taken.

	Sentence Completions	*Reading Comprehension*
EXCELLENT	16–19	40–48
GOOD	13–15	35–39
FAIR	9–12	26–34
POOR	5–8	17–25
VERY POOR	0–4	0–16

SAT CRITICAL READING SCORE/ PERCENTILE CONVERSION TABLE

Critical Reading

SAT scaled verbal score	Percentile rank
800	99.7+
790	99.5
740–780	99
700–730	97
670–690	95
640–660	91
610–630	85
580–600	77
550–570	68
510–540	57
480–500	46
440–470	32
410–430	21
380–400	13
340–370	6
300–330	2
230–290	1
200–220	0–0.5

Explanatory Answers for
Practice Test 1

Section 1: Critical Reading

As you read these Explanatory Answers, refer to Sixteen Verbal (Critical Reading) Strategies (beginning on page 1) whenever a specific strategy is referred to in the answer. Of particular importance are the following Master Verbal Strategies:

Sentence Completion Master Strategy 1—page 3.
Sentence Completion Master Strategy 2—page 4.
Reading Comprehension Master Strategy 2—page 24.

Note: All Reading questions use Reading Comprehension Strategies 1, 2, and 3 as well as other strategies indicated.

1. Choice D is correct. See **Sentence Completion Strategy 2**. Examine the first word of each choice. Choice (B) pacifism and Choice (E) oblivion are incorrect choices because a rising tide of pacifism or oblivion in public education does *not* make good sense. Now consider the other choices. Choice (A) compromise . . inept and Choice (C) ambiguity . . average do *not* make good sense in the sentence. Choice (D) mediocrity . . dedicated *does* make good sense.

2. Choice C is correct. See **Sentence Completion Strategy 2**. First we eliminate Choice (A) foretold, Choice (B) impossible, and Choice (E) glaring. Reason: These choices do not make sense in the sentence up to the word "eclipses." We further eliminate Choice (D) true . . rational, because it does not make sense for anyone to consider an eclipse rational. Only Choice (C) understandable . . magical makes sense.

3. Choice D is correct. The fact that the girl had become more self-confident indicates that she would be more active in participating in a conversation. If you used **Sentence Completion Strategy 3**—trying to complete the sentence *before* looking at the five choices—you might have come up with any of the following appropriate words:

starting	beginning
launching	originating

    The other choices are, therefore, incorrect.

4. Choice D is correct. See **Sentence Completion Strategy 2**.

STEP 1

Let us first examine the first words of each choice. We can then eliminate Choice (B) confuse and Choice (E) misconstrue because it does *not* make sense to say that an authority would be able to "confuse" or "misconstrue" something in a book. So Choices B and E are incorrect.

STEP 2

Let us now consider the remaining choices. Choice (A) understand . . simple and Choice (C) read . . useless do *not* make sense in the sentence. Therefore, these choices are incorrect. Choice (D) comprehend . . complex *does* make sense.

5. Choice B is correct. See **Sentence Completion Strategy 4**. The words "not only" constitute a Support indicator. The second part of the sentence is, therefore, expected to reinforce the first part of the sentence. Choice (B) reject . . refused supplies the two words that provide a sentence that makes sense. Choices A, C, D, and E are incorrect because their word pairs do not produce sentences that make sense.

6. Choice A is correct. See **Sentence Completion Strategy 3**. If you used this strategy of trying to complete the sentence *before* looking at the five choices, you might have come up with any of the following appropriate words:

   persistence   perseverance
   steadfastness   indefatigability

   These words all mean the same as Choice (A) tenacity. Accordingly, Choices B, C, D, and E are incorrect.

7. Choice C is correct. See **Sentence Completion Strategy 4**. The adverb "ironically" means in a manner so that the opposite of what is expected takes place. So we have an Opposition indicator here. Choice (C) weaken is, of course, the opposite of strengthen. Accordingly, Choices A, B, D, and E are incorrect.

8. Choice B is correct. See **Sentence Completion Strategy 4**. The words "in spite of" constitute an Opposition indicator. We can then expect an opposing idea to complete the sentence. The word "baffled" means "puzzled" or "unable to comprehend." Choice (B) baffled gives us the word that brings out the opposition thought we expect in the sentence. Choices A, C, D, and E do not give us a sentence that makes sense.

9. Choice E is correct. See the beginning sentence which states: "the greatest acrobats on earth" introducing the monkeys which in line 4 are called "ceboids." The whole passage is about the "ceboid acrobats."

10. Choice C is correct. See lines 14–19 where the comparisons are made.

11. Choice B is correct. See lines 1–3. Note that even if you didn't know the meaning of "deprecate," you could figure that the word imparted a negative connotation since the prefix "de" means "away from" and is negative. Also don't get lured into Choice D just because "Babel" was mentioned.

12. Choice B is correct. See line 4: ". . . influence is most dangerous . . ."

13. Choice D is correct. The second paragraph states that "the other classes . . . adopted many of the outward characteristics of the aristocracy."

14. Choice C is correct. The second paragraph implies that the bourgeoisie was "rising to political power" and rivaling the power of the aristocracy.

15. Choice B is correct. The third and fifth paragraphs describe the castles as "strongholds" and "fortified houses."

16. Choice A is correct. This information is given in paragraph 3, where it states that "the Magyar armies" harried central Europe.

17. Choice C is correct. The fourth paragraph relates how "power passed into the hands of warriors invested by the monarchy and the Church with lands."

18. Choice D is correct. Paragraph 2 states, "Noblemen who became bishops or who founded new Orders helped to implant aristocratic principles . . . deep within . . . the Church."

19. Choice C is correct. Given the context of the rest of the sentence, it can be seen that Choice C is correct. See also **Reading Comprehension Strategy 5**.

20. Choice B is correct. The last paragraph states that hunting was a rehearsal for war and it made up "for the lack of butcher's meat."

21. Choice C is correct. See paragraph 2: "Even the unarmed peasantry . . . long remained tenaciously loyal to their lords, held to their allegiance by that combination of love and fear, **amor et timor . . .**"

22. Choice A is correct. See paragraph 4: ". . . warriors . . . undertook . . . to protect the unarmed peasantry."

23. Choice B is correct. See paragraph 4: "It was recognized in theory that the Church and the monarchy were the principal powers and that they were bound by the nature of their office to ensure peace and security . . . but . . . they were too weak, too torn by internal conflicts to fulfill their obligations."

24. Choice D is correct. Given the context of the rest of the sentence, it would appear that because of the word "themselves," "retinue" must refer to humans. It is more likely that it refers to "attendants" than to "family." See also **Reading Comprehension Strategy 5**.

Explanatory Answers for Practice Test 1 (continued)

Section 2: Critical Reading

As you read these Explanatory Answers, refer to Sixteen Verbal (Critical Reading) Strategies (beginning on page 1) whenever a specific strategy is referred to in the answer. Of particular importance are the following Master Verbal Strategies:

Sentence Completion Master Strategy 1—page 3.
Sentence Completion Master Strategy 2—page 4.
Reading Comprehension Master Strategy 2—page 24.

Note: All Reading questions use Reading Comprehension Strategies 1, 2, and 3 as well as other strategies indicated.

1. Choice D is correct. See **Sentence Completion Strategy 4**. The words "in addition to" constitute a Support indicator. We can then expect an additional favorable word to complete the sentence. That word is dapper (Choice D), meaning "neatly dressed." Choices A, B, C, and E are incorrect because they do not make good sense in the sentence.

2. Choice D is correct. See **Sentence Completion Strategy 2**. Examine the first word of each choice. We eliminate Choice (C) motor and Choice (E) reciprocal because motor curbs and reciprocal curbs do not make good sense in the opening clause of the sentence. Now we consider Choice (A) profitable . . drive, which does not make sentence sense; Choice (B) flexible . . produce, which also does *not* make sentence sense; and Choice (D) export . . ship, which *does* make sentence sense.

3. Choice A is correct. See **Sentence Completion Strategy 1**. Photographs of starving children demonstrate something. The logical choice among all the choices constitutes the results of consequences of drought, poor land, and overpopulation. The other choices are incorrect because they do not make sense in the sentence.

4. Choice D is correct. See **Sentence Completion Strategy 2**. Examine the first words of each choice. We can eliminate Choice (B) advantages . . because it doesn't make sense in the sentence. The first words of the other four choices *do* make sense, so let us proceed to fill the two spaces for each of these remaining choices. Only Choice (D) tensions . . security makes good sentence sense.

5. Choice B is correct. If you used **Sentence Completion Strategy 3**, you might have come up with any of the following words:

    refused   repudiated   shunned

    These words all mean about the same as the correct Choice (B) rejected.

6. (D) See lines 5–8: ". . . individual attention . . . creating a more efficient learning environment." Note that what is contained in Choice A (flexible standards), Choice B (parent and child), Choice C (travel time), and Choice E (conditions in learning environment) are all mentioned but an effective learning condition is not based upon them.

7. (B) Choice A is addressed in lines 10–14. Choice C is addressed in lines 16–19. Choice D is addressed in lines 14–16 (varied feedback). Choice E is addressed in lines 10–12 (diversity). For Choice B, multi-cultural ways are not mentioned in the passage and even though there may be many students, those students may all be of one culture.

8. (E) The criterion which appears in both passages is the learning experience. See lines 5–8 and lines 11–14.

9. (C) What is missing in home schooling is the interaction with other students as stated in lines 12–14. Thus interaction with students on a regular basis would fill the void. Note in Choice B, the "occasional" work may not be adequate. In Choice D, in spending one-half time at home and one-half time in school it may be difficult and awkward to coordinate or relate what is taught or developed at home and what is taught or developed at school.

10. Choice D is correct. See lines 19–21: "The cry for freedom . . . the birth of the New Man." Choice A is incorrect. Although the author may agree to what the choice says, he does not actually state or imply such. Choice B is incorrect because nowhere in the passage is Choice B stated or implied. Choice C is incorrect. See lines 31–32: "African-American literature rejects the despair and cynicism; it is a literature of realistic hope and life-affirmation." Choice E is incorrect. See lines 42–43: ". . . life should not be a sedate waltz or foxtrot . . . "

11. Choice A is correct. See lines 38–42: ". . . . life should be vivacious, exuberant, wholesomely uninhibited . . . and man should be loving." Choice B is incorrect because nowhere does the passage indicate that Choice B is true. Choice C is incorrect. Although lines 41–42 state that "life should be passionately lived and man should be loving," these lines do not mean that people should demonstrate their passions in public whenever the urge is there. Choice D is incorrect. Nowhere does the passage recommend Choice D. Choice E is incorrect. Although lines 7–12 state "In African-American literature . . . the rage of the oppressed," the passage does not state or imply that the ancestors of those who have been oppressed should be enraged.

12. Choice D is correct. Let us consider each item. Item I is incorrect because the passage nowhere expresses the need for *nonviolent* opposition to racism. Item II is correct. See lines 48–53: "Black literature in America [African-American literature] is . . . finding deep joy in humanity." Item III is correct. See lines 36–42: "African-American literature is a statement . . . . and man should be loving." Accordingly, only

Choices II and III are correct. Therefore, Choice D is correct, and Choices A, B, C, and E are incorrect.

13. Choice B is correct. See lines 28–32: "Like the spirituals . . . realistic hope and life-affirmation." Choice A is incorrect. See lines 7–18: "In African-American literature . . . the burden of protest." Although an indication of anger is present in the passage, it is not dominant. Moreover, nowhere in the passage is there evidence of vindictiveness. Choice C is incorrect because forgiveness and charity are not referred to in the passage. Choice D is incorrect. See lines 28–36: "Like the spirituals . . . goodness will prevail." Choice E is incorrect. Although the passage refers to *grief* in line 16 and also *cruelty* in line 45, grief and cruelty do not represent the tone of the passage.

14. Choice E is correct. See lines 27–28: ". . . for a human world."

15. Choice C is correct. It can be seen from the context of the sentence that the word "iniquity" must mean something bad (the word is preceded by "investigation" and is in contrast to "an investigation . . . potential godliness," which appears in the same sentence). See also **Reading Comprehension Strategy 5**.

16. Choice A is correct. See lines 81–82: " . . . as Dr. Skinner argues, that one can extrapolate from pigeons to people . . ." Choice B is incorrect because, though Skinner agrees that introspection may be of some use (lines 17–21), nowhere does the article indicate that he suggests wide use of the introspective method. Choice C is incorrect since Skinner, so the author says (lines 84–86), "has not satisfactorily rebutted . . . rather than scientific." Choice D is incorrect because lines 92–94 state that ". . . Skinner predicts . . . impending disaster." Choice E is incorrect because there is nothing in the passage to indicate this statement. Incidentally, this point of view (Choice E) is held by Noam Chomsky of linguistics fame.

17. Choice A is incorrect. See line 94 to the end of the passage: "Two key concepts . . . not so reassuring." Choice B is incorrect. See lines 13–16: ". . . an earlier stage of . . . influence of mentalism." Choice C is incorrect. See lines 66–74: "It is a veritable . . . to external stimuli." Choice D is incorrect since mentalism evolved before methodological and radical behaviorism. See lines 12–20: "What such people . . . its possible usefulness." Choice E is correct. The passage, from line 69 to the end, brings out weaknesses in Skinner's presentation.

18. Choice D is correct. Skinner, in lines 30–31, says "... few would contend that behavior is 'endlessly malleable.'" Also, see lines 41–48: "Contingencies of reinforcement ... likely to occur." In effect, Skinner is saying that behavior cannot always, by plan or design, be altered or influenced; behavior must depend, to some extent, on the element of chance.

19. Choice D is correct. Skinner is known for his experiments with pigeons. Also, rats have been used frequently by behaviorists in experimentation. See lines 75–84. In addition, see lines 43–45: "In both natural ... is crucial." The other choices are not relevant to Darwin or his work.

20. Choice A is correct. From the context in the rest of the sentence where "extrapolate" appears, choice A fits best. Note, the word "extrapolate" is derived from the Latin "extra" (outside) and "polire" (to polish). See also **Reading Comprehension Strategy 5**.

21. Choice A is incorrect because Choice A is true according to line 17. Choice B is incorrect because Choice B is true according to lines 74–80. Choice C is correct because Choice C is *not* true according to lines 75–80. Choice D is incorrect because Choice D is true according to lines 12–20. Choice E is incorrect because Choice E is true according to lines 65–69.

22. Choice A is incorrect. See lines 22–25: "... to those who object ... Skinner expresses puzzlement." Choice B is correct because Skinner, a radical behaviorist, though believing that environmental influences are highly important in shaping human behavior, nevertheless states in lines 41–45: "Contingencies of reinforcement ... is crucial." Operant conditioning is, according to behaviorists, a vital aspect of learning. Choice C is incorrect. Although Skinner accepts introspection (lines 18–21) as part of his system, nowhere does he place primary importance on introspection. Choice D is incorrect. Though Skinner may agree with this choice, nowhere in the passage does he state or imply this opinion. Choice E is incorrect. The word "malleable" means capable of being shaped or formed—from the Latin "malleare," meaning "to hammer." The quote in the stem of the question says, in effect, that few people would say that behavior can always be shaped.

23. Choice A is correct. I is correct; see the eighth paragraph, last sentence. II is incorrect; don't be fooled by what is in the third sentence of the eighth paragraph. It does not refer to *scientistic* areas. III is incorrect; see the third sentence in the eighth paragraph.

24. Choice D is correct. Given the context of the sentence and the sentences preceding and succeeding it, "veritable" means "true." One may also note the "ver" in "veritable" and may associate that with the word "verify," which also means true. This is the association strategy, which can be used to figure out clues to meanings of words. See also **Reading Comprehension Strategy 5**.

Explanatory Answers for Practice Test 1 (continued)

Section 3: Critical Reading

As you read these Explanatory Answers, refer to Sixteen Verbal (Critical Reading Strategies (beginning on page 1) whenever a specific Strategy is referred to in the answer. Of particular importance are the following Master Verbal Strategies:

Sentence Completion Master Strategy 1—page 3.
Sentence Completion Master Strategy 2—page 4.
Reading Comprehension Master Strategy 2—page 24.

Note: All Reading questions use Reading Comprehension Strategies 1, 2, and 3 as well as other strategies indicated.

1. Choice E is correct. See **Sentence Completion Strategy 2**. Examine the first words of each choice. We eliminate Choice (B) expedite (meaning "to speed up") and Choice (D) drench (which means "to wet through and through") because the parked vehicles do not expedite or drench the flow of traffic. Now we consider Choices A, C, and E. The only word pair that makes good sentence sense is Choice (E) impede . . flout. The word "impede" means "to block up or obstruct," and the word "flout" means "scoff at or show contempt for."

2. Choice E is correct. See **Sentence Completion Strategy 2**. Examine the first words of each choice. We eliminate Choice (D) recording because the film rental business is not recording. Now we consider the four remaining word pairs. The only choice that makes sense in the sentence is Choice (E) booming . . leisure.

3. Choice E is correct. See **Sentence Completion Strategy 2**. Look at the first word of each choice. The first words in Choices B, C, and D do not sound right when inserted in the first blank of the sentence. Thus we can eliminate Choices B, C, and D. Now try both words in the remaining Choices, A and E. Choice E is the only one that works.

4. Choice E is correct. See **Sentence Completion Strategy 1**. Try each choice. The *apparent contradiction* of scarcity amidst plenty characterizes even a rich country in a time of inflation.

5. Choice C is correct. See **Sentence Completion Strategy 1**. The word "generate" (meaning "to produce") completes the sentence so that it makes good sense. The other choices don't do that.

6. Choice D is correct. See **Sentence Completion Strategy 1**. Try each choice. The sentence implies that he retained the belief until his death; hence he was *stubborn* or unchanging in his belief.

7. Choice C is correct. Throughout Passage 1, the author is bringing out the fact that violence is widely shown and well received on television. For example: Line 1: "Violence is alive and well on television." Lines 4–6: ". . . as a result of . . . the horror of violence." Lines 14–15: "Violence on TV . . . in recent years." Although Choices A, B, D, and E are discussed or implied in the passage, none of these choices summarizes the content of the passage as a whole. Therefore, these choices are incorrect.

8. Choice D is correct. See lines 35–39: "The simple gunfight . . . for hundreds to die." Accordingly, Choice A is incorrect. Choices B and C are incorrect because there is no violence shown on the screen in these choices. Choice E is incorrect because the violence of a double murder by a jealous husband hardly compares in intensity with the violence of a bomb exploding in a bus carrying a busload of innocent civilians.

9. Choice E is correct. See lines 35–39: "The simple gunfight of the past . . . for hundreds to die." Choice A is incorrect because, though the statement may be true, the passage nowhere indicates that TV programs generally are different today from what they were a generation ago. Choice B is incorrect. See lines 44–46: "Many people . . . the way of the world." Choice C is incorrect. See lines 14–16: "Violence on TV . . . and more action series," Choice D is incorrect. See lines 46–49: "It is high time . . . viewing televised violence." No mention is made in the passage that broadcasting stations are doing any warning or notifying about the dangers of showing violence on TV.

10. Choice C is correct. The cruelties of our prison system are referred to in lines 75–82: ". . . just as so much of our current violence is socially acceptable . . . classes of society." The horrors of our prisons were current at the time the author wrote this article, and they are current today. The violence spoken about in Choices A, B, and D were socially acceptable at the time they occurred in the past. The question asks for an illustration of *current* "socially acceptable" violence. Accordingly, Choices A, B, and D are incorrect. Choice E, though it refers to current violence, is *not* socially acceptable. See lines 83–88: "What we have now . . . familiar 'crime in the streets.'" Therefore, Choice E is incorrect.

11. Choice A is correct. The author's definition of violence is extremely broad—including not only acts of force but also the social infliction of harm as in "exploiting women and children in textile mills and sweatshops" (lines 68–70). Passage 2 refers to acts of violence other than those expressed in Choices B and C. Therefore, these choices are incorrect. One could easily cite illegal conduct on the part of the government or a citizen that is *not* of a violent nature. Therefore, Choice D is incorrect. The FBI could conceivably commit an act of violence. The author would not condone this. See lines 92–94: "But now, too, official violence . . . numerous sympathizers." Therefore, Choice E is incorrect.

12. Choice A is correct. The author of Passage 2 describes current violence as "acceptable neither to the authorities nor to the victims" [Item I]. Item II and Item III are not indicated anywhere in the passage. Therefore, only Choice A is correct.

13. Choice C is correct. It indicates the only form of violence that is *not* mentioned in Passage 2. The following line references are given to indicate that Choices A, B, D, and E represent forms of violence that *are* mentioned in the passage. Choice A—see lines 57–59: ". . . the lawlessness . . . during Reconstruction and after." Choice B—see lines 51–52: ". . . our almost . . . against the Indians." Choice D—see lines 52–54: ". . . and all the others . . . Mexicans in Texas." Choice E—see lines 55–56: ". . . the pervasive violence of slavery."

14. Choice D is correct. The author, throughout Passage 2, expresses opposition to any type of violence—whether one engages in violence or tolerates it. Therefore, Choice D is correct because the author would not approve of the violence practiced by football players. Accordingly, Choices A, B, C, and E are incorrect. Although Choice A involves violence, a person who tries to prevent a mugging is obviously opposed to the violence of the mugger.

15. Choice C is correct. In the context of the rest of the sentence in lines 3 and line 55, you can see that "pervasiveness" means "seeping through." Note that Choice A is incorrect because in lines 2–3, the word "variety" is used and would be redundant if repeated. This is also true for Choice B, "televised." See also **Reading Comprehension Strategy 5**.

16. Choice E is correct. See lines 19–20, 25, and 28.

17. Choice A is correct. The author's attitude in Passage 2 is that violence as shown historically is "a way of life." Thus if violence were curtailed on television, it would still exist elsewhere and continue to exist.

18. Choice D is correct. Only the author of Passage 1 proposes a direct resolution—lines 46–49. The statement in Choice A is *true*. See lines 92–101. The statement in Choice B is *true*. See lines 33–37 and 50–60. The statement in Choice C is *true*. The author of Passage 1 primarily talks only about televised violence, whereas the author of Passage 2 refers to corporate violence, air pollution, prison violence, and the like. The statement in Choice E is *true*. See lines 44–46 and lines 50–64.

19. Choice C is correct. It can be seen from what precedes in Passage 2 that "polarization" must mean some very great opposing viewpoints. Don't be lured into Choice A, thinking that polarization has to do with electrical current; or Choice B, that polarization has to do with governments, since society was discussed; or Choice D, that polarization has to do with religion because religious dissent was mentioned; or Choice E, that polarization has to do with climate because we have a north and south pole. See also **Reading Comprehension Strategy 5**.

What You Must Do Now to Raise Your SAT Critical Reading Score

1. a) Follow the test directions on page 191 to determine your scaled score for the SAT Test you've just taken. These results will give you a good idea about whether or not you ought to study hard in order to achieve a certain score on the actual SAT.

   b) Using your Test correct answer count as a basis, indicate for yourself your areas of strength and weakness as revealed by the "Chart for Self-Appraisal" on page 192.

2. Eliminate your weaknesses in each of the SAT test areas (as revealed in the "Chart for Self-Appraisal") by taking the following Giant Steps toward SAT success.

Critical Reading Part

Giant Step 1

Take advantage of the Critical Reading Strategies that begin on page 1. Read again the Explanatory Answer for each of the Critical Reading questions that you got wrong. Refer to the Critical Reading Strategy that applies to each of your incorrect answers. Learn each of these Critical Reading Strategies thoroughly. These strategies are crucial if you want to raise your SAT Critical Reading score substantially.

Giant Step 2

You can improve your vocabulary by doing the following:

1. Study "Word Building with Roots, Prefixes, and Suffixes," beginning on page 70.

2. Learn the "Hot Prefixes and Roots" on page 84.

3. Read through "A List of Words Appearing More Than Once on SAT Exams" on page 90.

4. Look through the "Most Important/Frequently Used SAT Words and Their Opposites" on page 92.

5. Take the Vocabulary Practice Tests on page 158.

6. Read as widely as possible—not only novels. Non-fiction is important too . . . and don't forget to read newspapers and magazines.

7. Listen to people who speak well. Tune in to worthwhile TV programs also.

8. Use the dictionary frequently and extensively—at home, on the bus, at work, etc.

9. Play word games—for example, crossword puzzles, anagrams, and Scrabble. Another game is to compose your own Sentence Completion questions. Try them on your friends.

Giant Step 3

After you have done some of the tasks you have been advised to do in the suggestions above, proceed to Practice Test 2, beginning on page 203.

After taking Practice Test 2, concentrate on the weaknesses that still remain.

If you do the job *right* and follow the steps listed above, you are likely to raise your SAT score on each of the Critical Reading parts of the test 150 points—maybe 200 points—and even more.

> I am the master of my fate;
> I am the captain of my soul.
>
> —From the poem "Invictus"
> by William Ernest Henley

SAT Critical Reading
Practice Test 2

Start with number 1 for each new section. If a section has fewer questions than answer spaces, leave the extra answer spaces blank. Be sure to erase any errors or stray marks completely.

SECTION 1

1 Ⓐ Ⓑ Ⓒ Ⓓ Ⓔ	11 Ⓐ Ⓑ Ⓒ Ⓓ Ⓔ	21 Ⓐ Ⓑ Ⓒ Ⓓ Ⓔ	31 Ⓐ Ⓑ Ⓒ Ⓓ Ⓔ
2 Ⓐ Ⓑ Ⓒ Ⓓ Ⓔ	12 Ⓐ Ⓑ Ⓒ Ⓓ Ⓔ	22 Ⓐ Ⓑ Ⓒ Ⓓ Ⓔ	32 Ⓐ Ⓑ Ⓒ Ⓓ Ⓔ
3 Ⓐ Ⓑ Ⓒ Ⓓ Ⓔ	13 Ⓐ Ⓑ Ⓒ Ⓓ Ⓔ	23 Ⓐ Ⓑ Ⓒ Ⓓ Ⓔ	33 Ⓐ Ⓑ Ⓒ Ⓓ Ⓔ
4 Ⓐ Ⓑ Ⓒ Ⓓ Ⓔ	14 Ⓐ Ⓑ Ⓒ Ⓓ Ⓔ	24 Ⓐ Ⓑ Ⓒ Ⓓ Ⓔ	34 Ⓐ Ⓑ Ⓒ Ⓓ Ⓔ
5 Ⓐ Ⓑ Ⓒ Ⓓ Ⓔ	15 Ⓐ Ⓑ Ⓒ Ⓓ Ⓔ	25 Ⓐ Ⓑ Ⓒ Ⓓ Ⓔ	35 Ⓐ Ⓑ Ⓒ Ⓓ Ⓔ
6 Ⓐ Ⓑ Ⓒ Ⓓ Ⓔ	16 Ⓐ Ⓑ Ⓒ Ⓓ Ⓔ	26 Ⓐ Ⓑ Ⓒ Ⓓ Ⓔ	36 Ⓐ Ⓑ Ⓒ Ⓓ Ⓔ
7 Ⓐ Ⓑ Ⓒ Ⓓ Ⓔ	17 Ⓐ Ⓑ Ⓒ Ⓓ Ⓔ	27 Ⓐ Ⓑ Ⓒ Ⓓ Ⓔ	37 Ⓐ Ⓑ Ⓒ Ⓓ Ⓔ
8 Ⓐ Ⓑ Ⓒ Ⓓ Ⓔ	18 Ⓐ Ⓑ Ⓒ Ⓓ Ⓔ	28 Ⓐ Ⓑ Ⓒ Ⓓ Ⓔ	38 Ⓐ Ⓑ Ⓒ Ⓓ Ⓔ
9 Ⓐ Ⓑ Ⓒ Ⓓ Ⓔ	19 Ⓐ Ⓑ Ⓒ Ⓓ Ⓔ	29 Ⓐ Ⓑ Ⓒ Ⓓ Ⓔ	39 Ⓐ Ⓑ Ⓒ Ⓓ Ⓔ
10 Ⓐ Ⓑ Ⓒ Ⓓ Ⓔ	20 Ⓐ Ⓑ Ⓒ Ⓓ Ⓔ	30 Ⓐ Ⓑ Ⓒ Ⓓ Ⓔ	40 Ⓐ Ⓑ Ⓒ Ⓓ Ⓔ

SECTION 2

1 Ⓐ Ⓑ Ⓒ Ⓓ Ⓔ	11 Ⓐ Ⓑ Ⓒ Ⓓ Ⓔ	21 Ⓐ Ⓑ Ⓒ Ⓓ Ⓔ	31 Ⓐ Ⓑ Ⓒ Ⓓ Ⓔ
2 Ⓐ Ⓑ Ⓒ Ⓓ Ⓔ	12 Ⓐ Ⓑ Ⓒ Ⓓ Ⓔ	22 Ⓐ Ⓑ Ⓒ Ⓓ Ⓔ	32 Ⓐ Ⓑ Ⓒ Ⓓ Ⓔ
3 Ⓐ Ⓑ Ⓒ Ⓓ Ⓔ	13 Ⓐ Ⓑ Ⓒ Ⓓ Ⓔ	23 Ⓐ Ⓑ Ⓒ Ⓓ Ⓔ	33 Ⓐ Ⓑ Ⓒ Ⓓ Ⓔ
4 Ⓐ Ⓑ Ⓒ Ⓓ Ⓔ	14 Ⓑ Ⓒ Ⓓ Ⓔ	24 Ⓐ Ⓑ Ⓒ Ⓓ Ⓔ	34 Ⓐ Ⓑ Ⓒ Ⓓ Ⓔ
5 Ⓐ Ⓑ Ⓒ Ⓓ Ⓔ	15 Ⓐ Ⓑ Ⓒ Ⓓ Ⓔ	25 Ⓐ Ⓑ Ⓒ Ⓓ Ⓔ	35 Ⓐ ⒷⒹ Ⓒ Ⓔ
6 Ⓐ Ⓑ Ⓒ Ⓓ Ⓔ	16 Ⓐ Ⓑ Ⓒ Ⓓ Ⓔ	26 Ⓐ Ⓑ Ⓒ Ⓓ Ⓔ	36 Ⓐ Ⓑ Ⓒ Ⓓ Ⓔ
7 Ⓐ Ⓑ Ⓒ Ⓓ Ⓔ	17 Ⓐ Ⓑ Ⓒ Ⓓ Ⓔ	27 Ⓐ Ⓑ Ⓒ Ⓓ Ⓔ	37 Ⓐ Ⓑ Ⓒ Ⓓ Ⓔ
8 Ⓐ Ⓑ Ⓒ Ⓓ Ⓔ	18 Ⓐ Ⓑ Ⓒ Ⓓ Ⓔ	28 Ⓐ Ⓑ Ⓒ Ⓓ Ⓔ	38 Ⓐ Ⓑ Ⓒ Ⓓ Ⓔ
9 Ⓐ Ⓑ Ⓒ Ⓓ Ⓔ	19 Ⓐ Ⓑ Ⓒ Ⓓ Ⓔ	29 Ⓐ Ⓑ Ⓒ Ⓓ Ⓔ	39 Ⓐ Ⓑ Ⓒ Ⓓ Ⓔ
10 Ⓐ Ⓑ Ⓒ Ⓓ Ⓔ	20 Ⓐ Ⓑ Ⓒ Ⓓ Ⓔ	30 Ⓐ Ⓑ Ⓒ Ⓓ Ⓔ	40 Ⓐ Ⓑ Ⓒ Ⓓ Ⓔ

SECTION 3

1 Ⓐ Ⓑ Ⓒ Ⓓ Ⓔ	11 Ⓐ Ⓑ Ⓒ Ⓓ Ⓔ	21 Ⓐ Ⓑ Ⓒ Ⓓ Ⓔ	31 Ⓐ Ⓑ Ⓒ Ⓓ Ⓔ
2 Ⓐ Ⓑ Ⓒ Ⓓ Ⓔ	12 Ⓐ Ⓑ Ⓒ Ⓓ Ⓔ	22 Ⓐ Ⓑ Ⓒ Ⓓ Ⓔ	32 Ⓐ Ⓑ Ⓒ Ⓓ Ⓔ
3 Ⓐ Ⓑ Ⓒ Ⓓ Ⓔ	13 Ⓐ Ⓑ Ⓒ Ⓓ Ⓔ	23 Ⓐ Ⓑ Ⓒ Ⓓ Ⓔ	33 Ⓐ Ⓑ Ⓒ Ⓓ Ⓔ
4 Ⓐ Ⓑ Ⓒ Ⓓ Ⓔ	14 Ⓐ Ⓑ Ⓒ Ⓓ Ⓔ	24 Ⓐ Ⓑ Ⓒ Ⓓ Ⓔ	34 Ⓐ Ⓑ Ⓒ Ⓓ Ⓔ
5 Ⓐ Ⓑ Ⓒ Ⓓ Ⓔ	15 Ⓐ Ⓑ Ⓒ Ⓓ Ⓔ	25 Ⓐ Ⓑ Ⓒ Ⓓ Ⓔ	35 Ⓐ ⒷⒹ Ⓒ Ⓔ
6 Ⓐ Ⓑ Ⓒ Ⓓ Ⓔ	16 Ⓐ Ⓑ Ⓒ Ⓓ Ⓔ	26 Ⓐ Ⓑ Ⓒ Ⓔ	36 Ⓐ Ⓑ Ⓒ Ⓓ Ⓔ
7 Ⓐ Ⓑ Ⓒ Ⓓ Ⓔ	17 Ⓐ Ⓑ Ⓒ Ⓓ Ⓔ	27 Ⓐ Ⓑ Ⓒ Ⓓ Ⓔ	37 Ⓐ Ⓑ Ⓒ Ⓓ Ⓔ
8 Ⓐ Ⓑ Ⓒ Ⓓ Ⓔ	18 Ⓐ Ⓑ Ⓒ Ⓓ Ⓔ	28 Ⓐ Ⓑ Ⓒ Ⓓ Ⓔ	38 Ⓐ Ⓑ Ⓒ Ⓓ Ⓔ
9 Ⓐ Ⓑ Ⓒ Ⓓ Ⓔ	19 Ⓐ Ⓑ Ⓒ Ⓓ Ⓔ	29 Ⓐ Ⓑ Ⓒ Ⓓ Ⓔ	39 Ⓐ Ⓑ Ⓒ Ⓓ Ⓔ
10 Ⓐ Ⓑ Ⓒ Ⓓ Ⓔ	20 Ⓐ Ⓑ Ⓒ Ⓓ Ⓔ	30 Ⓐ Ⓑ Ⓒ Ⓓ Ⓔ	40 Ⓐ Ⓑ Ⓒ Ⓓ Ⓔ

SECTION 1

Time: 25 Minutes—Turn to Section 1 (page 204) of your answer sheet to answer the questions in this section.
24 Questions

Directions: For each question in this section, select the best answer from among the choices given and fill in the corresponding circle on the answer sheet.

Each sentence below has one or two blanks, each blank indicating that something has been omitted. Beneath the sentence are five words or sets of words labeled A through E. Choose the word or set of words that, when inserted in the sentence, best fits the meaning of the sentence as a whole.

Example:

Hoping to _____ the dispute, negotiators proposed a compromise that they felt would be _____ to both labor and management.

(A) enforce . . useful
(B) end . . divisive
(C) overcome . . unattractive
(D) extend . . satisfactory
(E) resolve . . acceptable

Ⓐ Ⓑ Ⓒ Ⓓ ●

1. Athens was ruled not by kings and emperors as was common among other _____ at the time, but by a citizenry, which _____ fully in the affairs of the city.

   (A) committees . . cooperated
   (B) tribes . . engaged
   (C) cities . . revolutionized
   (D) populations . . applied
   (E) societies . . participated

2. Fossils are _____ in rock formations that were once soft and have _____ with the passage of time.

   (A) abolished . . corresponded
   (B) interactive . . communicated
   (C) preserved . . hardened
   (D) created . . revived
   (E) discounted . . deteriorated

3. The social-cultural trends of the 1960s _____ not only the relative affluence of the postwar period but also the coming to maturity of a generation that was a product of that _____ .

   (A) dominated . . movement
   (B) reflected . . prosperity
   (C) accentuated . . depression
   (D) cautioned . . decade
   (E) accepted . . revolution

4. Rotation of crops helps to _____ soil fertility and soil usefulness for a long period of time.

   (A) conserve
   (B) disperse
   (C) employ
   (D) research
   (E) shorten

5. Some illnesses, such as malaria, which have been virtually eliminated in the United States, are still _____ in many places abroad.

   (A) discussed
   (B) prevalent
   (C) scarce
   (D) unknown
   (E) hospitalized

6. With lack of _____ , almost anyone can develop the disease we call alcoholism, just as any of us can contract pneumonia by _____ exposing ourselves to its causes.

   (A) advice . . carefully
   (B) control . . foolishly
   (C) opportunity . . knowingly
   (D) sympathy . . fortunately
   (E) conscience . . happily

7. Use of air conditioners and other electrical apparatus had to be _____ that summer because of the _____ of the generating system.

   (A) postulated . . reaction
   (B) curtailed . . inefficiency
   (C) implemented . . residuals
   (D) augmented . . responsiveness
   (E) manipulated . . intensity

8. The Bavarians consider beer their national beverage, yet at the same time they do not view it as a drink but rather as _____ bread—a staple food.

   (A) fresh
   (B) liquid
   (C) stale
   (D) bitter
   (E) costly

Each passage below is followed by questions based on its content. Answer the questions on the basis of what is stated or implied in each passage and in any introductory material that may be provided.

Questions 9–10 are based on the following passage.

Despite the many categories of the historian, there are only two ages of man. The first age, the age from the beginnings of recorded time to the present, is the age of the cave man. It is the age of war.
5 It is today. The second age, still only a prospect, is the age of civilized man. The test of civilized man will be represented by his ability to use his inventiveness for his own good by substituting world law for world anarchy. That second age is still within
10 the reach of the individual in our time. It is not a part-time job, however. It calls for total awareness, total commitment.

9. The title below that best expresses the ideas of this passage is:

   (A) The historian at work
   (B) The dangers of all-out war
   (C) The power of world anarchy
   (D) Mankind on the threshold
   (E) The decline of civilization

10. The author's attitude toward the possibility of man's reaching an age of civilization is one of

   (A) limited hope
   (B) complete despair
   (C) marked uncertainty
   (D) complacency
   (E) anger

Questions 11–12 are based on the following passage.

Readers in the past seem to have been more patient than the readers of today. There were few diversions, and they had more time to read novels of a length that seems to us now inordinate. It may be
5 that they were not irritated by the digressions and irrelevances that interrupted the narration. But some of the novels that suffer from these defects are among the greatest that have ever been written. It is deplorable that on this account they should be
10 less and less read.

11. The title below that best expresses the ideas of this passage is:

   (A) Defects of today's novels
   (B) Novel reading then and now
   (C) The great novel
   (D) The impatient reader of novels
   (E) Decline in education

12. The author implies that

   (A) authors of the past did not use narration to any extent
   (B) great novels are usually long
   (C) digressions and irrelevances are characteristic of modern novels
   (D) readers of the past were more capable
   (E) people today have more pastimes than formerly

Questions 13–24 are based on the following passage.

This passage describes the relationship between age and income throughout various periods of American history and the effects this trend will have on the various population groups in the future.

The relationship between age and income is only casually appreciated by recent theories on the purported redistribution of income. It is known, of course, that the average person's income begins to
5   decline after he is fifty-five years of age, and that it declines sharply after sixty-five. For example as early as in 1957, 58 percent of the spending units headed by persons sixty-five years and older earned less than $2,000. The relationship between old age
10 and low income has often been considered a reflection of sociological rather than economic factors— and therefore not to be included in any study of the economy. Actually, the character of the relationship is too integrated to be dissected. However, its
15 significance is mounting with the increase in the number of older persons. The lowest-income groups include a heavy concentration of older persons—in 1957, one-third of all spending units in the $0–$2,000 class were headed by persons
20 sixty-five years and older; in 1948, it was 28 percent.

But in economic planning and social policy, it must be remembered that, with the same income, the sixty-five-or-more spending unit will not spend
25 less or need less than the younger spending unit, even though the pressure to save is greater than on the young. The functional ethos of our economy dictates that the comparatively unproductive old-age population should consume in accordance with
30 their output rather than their requirements. Most social scientists have accepted these values; they have assumed that the minimum economic needs of the aged should be lower than those of the younger family. But it is precisely at retirement that personal
35 requirements and the new demands of leisure call for an even larger income if this period is to be something more enjoyable than a wait for death.

The relationship between age and income is seen most clearly in the unionized blue-collar-
40 worker. Except for layoffs, which his seniority minimizes, and wage increments for higher productivity, awarded in many industries, his income range is determined by his occupation. But within that income range, the deciding factor is the man's
45 age. After forty-five, the average worker who loses his job has more difficulty in finding a new one. Despite his seniority, the older worker is likely to be downgraded to a lower-paying job when he can no longer maintain the pace set by younger men.
50 This is especially true of unskilled and semiskilled workers. The early and lower income period of a person's working life, during which he acquires his basic vocational skills, is most pronounced for the skilled, managerial, or professional worker. Then,
55 between the ages of twenty-five and fifty, the average worker receives his peak earnings. Meanwhile, his family expenses rise, there are children to support and basic household durables to obtain. Although his family's income may rise substantially
60 until he is somewhere between thirty-five and forty-five, per capita consumption may drop at the same time. For the growing, working-class family, limited in income by the very nature of the breadwinner's occupation, the economic consequences of this
65 parallel rise in age, income, and obligations are especially pressing. Many in the low-income classes are just as vulnerable to poverty during middle age, when they have a substantially larger income, as in old age. As family obligations finally do begin
70 declining, so does income. Consequently, most members of these classes never have an adequate income.

Thus we see that, for a time, increasing age means increasing income, and therefore a probable boost
75 in income-tenth position. Although there are no extensive data in the matter, it can be confidently asserted that the higher income-tenths have a much greater representation of spending units headed by persons aged thirty-five to fifty-five than do the
80 lower-income-tenths. This is demonstrably the case among the richest 5 percent of the consumer units. The real question is: To what extent does distribution of income-tenths within a certain age group deviate from distribution of income-tenths
85 generally? Although information is not as complete as might be desired, there is more than enough to make contingent generalizations. Detailed data exist on income distribution by tenths and by age for 1935– 36 and 1948, and on income-size distribution by age
90 for the postwar years. They disclose sharp income inequalities within every age group (although more moderate in the eighteen-to-twenty-five category)— inequalities that closely parallel the overall national income pattern. The implication is clear: A spending
95 unit's income-tenth position *within his age category* varies much less, if at all, and is determined primarily by his occupation.

In other words, in America, the legendary land of economic opportunity where any man can
100 work his way to the top, there is only slight income mobility outside the natural age cycle of rising, then falling income. Since most of the sixty-five-and-over age group falls into the low-income brackets and constitutes the largest segment of the $0–$2,000
105 income class, it is of obvious importance in analyzing future poverty in the United States to examine the growth trends of his group. The sixty-five-and-over population composed 4.0 percent of the total

population in 1900, 5.3 percent in 1930, 8.4 percent
110 in 1955, and will reach an estimated 10.8 percent
in 2010. Between 1900 and 2010, the total national
population is expected to increase 276 percent,
but those from ages forty-five through sixty-four
are expected to increase 416 percent, and those
115 sixty-five and over are expected to increase 672 percent. Between 1990 and 2010, the population aged
eighteen to twenty-five is also expected to grow far
more rapidly than the middle-aged population. With
the more rapid expansion of these two low-income
120 groups, the young and the old, in the years immediately ahead, an increase in the extent of poverty is
probable.

13. According to the passage, most social scientists
erroneously assume that

(A) personal expenses increase with the age of the
spending unit
(B) the needs of the younger spending unit are
greater than those of the aged
(C) the relationship between old age and low
income is an economic and not a sociological
problem
(D) members of the old-age population should consume in accordance with their requirements
(E) leisure living requires increased income

14. The word "appreciated" in line 2 most nearly
means

(A) had artistic interest
(B) increased in value
(C) had curiosity
(D) had gratitude
(E) understood

15. It can be inferred that in the 35–55 age category

(A) income-tenth positions vary greatly
(B) income-tenth positions vary very little
(C) earning potential does not resemble the over-
all national income pattern
(D) occupations have little bearing on the income-
tenth position
(E) there is great mobility between income-tenth
positions

16. The author believes which of the following?

I. The aged will continue to increase as a percentage of the total population.
II. Income inequalities decrease with increasing
age.
III. Managerial and professional workers have
greater income mobility than blue-collar
workers.

(A) I only
(B) II only
(C) III only
(D) I and II only
(E) I and III only

17. In the passage the term "functional ethos" in line
27 means

(A) national group
(B) ethnic influence
(C) prevailing ideology
(D) biased opinion
(E) practical ethics

18. The article states that the old-age population

(A) has increased because of longer life expectancy
(B) exceeds all but the 18–25 age group in growth
rate
(C) is well represented among the higher income-
tenths
(D) is increasing as a percentage of the low
income-tenths
(E) has its greatest numbers among the middle
income group

19. According to the author, aside from the natural age
cycle, economic opportunity in America is greatly
limited by

I. occupation
II. income inequality within every group
III. class

(A) I only
(B) II only
(C) III only
(D) I and III only
(E) I and II only

20. The word "ethos" in line 27 most nearly means

(A) the character of a group of people
(B) economic–sociological ramifications
(C) the productivity of all age groups
(D) the management of large corporations
(E) the social scientists who deal with the economy

21. According to the passage, the older, unionized blue-collar workers are

   (A) assured constant salary until retirement
   (B) given preference over new workers because of seniority
   (C) likely to receive downgraded salary
   (D) more susceptible to layoff after 40
   (E) encouraged to move to slower-paced but equal-paying jobs

22. The article states that the average worker finds that

   (A) as family obligations begin escalating, income begins to decline
   (B) he reaches economic stability at middle age because of the parallel rise in age, obligations, and income
   (C) he earns least while he is acquiring vocational skills
   (D) he reaches peak earning power between the ages of 40 and 65
   (E) his wage gains coincide with the decline of family needs

23. It can be inferred that one could most accurately predict a person's income from

   (A) his age
   (B) his natural age cycle
   (C) his occupation
   (D) his occupation and age
   (E) his seniority position

24. Which lines in the passage illustrate the author's sarcasm?

   (A) lines 22–27
   (B) lines 51–54
   (C) lines 73–75
   (D) lines 111–114
   (E) lines 118–122

STOP
If you finish before time is called, you may check your work on this section only.
Do not turn to any other section in the test.

Take a 1 minute break
before starting section 2

SECTION 2

Time: 25 Minutes—Turn to Section 2 (page 204) of your answer sheet to answer the questions in this section.
24 Questions

Directions: For each question in this section, select the best answer from among the choices given and fill in the corresponding circle on the answer sheet.

Each sentence below has one or two blanks, each blank indicating that something has been omitted. Beneath the sentence are five words or sets of words labeled A through E. Choose the word or set of words that, when inserted in the sentence, best fits the meaning of the sentence as a whole.

Example:

Hoping to _____ the dispute, negotiators proposed a compromise that they felt would be _____ to both labor and management.

(A) enforce . . useful
(B) end . . divisive
(C) overcome . . unattractive
(D) extend . . satisfactory
(E) resolve . . acceptable

Ⓐ Ⓑ Ⓒ Ⓓ ●

1. The Forest Service warned that the spring forest fire season was in full swing and urged that _____ caution be exercised in wooded areas.

   (A) moderate
   (B) scant
   (C) customary
   (D) extreme
   (E) reasonable

2. The Classical age of Greek art ended with the defeat of Athens by Sparta; the _____ effect of the long war was the weakening and _____ of the Greek spirit.

   (A) cumulative . . corrosion
   (B) immediate . . storing
   (C) imagined . . cooperation
   (D) delayed . . rebuilding
   (E) intuitive . . cancelation

3. Mary, bored by even the briefest periods of idleness, was _____ switching from one activity to another.

   (A) hesitantly
   (B) lazily
   (C) slowly
   (D) surprisingly
   (E) continually

4. The bee _____ the nectar from the different flowers and then _____ the liquid into honey.

   (A) consumes . . conforms
   (B) observes . . pours
   (C) rejects . . solidifies
   (D) crushes . . injects
   (E) extracts . . converts

5. The plan turned out to be _____ because it would have required more financial backing than was available.

   (A) intractable
   (B) chaotic
   (C) irreversible
   (D) untenable
   (E) superfluous

The passages below are followed by questions based on their content; questions following a pair of related passages may also be based on the relationship between the paired passages. Answer the questions on the basis of what is stated or implied in the passages and in any introductory material that may be provided.

Questions 6–9 are based on the following passages.

Passage 1

All the arts contain some preposterous fiction, but the theatre is the most preposterous of all. Imagine asking us to believe that we are in Venice in the sixteenth century, and that Mr. Billington
5   is a Moor, and that he is about to stifle the much admired Miss Huckaby with a pillow; and imagine trying to make us believe that people ever talked in blank verse—more than that: that people were ever so marvelously articulate. The theatre is a lily that
10 inexplicably arises from a jungle of weedy falsities. Yet it is precisely from the tension produced by all this absurdity that it is able to create such poetry, power, enchantment and truth.

Passage 2

The theater is a venue for the most realistic and
15 direct fiction ever imagined. So many of the contemporary plays make us realize how we are living our lives and perhaps how we should change them. From these "reality shows" we can feel all the poverty, despair and unfairness in our world which
20 then affords us the opportunity for change for the better.

6. Which statement best illustrates the author's meaning when he says, "The theatre is a lily that inexplicably arises from a jungle of weedy falsities"?

 (A) The theatre is the "flower" among the arts.
 (B) The theatre helps to raise public taste to a higher level.
 (C) The theatre can create an illusion of truth from improbable situations.
 (D) The theatre has overcome the unsavory reputation of earlier periods.
 (E) In the theatre, real acting talent can be developed from unpromising material.

7. The author's feeling toward contemporary plays is that they

 (A) have no value for the spectator
 (B) they can be appreciated by everyone
 (C) they elicit the negative aspects of life
 (D) they have a long-lasting effect on us
 (E) they do not deal with poetry or truth

8. The two passages are similar in that

 (A) both describe specific examples from specific plays
 (B) both are completely objective in their respective arguments
 (C) both authors of them believe that they depict the accuracy of the particular time
 (D) both authors show the same intensity and passion in their argument
 (E) both show that something positive can come out of something negative

9. Which of the following is true?

 (A) One author would not disagree with the other's premise.
 (B) The author of Passage 1 despises all characters in 16th century plays.
 (C) The author of Passage 1 believes that people in the 16th century were very articulate.
 (D) Analogies to objects and places is a literary device used in only one passage.
 (E) The author of Passage 2 believes that the theater compromises reality.

Questions 10–15 are based on the following passage.

The following passage deals with adjustment to one's surroundings and the terms and theory associated with such adjustment.

As in the case of so many words used by the biologist and physiologist, the word acclimatization is hard to define. With increase in knowledge and understanding, meanings of words change. Originally the term
5 acclimatization was taken to mean only the ability of human beings or animals or plants to accustom themselves to new and strange climatic conditions, primarily altered temperature. A person or a wolf moves to a hot climate and is uncomfortable there,
10 but after a time is better able to withstand the heat. But aside from temperature, there are other aspects of climate. A person or an animal may become adjusted to living at higher altitudes than those it was originally accustomed to. At really high altitudes, such as
15 aviators may be exposed to, the low atmospheric pressure becomes a factor of primary importance In changing to a new environment, a person may, therefore, meet new conditions of temperature or pressure, and in addition may have to contend with different
20 chemical surroundings. On high mountains, the amount of oxygen in the atmosphere may be relatively small; in crowded cities, a person may become exposed to relatively high concentrations of carbon dioxide or even carbon monoxide, and in various
25 areas may be exposed to conditions in which the water content of the atmosphere is extremely high or extremely low. Thus in the case of humans, animals, and even plants, the concept of acclimatization includes the phenomena of increased toleration of
30 high or low temperature, of altered pressure, and of changes in the chemical environment.

Let us define acclimatization, therefore, as the process in which an organism or a part of an organism becomes inured to an environment which
35 is normally unsuitable to it or lethal for it. By and large, acclimatization is a relatively slow process. The term should not be taken to include relatively rapid adjustments such as our sense organs are constantly making. This type of adjustment is
40 commonly referred to by physiologists as "adaptation." Thus our touch sense soon becomes accustomed to the pressure of our clothes and we do not feel them; we soon fail to hear the ticking of a clock; obnoxious orders after a time fail to make
45 much impression on us, and our eyes in strong light rapidly become insensitive. The fundamental fact about acclimatization is that all animals and plants have some capacity to adjust themselves to changes in their environment. This is one of the most
50 remarkable characteristics of living organisms, a characteristic for which it is extremely difficult to find explanations.

10. According to the reading selection, all animals and plants

(A) have an ability for acclimatization.
(B) can adjust to only one change in the environment at a time.
(C) are successful in adjusting themselves to changes in their environments.
(D) can adjust to natural changes in the environment but not to artificially induced changes.
(E) that have once acclimatized themselves to an environmental change can acclimatize themselves more rapidly to subsequent changes.

11. It can be inferred from the reading selection that

(A) every change in the environment requires acclimatization by living things.
(B) plants and animals are more alike than they are different.
(C) biologists and physiologists study essentially the same things.
(D) the explanation of acclimatization is specific to each plant and animal.
(E) as science develops, the connotation of terms may change.

12. According to the reading selection, acclimatization

(A) is similar to adaptation.
(B) is more important today than it formerly was.
(C) involves positive as well as negative adjustment.
(D) may be involved with a part of an organism but not with the whole organism.
(E) is more difficult to explain with the more complex present-day environment than formerly.

13. By inference from the reading selection, which one of the following would *not* require the process of acclimatization?

(A) an ocean fish placed in a lake
(B) a skin diver making a deep dive
(C) an airplane pilot making a high-altitude flight
(D) a person going from daylight into a darkened room
(E) a businessman moving from Denver, Colorado, to New Orleans, Louisiana

14. The word "inured" in line 34 most likely means

(A) exposed
(B) accustomed
(C) attracted
(D) associated
(E) in love with

15. According to the passage, a major distinction between acclimatization and adaptation is that acclimatization

(A) is more important than adaptation.
(B) is relatively slow and adaptation is relatively rapid.
(C) applies to adjustments while adaptation does not apply to adjustments.
(D) applies to terrestrial animals and adaptation to aquatic animals.
(E) is applicable to all animals and plants and adaptation only to higher animals and man.

Questions 16–24 are based on the following passage.

The following passage is about the Chinese Empire, the forces that kept the Empire together, its culture, and its philosophy.

First of all, it is important to note that the old China was an empire rather than a state. To the Chinese and their rulers, the word China did not exist and to them it would have been meaningless. They
5 sometimes used a term which we translate "the Middle Kingdom." To them there could be only one legitimate ruler for all civilized mankind. All others were rightly subordinate to him and should acknowledge his suzerainty. From this standpoint,
10 there could not, as in Europe, be diplomatic relations between equal states, each of them sovereign. When, in the nineteenth century, Europeans insisted upon intercourse with China on the basis of equality, the Chinese were at first amused and then
15 scandalized and indignant. Centuries of training had bred in them the conviction that all other rulers should be tributary to the Son of Heaven.

The tie which bound this world-embracing empire together, so the Chinese were taught to
20 believe, was as much cultural as political. As there could be only one legitimate ruler to whom all mankind must be subject, so there could be only one culture that fully deserved to be called civilized. Other cultures might have worth, but ultimately
25 they were more or less barbarous. There could be only one civilization, and that was the civilization of the Middle Kingdom. Beginning with the Han, the ideal of civilization was held to be Confucian. The Confucian interpretation of civilization was adopted
30 and inculcated as the norm. Others might be tolerated, but if they seriously threatened the Confucian institutions and foundations of society they were to be curbed and, perhaps, exterminated as a threat to the highest values.
35 Since the bond of the Empire was cultural and since the Empire should include all civilized mankind, racial distinctions were not so marked as in most other parts of the world. The Chinese did not have so strong a sense of being of different
40 blood from non-Chinese as twentieth-century conceptions of race and nation later led them to develop. They were proud of being "the sons of Han" or "the men of T'ang," but if a people fully adopted Chinese culture no great distinction was perceived between
45 them and those who earlier had been governed by that culture.

This helps to account for the comparative contentment of Chinese under alien rulers. If, as was usually the case, these invading conquerors
50 adopted the culture of their subjects and governed through the accustomed machinery and by traditional Confucian principles, they were accepted as legitimate Emperors. Few of the non-Chinese dynasties completely made this identification. This
55 probably in part accounts for such restiveness as the Chinese showed under their rule. For instance, so long as they were dominant, the Manchus, while they accepted much of the Chinese culture and prided themselves on being experts in it and posed
60 as its patrons, never completely abandoned their distinctive ancestral ways.

The fact that the tie was cultural rather than racial helps to account for the remarkable homogeneity of the Chinese. Many different ethnic strains
65 have gone to make up the people whom we call the Chinese. Presumably in the Chou and probably, earlier, in the Shang, the bearers of Chinese culture were not a single race. As Chinese culture moved southward it encountered differing cultures
70 and, almost certainly, divergent stocks. The many invaders from the north and west brought in more variety. In contrast with India, where caste and religion have tended to keep apart the racial strata, in China assimilation made great progress.
75 That assimilation has not been complete. Today the discerning observer can notice differences even among those who are Chinese in language and customs, and in many parts of China Proper there are groups who preserve not only their racial
80 but also their linguistic and cultural identity. Still, nowhere else on the globe is there so numerous a people who are so nearly homogeneous as are the Chinese.

This homogeneity is due not merely to a common
85 cultural tie, but also to the particular kind of culture which constitutes that tie. Something in the Chinese tradition recognized as civilized those who conformed to certain ethical standards and social customs. It was the fitting into Confucian patterns of conduct and of
90 family and community life rather than blood kinship or ancestry which labeled one as civilized and as Chinese.

16. The force that kept the Chinese Empire together was largely

(A) religious
(B) military
(C) economic
(D) a fear of invasion from the north and west
(E) the combination of a political and a cultural bond

17. The reason China resisted having diplomatic relations with European nations was that

(A) for centuries the Chinese had believed that their nation must be supreme among all other countries
(B) the Chinese saw nothing of value in European culture
(C) China was afraid of European military power
(D) such relations were against the teachings of the Son of Heaven
(E) the danger of disease was ever present when foreigners arrived

18. Confucianism stresses, above all,

(A) image worship
(B) recognition of moral values
(C) division of church and state
(D) acceptance of foreigners
(E) separation of social classes

19. Han and T'ang were Chinese

(A) philosophers
(B) holidays
(C) dynasties
(D) generals
(E) religions

20. If the unifying force in the Chinese empire had been racial, it is likely that

(A) China would have never become great
(B) China would be engaged in constant warfare
(C) China would have become a highly industrialized nation
(D) there would have been increasing discontent under foreign rulers
(E) China would have greatly expanded its influence

21. A problem of contemporary India that does not trouble China is

(A) overpopulation
(B) the persistence of the caste system
(C) a lack of modern industrial development
(D) a scarcity of universities
(E) a low standard of living

22. The Manchus encountered some dissatisfaction within the empire because

(A) of their tyrannical rule
(B) they retained some of their original cultural practices
(C) they were of a distinctly foreign race
(D) of the heavy taxes they levied
(E) they rejected totally Chinese culture

23. The Chinese are basically a homogeneous people because

(A) different races were able to assimilate to a great degree
(B) there has always been only one race in China
(C) the other races came to look like the Chinese because of geographical factors
(D) all other races were forcibly kept out of China
(E) of their antipathy toward intermarriage

24. The word "restiveness" in line 55 means

(A) authority
(B) happiness
(C) impatience
(D) hyperactivity
(E) quietude

STOP

If you finish before time is called, you may check your work on this section only.
Do not turn to any other section in the test.

SECTION 3

Time: 20 Minutes—Turn to Section 3 (page 204) of your answer sheet to answer the questions in this section.
19 Questions

Directions: For each question in this section, select the best answer from among the choices given and fill in the corresponding circle on the answer sheet.

Each sentence below has one or two blanks, each blank indicating that something has been omitted. Beneath the sentence are five words or sets of words labeled A through E. Choose the word or set of words that, when inserted in the sentence, best fits the meaning of the sentence as a whole.

Example:

Hoping to _____ the dispute, negotiators proposed a compromise that they felt would be _____ to both labor and management.

(A) enforce . . useful
(B) end . . divisive
(C) overcome . . unattractive
(D) extend . . satisfactory
(E) resolve . . acceptable

Ⓐ Ⓑ Ⓒ Ⓓ ●

1. Joining _____ momentum for reform in intercollegiate sports, university presidents have called for swift steps to correct imbalances between classwork and _____ .

   (A) a maximum . . studies
   (B) a rational . . awards
   (C) an increasing . . athletics
   (D) an exceptional . . professors
   (E) a futile . . contests

2. Thinking nothing can be done, many victims of arthritis ignore or delay _____ countermeasures, thus aggravating the problem.

   (A) tardy
   (B) injurious
   (C) characteristic
   (D) weird
   (E) effective

3. A strange and _____ fate seemed to keep him helpless and unhappy, despite occasional interludes of _____ .

   (A) malevolent . . conflict
   (B) bizarre . . disenchantment
   (C) virulent . . tension
   (D) ineluctable . . serenity
   (E) intriguing . . inactivity

4. Samuel Clemens chose the _____ Mark Twain as a result of his knowledge of riverboat piloting.

   (A) protagonist
   (B) pseudonym
   (C) mountebank
   (D) hallucination
   (E) misanthrope

5. For years a vocalist of spirituals, Marian Anderson was finally recognized as _____ singer when the Metropolitan Opera House engaged her.

   (A) a versatile
   (B) an unusual
   (C) an attractive
   (D) a cooperative
   (E) a mediocre

6. Leonardo da Vinci _____ the law of gravity two centuries before Newton and also made the first complete _____ charts of the human body.

   (A) examined . . colorful
   (B) anticipated . . anatomical
   (C) avoided . . meaningful
   (D) realized . . explanatory
   (E) suspected . . mural

The two passages below are followed by questions based on their content and on the relationship between the two passages. Answer the questions on the basis of what is stated or implied in the passages and in any introductory material that may be provided.

Questions 7–19 are based on the following passages.

The following two passages describe two views of the make-up and character of an artist.

Passage 1

The special quality which makes an artist of any worth might be defined, indeed, as an extraordinary capacity for irritation, a pathological sensitiveness to environmental pricks and stings. He differs
5 from the rest of us mainly because he reacts sharply and in an uncommon manner to phenomena which leave the rest of us unmoved, or, at most, merely annoy us vaguely. He is, in brief, a more delicate fellow than we are, and hence less fitted to prosper
10 and enjoy himself under the conditions of life which he and we must face alike. Therefore, he takes to artistic endeavor, which is at once a criticism of life and an attempt to escape from life.

So much for the theory of it. The more the
15 facts are studied, the more they bear it out. In those fields of art, at all events, which concern themselves with ideas as well as with sensations it is almost impossible to find any trace of an artist who was not actively hostile to his environment,
20 and thus an indifferent patriot. From Dante to Tolstoy and from Shakespeare to Mark Twain the story is ever the same. Names suggest themselves instantly: Goethe, Heine, Shelley, Byron, Thackeray, Balzac, Rabelais, Cervantes, Swift,
25 Dostoevsky, Carlyle, Moliere, Pope—all bitter critics of their time and nation, most of them piously hated by the contemporary 100 percenters, some of them actually fugitives from rage and reprisal.

Dante put all of the patriotic Italians of his day
30 into Hell, and showed them boiling, roasting and writhing on hooks. Cervantes drew such a devastating picture of the Spain that he lived in that it ruined the Spaniards. Shakespeare made his heroes foreigners and his clowns Englishmen.
35 Goethe was in favor of Napoleon. Rabelais, a citizen of Christendom rather than of France, raised a cackle against it that Christendom is still trying in vain to suppress. Swift, having finished the Irish and then the English, proceeded to finish the
40 whole human race. The exceptions are few and far between, and not many of them will bear examination. So far as I know, the only eminent writer in

English history who was also a 100% Englishman, absolutely beyond suspicion, was Samuel Johnson.
45 But was Johnson actually an artist? If he was, then a kazoo-player is a musician. He employed the materials of one of the arts, to wit, words, but his use of them was mechanical, not artistic. If Johnson were alive today, he would be a United States Senator, or
50 a university president. He left such wounds upon English prose that it was a century recovering from them.

Passage 2

For the ease and pleasure of treading the old road, accepting the fashions, the education, the religion
55 of society, he takes the cross of making his own, and, of course, the self-accusation, the faint heart, the frequent uncertainty and loss of time, which are the nettles and tangling vines in the way of the self-relying and self-directed, and the state of virtual
60 hostility in which he seems to stand to society, and especially to educated society. For all this loss and scorn, what offset? The artist is to find consolation in exercising the highest functions of human nature. The artist is one who raises himself from
65 private consideration and breathes and lives on public and illustrious thoughts. The artist is the world's eye. He is the world's heart. He is to resist the vulgar prosperity that retrogrades ever to barbarism, by preserving and communicating heroic
70 sentiments, noble biographies, melodious verse, and the conclusions of history. Whatsoever oracles the human heart, in all emergencies, in all solemn hours, has uttered as its commentary on the world of actions—these he shall receive and impart. And
75 whatsoever new verdict Reason from her inviolable seat pronounces on the passing men and women and events of today—this he shall hear and promulgate.

These being his functions, it becomes the
80 artist to feel all confidence in himself, and to defer never to the popular cry. He and he only knows the world. The world of any moment is the merest appearance. Some great decorum, some fetish of a government, some ephemeral trade, or war, or man,
85 is cried up by half mankind and cried down by the other half, as if all depended on this particular up or down. The odds are that the whole question is not worth the poorest thought which the scholar has lost in listening to the controversy. Let her not
90 quit her belief that a popgun is a popgun, though

the ancient and honorable of the earth affirm it to be the crack of doom. In silence, in steadiness, in severe abstraction, let him hold by himself; add observation to observation, patient of neglect,
95 patient of reproach, and bide his own time—happy enough if he can satisfy himself alone that this day he has seen something truly. Success treads on every right step. For the instinct is sure, that prompts him to tell his brother what he thinks.
100 The artist then learns that in going down into the secrets of his own mind he has descended into the secrets of all minds. He learns that the artist who has mastered any law in his private thoughts is master to that extent of all translated. The poet, in utter
105 solitude remembering his spontaneous thoughts and recording them, is found to have recorded that which men in crowded cities find true for them also. The orator distrusts at first the fitness of his frank confessions, his want of knowledge of the persons
110 he addresses, until he finds that he is the complement of his hearers—that they drink his words because he fulfills for them their own nature; the deeper he dives into his privatest, secretest presentiment, to his wonder he finds this is the most
115 acceptable, most public, and universally true. The people delight in it; the better part of every man feels. This is my music; this is myself.

7. Which of the following quotations is related most closely to the principal idea of Passage 1?

   (A) "All nature is but art unknown to thee, All chance, direction which thou canst not see."
   (B) "When to her share some human errors fall, Look on her face and you'll forget them all."
   (C) "All human things are subject to decay, "And, when fate summons, monarchs must obey."
   (D) "A little learning is a dangerous thing, Drink deep or taste not the Pierian spring."
   (E) "Great wits are sure to madness near allied, And thin partitions do their bounds divide."

8. The author of Passage 1 seems to regard the artist as

   (A) the best representative of his time
   (B) an unnecessary threat to the social order
   (C) one who creates out of discontent
   (D) one who truly knows how to enjoy life
   (E) one who is touched with genius

9. It can be inferred that the author of Passage 1 believes that United States Senators and university presidents

   (A) must be treated with respect because of their position
   (B) are to be held in low esteem
   (C) are generally appreciative of the great literary classics
   (D) have native writing ability
   (E) have the qualities of the artist

10. All of the following ideas about artists are mentioned in Passage 1 *except* that

   (A) they are irritated by their surroundings
   (B) they are escapists from reality
   (C) they are lovers of beauty
   (D) they are hated by their contemporaries
   (E) they are critical of their times

11. Which of the following best describes Passage 1 author's attitude toward artists?

   (A) sharply critical
   (B) sincerely sympathetic
   (C) deeply resentful
   (D) mildly annoyed
   (E) completely delighted

12. It is a frequent criticism of the artist that he lives by himself, in an "ivory tower," remote from the problems and business of the world. Which of these below constitutes the best refutation by the writer of Passage 2 to the criticism here noted?

   (A) The world's concerns being ephemeral, the artist does well to renounce them and the world.
   (B) The artist lives in the past to interpret the present.
   (C) The artist at his truest is the spokesman of the people.
   (D) The artist is not concerned with the world's doings because he is not selfish and therefore not engrossed in matters of importance to himself and neighbors.
   (E) The artist's academic researches of today are the businessman's practical products of tomorrow.

13. The artist's road is rough, according to Passage 2. Which of these is the artist's greatest difficulty?

   (A) The artist must renounce religion.
   (B) The artist must pioneer new approaches.
   (C) The artist must express scorn for and hostility to society.
   (D) The artist is uncertain of his course.
   (E) There is a pleasure in the main-traveled roads in education, religion, and all social fashions.

14. When the writer of Passage 2 speaks of the "world's eye" and the "world's heart" he means

(A) the same thing
(B) culture and conscience
(C) culture and wisdom
(D) a scanning of all the world's geography and a deep sympathy for every living thing
(E) mind and love

15. By the phrase "nettles and tangling vines" (line 58) the author probably refers to

(A) "self-accusation" and "loss of time"
(B) "faint heart" and "self-accusation"
(C) "the slings and arrows of outrageous fortune"
(D) a general term for the difficulties of a scholar's life
(E) "self-accusation" and "uncertainty"

16. The various ideas in Passage 2 are best summarized in which of these groups?

I. truth versus society
the artist and books
the world and the artist
II. the ease of living traditionally
the glory of an artist's life
true knowledge versus trivia
III. the hardships of the scholar
the artist's functions
the artist's justifications for disregarding the world's business

(A) I and III together
(B) I only
(C) III only
(D) I, II, and III together
(E) I and II together

17. "seems to stand" (line 60) means

(A) is
(B) ends probably in becoming
(C) gives the false impression of being
(D) is seen to be
(E) the quicksands of time

18. The difference between the description of the artist in Passage 1 as compared with the artist in Passage 2 is that

(A) one is loyal to his fellow men and women whereas the other is opposed to his or her environment
(B) one is sensitive to his or her environment whereas the other is apathetic
(C) one has political aspirations; the other does not
(D) one has deep knowledge; the other has superficial knowledge
(E) one could be proficient in a field other than art; the other could create only in his or her present field

19. Which of the following describes statements that refer to the *same* one artist (either the one in Passage 1 *or* the one in Passage 2)?

I. This artist's thoughts are also the spectator's thoughts.
This artist lives modestly and not luxuriously.
II. This artist admires foreigners over his own countrymen.
This artist reacts to many things that most people would be neutral to.
III. This artist is happy to be at his best. This artist accepts society.

(A) I only
(B) II only
(C) III only
(D) I and III only
(E) I, II, and III

STOP
If you finish before time is called, you may check your work on this section only.
Do not turn to any other section in the test.

Answer Key for the SAT Practice Test 2 (Critical Reading and Writing)

Critical Reading

Section 1	Correct Answer		Section 2	Correct Answer		Section 3	Correct Answer
1	E		1	D		1	C
2	C		2	A		2	E
3	B		3	E		3	D
4	A		4	E		4	B
5	B		5	D		5	A
6	B		6	C		6	B
7	B		7	C		7	E
8	B		8	E		8	C
9	D		9	D		9	B
10	A		10	A		10	C
11	B		11	E		11	B
12	E		12	A		12	C
13	B		13	D		13	B
14	E		14	B		14	C
15	A		15	B		15	E
16	E		16	E		16	C
17	C		17	A		17	C
18	D		18	B		18	A
19	D		19	C		19	E
20	A		20	D			
21	C		21	B			
22	C		22	B		Number correct	
23	C		23	A			
24	D		24	C			
						Number incorrect	

Number correct

Number incorrect

Number correct

Number incorrect

Scoring the SAT Practice Test 1
Check your responses with the correct answers on the previous page. Fill in the blanks below and do the calculations to get your critical reading raw scores. Use the table to find your critical reading scaled scores.

Get Your Critical Reading Sore
How many critical reading questions did you get **right?**

Section 1: Questions 1–24   _____

Section 2: Questions 1–24   +   _____

Section 3: Questions 1–19   +   _____

        Total   =   _____ **(A)**

How many critical reading questions did you get **wrong?**

Section 1: Questions 1–24   _____

Section 2: Questions 1–24   +   _____

Section 3: Questions 1–19   +   _____

        Total   =   _____ **(B)**

       $\times$ 0.25   =   _____

       A–B   =   _____

        Critical Reading Raw Score

Round critical reading raw score to the nearest whole number.

_____

Use the Score Conversion Table to find your critical reading scaled score.

_____

SAT Score Conversion Table

Raw Score	Critical Reading Scaled Score	Raw Score	Critical Reading Scaled Score
67	800	31	510
66	800	30	510
65	790	30	510
64	770	30	510
63	750	27	490
62	740	26	480
61	730	25	480
60	720	24	470
59	700	23	460
58	690	22	460
57	690	21	450
56	680	20	440
55	670	19	440
54	660	18	430
53	650	17	420
52	650	16	420
51	640	15	410
50	630	14	400
49	620	13	400
48	620	12	390
47	610	11	380
46	600	10	370
45	600	9	360
44	590	8	350
43	590	7	340
42	580	6	330
41	570	5	320
40	570	4	310
39	560	3	300
38	550	2	280
37	550	1	270
36	540	0	250
35	540	−1	230
34	530	−2	210
33	520	−3	200
32	520	−4	200
		and below	

This table is for use only with the test in this book.

CHART FOR SELF-APPRAISAL BASED ON THE PRACTICE TEST YOU HAVE JUST TAKEN

The Self-Appraisal Chart below tells you quickly where your SAT strengths and weaknesses lie. Check or circle the appropriate box in accordance with the number of your correct answers for each area of the Practice Test you have just taken.

	Sentence Completions	Reading Comprehension
EXCELLENT	16–19	40–48
GOOD	13–15	35–39
FAIR	9–12	26–34
POOR	5–8	17–25
VERY POOR	0–4	0–16

SAT Critical Reading Score/Percentile Conversion Table

Critical Reading

SAT scaled verbal score	Percentile rank
800	99.7+
790	99.5
740–780	99
700–730	97
670–690	95
640–660	91
610–630	85
580–600	77
550–570	68
510–540	57
480–500	46
440–470	32
410–430	21
380–400	13
340–370	6
300–330	2
230–290	1
200–220	0–0.5

Explanatory Answers for Practice Test 2

Section 1: Critical Reading

As you read these Explanatory Answers, refer to Sixteen Verbal (Critical Reading) Strategies (beginning on page 1) whenever a specific strategy is referred to in the answer. Of particular importance are the following Master Verbal Strategies:

Sentence Completion Master Strategy 1—page 3.
Sentence Completion Master Strategy 2—page 4.
Reading Comprehension Master Strategy 2—page 24.

Note: All Reading questions use Reading Comprehension Strategies 1, 2, and 3 as well as other strategies indicated.

1. Choice E is correct. See **Sentence Completion Strategy 2.** Examine the first word of each choice. Choice (A) committees and Choice (B) tribes are incorrect because it is clear that committees and tribes cannot be equated with cities such as Athens. Now consider the other choices. Choice (E) societies . . participated is the only choice which has a word pair that makes sentence sense.

2. Choice C is correct. See **Sentence Completion Strategy 2.** Examine the first word of each choice. Choice (A) abolished and Choice (E) discounted do not make sense because we cannot say that fossils are abolished or discounted in rock formations. Now consider the other choices. Choice (C) preserved . . hardened is the only choice which has a word pair that makes sentence sense.

3. Choice B is correct. See **Sentence Completion Strategy 2.** Examine the first word of each choice. We eliminate Choice (A) dominated and Choice (D) cautioned because the trends do *not* dominate or caution affluence. Now consider the other choices. Choice (C) accentuated . . depression and Choice (E) accepted . . revolution do *not* make sentence sense. Choice (B) reflected . . prosperity *does* make sentence sense.

4. Choice A is correct. See **Sentence Completion Strategy 1.** The word "conserve" (meaning to "protect from loss") completes the sentence so that it makes good sense. The other choices don't do that.

5. Choice B is correct. See **Sentence Completion Strategy 1.** The word "prevalent" (meaning widely or commonly occurring) completed the sentence so that it makes good sense. The other choices don't do that.

6. Choice B is correct. Since this question has the two-blank choices, let us use **Sentence Completion Strategy 2.** When we use Step 1 of Strategy 2, we find a very unusual situation in this question—the first words in all five choices make sense: "With lack of" *advice* or *control* or *opportunity* or *sympathy* or *conscience*, "anyone can develop the disease of alcoholism . . ." Accordingly, we must go to Step 2 of Strategy 2 and consider *both* words of each choice. When we do so, we find that only Choice (B) control . . foolishly makes good sentence sense.

7. Choice B is correct. See **Sentence Completion Strategy 4.** "Because" is a *result indicator*. Since the generating system was not functioning efficiently, the use of electricity had to be *diminished* or *curtailed*.

8. Choice B is correct. See **Sentence Completion Strategy 1.** Something staple, such as bread, is in constant supply and demand. Beer, then, is considered a liquid bread by the Bavarians. Choices A, C, D, and E do not make good sense in the sentence.

9. Choice D is correct. One can see from the gist of the whole passage that the author is warning the reader of the dangers of anarchy and war. See line 4: "It is the age of war" and the need for "the age of civilized man" (line 6). Thus Choice D would be best.

10. Choice A is correct. See lines 11–12 where the author says that "It calls for total awareness, total commitment" indicating limited hope.

11. Choice B is correct. It can be seen that the author contrasts novel reading in the past with novel reading in the present throughout the passage. Although the author does mention a "defect in today's novels" (choice A), that is not the main consideration in the passage.

12. Choice E is correct. See lines 2–6: "there were few diversions . . . not irritated by the digressions and irrelevances. . . ." Do not be lured into Choice B: Although some great novels are long, not all are.

13. Choice B is correct. See paragraph 2: "Most social scientists . . . have assumed that the minimum economic needs of the aged should be lower than those of the younger family."

14. Choice E is correct. Given the context of the sentence and the next sentence, Choice E is the best. See also **Reading Comprehension Strategy 5.**

15. Choice A is correct. See paragraph 4: "[The data] disclose sharp income inequalities within every age group . . ."

16. Choice E is correct. For I, see paragraph 5: "Those sixty-five and over are expected to increase 672 percent." For III, see paragraph 3: "For the growing working-class family, limited in income by the very nature of the breadwinner's occupation . . ."

17. Choice C is correct. See paragraph 2: The sentence after the "functional ethos" sentence refers to "these values." See also **Reading Comprehension Strategy 5.**

18. Choice D is correct. See the last sentence in the passage: "With the more rapid expansion of these two low-income groups, the young and the old . . ."

19. Choice D is correct. For I, see paragraph 4: "A spending unit's income-tenth position *within his age category* varies much less, if at all, and is determined primarily by his occupation." For III, see paragraph 3: "For the growing working-class family, limited in income by the very nature of the breadwinner's occupation . . ."

20. Choice A is correct. From the context of the sentence, it can be seen that Choice A is the best. See also **Reading Comprehension Strategy 5.**

21. Choice C is correct. See paragraph 3: "Despite his seniority, the older worker is likely to be downgraded to a lower-paying job . . ."

22. Choice C is correct. See paragraph 3: "The early and lower income period of a person's working life, during which he acquires his basic vocational skills . . ."

23. Choice C is correct. See paragraph 4: "A spending unit's income-tenth position is . . . determined primarily by his occupation."

24. Choice D is correct. The phrase "the legendary land of economic opportunity where any man can work his way to the top" (lines 98–100), in contrast to what the author really believes, represents *sarcasm*.

Explanatory Answers for Practice Test 2 (continued)

Section 2: Critical Reading

As you read these Explanatory Answers, refer to Sixteen Verbal (Critical Reading) Strategies (beginning on page 1) whenever a specific strategy is referred to in the answer. Of particular importance are the following Master Verbal Strategies:

Sentence Completion Master Strategy 1—page 3.
Sentence Completion Master Strategy 2—page 4.
Reading Comprehension Master Strategy 2—page 24.

Note: All Reading questions use Reading Comprehension Strategies 1, 2, and 3 as well as other strategies indicated.

1. Choice D is correct. See **Sentence Completion Strategy 1.** The word "extreme" is the most appropriate among the five choices because the forest fire season is in *full swing*. The other choices are, therefore, not appropriate.

2. Choice A is correct. See **Sentence Completion Strategy 2.** Examine the first words of each choice. We eliminate Choice (C) imagined and Choice (E) intuitive. Reason: The effect of the long war was *not* imagined or intuitive (meaning knowing by a hidden sense). Now we consider Choice (B) immediate .. staring and Choice (D) delayed .. rebuilding. Neither word pair makes sense in the sentence. Choice (A) cumulative .. corrosion *does* make sense in the sentence.

3. Choice E is correct. See **Sentence Completion Strategy 3.** If you had tried to complete the sentence *before* looking at the five choices, you might have come up with any of the following words meaning "continually" or "regularly":

    constantly   always
    perpetually   persistently
    habitually

The other choices are, therefore, incorrect.

4. Choice E is correct. See **Sentence Completion Strategy 2.** Examine the first word of each choice. Choice (D) crushes is eliminated because it is not likely that the bee will crush the nectar from different flowers. Now consider each pair of words in the other choices. We find that Choice (E) extracts .. converts has the only word pair that makes sense in the sentence.

5. Choice D is correct. See **Sentence Completion Strategies 1 and 4.** The plan turned out to be impractical, unable to be logically supported. Note the root "ten" *to hold*, so "untenable" means *not holding*. Also note that the word "since" in the sentence is a *result indicator*.

6. Choice C is correct. In lines 9–10, the author is showing that through the "weedy falsities," truth can be created.

7. Choice C is correct. See the last lines 18–21 . . . "we can feel all the poverty, despair, and unfairness in our world . . ." For choice A, there may be value for the spectator: see line 17 "and perhaps how we should change them."

8. Choice E is correct. See lines 9–10, 15–18, and 18–21. This describes how something positive can come

out from something negative. In Choice A, although specific references (lines 4–6) are made, there are no specific references in Passage 2. In Choice B, there is no indication of both being completely objective, especially in Passage 1 line 2 where the author states that the theater is the "most preposterous of all." Choice C is incorrect in that in Passage 1, the author certainly does not believe in the accuracy of the time (16th century) whereas in Passage 2, the author does believe in the accuracy of the time. Choice D is incorrect in that it appears that the intensity and passion of the author's arguments in Passage 1 is far greater than that of the author's in Paragraph 2.

9. Choice D is correct. In lines 9–10 note the words "lily" (a flower) and "jungle" (a place) which are used as analogies. We do not see such analogies in Passage 2. In Choice A, both authors would disagree as the author in Passage 1 states that theater is fiction, not reality and the author in Passage 2 states that the theater is real. In Choice B, see lines 5–6: "the much admired Miss Huckaby." In Choice C, in lines 8–9, the author is sarcastic when he says that "people were ever so marvelously articulate." In Choice E, see lines 11–13: the author believes the contrary, that the theater is quite realistic.

10. Choice A is correct. See lines 46–49: "The fundamental fact . . . in their environment." Choices B, D, and E are incorrect because the passage does not indicate that these statements are true. Choice C is incorrect because it is only partially true. The passage does not state that *all* animals and plants are successful in adjusting themselves to changes in their environments.

11. Choice E is correct. See lines 4–8: "Originally the term acclimatization . . . altered temperature." Also see lines 11–13: "But aside from temperature . . . originally accustomed to." Choices A, B, C, and D are incorrect because one *cannot* infer from the passage what any of these choices state.

12. Choice A is correct. Acclimatization and adaptation are both forms of adjustment. Accordingly, these two processes are similar. The difference between the two terms, however, is brought out in lines 36–41: "By and large . . . as adaptation." Choice D is incorrect because the passage does not indicate what is expressed in Choice D. See lines 32–35: "Let us define acclimatization . . . lethal for it." Choices B, C, and E are incorrect because the passage does not indicate that any of these choices are true.

13. Choice D is correct. A person going from daylight

into a darkened room is an example of adaptation— not acclimatization. See lines 36–41: "By and large . . . as 'adaptation.' " Choices A, B, C, and E all require the process of acclimatization. Therefore, they are incorrect choices. An ocean fish placed in a lake (Choice A) is a chemical change. Choices B, C, and E are all pressure changes. Acclimatization, by definition, deals with chemical and pressure changes.

14. Choice B is correct. Given the context in the sentence, Choice B is the best. See also **Reading Comprehension Strategy 5**.

15. Choice B is correct. See lines 37–41: "The term [acclimatization] should not be taken . . . as 'adaptation.' " Choices A, D, and E are incorrect because the passage does not indicate that these choices are true. Choice C is partially correct in that acclimatization does apply to adjustments, but the choice is incorrect because adaptation also applies to adjustments. See lines 39–41: "This type of adjustment . . . as 'adaptation.' "

16. Choice E is correct. See paragraph 2 (beginning): "The tie which bound this world-embracing empire together . . . was as much cultural as political."

17. Choice A is correct. See paragraph 1 (end): "Centuries of training had bred in them the conviction that all other rulers should be tributary to the Son of Heaven."

18. Choice B is correct. See the last paragraph about the close relationship between "ethical standards" and "Confucian patterns."

19. Choice C is correct. The reader should infer from paragraphs 3 and 4 that Han and T'ang were dynasties—just as there was a Manchu dynasty.

20. Choice D is correct. The passage points out that since more emphasis was placed on being members of the same culture, rather than on being members of the same race, there was a "comparative contentment of Chinese under alien rulers" (paragraph 4: beginning).

21. Choice B is correct. See paragraph 5 (last sentence): "In contrast with India, where caste and religion have tended to keep apart the racial strata, in China assimilation made great progress."

22. Choice B is correct. Paragraph 4 (end) points out that the Manchus never gave up some of their ancestral ways, and this disturbed segments of the population.

23. Choice A is correct. The passage states that assimilation made great progress in China. (See the answer to question 21.)

24. Choice C is correct. From the context of the sentence and the sentence before and after it, it can be seen that "restiveness" must mean impatience or restlessness. See also **Reading Comprehension Strategy 5**.

Explanatory Answers for Practice Test 2 (continued)

Section 3: Critical Reading

As you read these Explanatory Answers, refer to Sixteen Verbal (Critical Reading) Strategies (beginning on page 1) whenever a specific strategy is referred to in the answer. Of particular importance are the following Master Verbal Strategies:

Sentence Completion Master Strategy 1—page 3.
Sentence Completion Master Strategy 2—page 4.
Reading Comprehension Master Strategy 2—page 24.

Note: All Reading questions use Reading Comprehension Strategies 1, 2, and 3 as well as other strategies indicated.

1. Choice C is correct. See **Sentence Completion Strategy 2.** Examine the first word of each choice. Choice (E) a futile does *not* make good sense because we do not refer to momentum as futile. Now consider the other choices. Choice (C) an increasing . . athletics is the only choice which has a word pair that makes sentence sense.

2. Choice E is correct. See **Sentence Completion Strategy 1.** The word "effective" (meaning "serving the purpose" or "producing a result") makes good sense in the sentence. The other choices don't do that.

3. Choice D is correct. See **Sentence Completion Strategy 4.** The word "despite" is an opposition indicator. A strange and inevitable or *ineluctable* fate seemed to keep him helpless and unhappy, despite occasional periods of calm, peacefulness or *serenity.*

4. Choice B is correct. See **Sentence Completion Strategies 1 and 4.** Try each choice, being aware that "result" is, of course, a result indicator: Samuel Clemens chose the pen name Mark Twain.

5. Choice A is correct. See **Sentence Completion Strategy 1.** The word "versatile" means capable of turning competently from one task or occupation to another. Clearly, Choice (A) versatile is the only correct choice.

6. Choice B is correct. See **Sentence Completion Strategy 2.** Examine the first words of each choice. We eliminate Choice (C) avoided and Choice (D) realized because it does not make sense to say that Leonardo realized or avoided the Law of Gravity. Now we consider Choice (A) examined . . colorful and Choice (E) suspected . . mural, neither of which makes sentence sense. Choice (B) anticipated . . anatomical is the only choice that makes sentence sense.

7. Choice E is correct. The author is stressing the point that the true artist—the person with rare creative ability and keen perception, or high intelligence— fails to communicate well with those about him— "differs from the rest of us" (lines 4–5). He is likely to be considered a "nut" by many whom he comes in contact with. "Great wits" in the Choice E quotation refers to the true artist. The quotation states, in effect, that there is a thin line between the true artist and the "nut." Choices A, B, C, and D are incorrect because they have little, if anything, to do with the main idea of the passage.

[Note: Choices C and E were composed by John Dryden (1631–1700), and Choices A, B, and D by Alexander Pope (1688–1744).]

8. Choice C is correct. See lines 9–11. The artist creates because he is "less fitted to prosper and enjoy himself under the conditions of life which he and we must face alike." Choices A and E are incorrect. Although they may be true, they are never mentioned in the passage. Choice B is incorrect because, although the artist may be a threat to the social order, he is by no means an unnecessary one. The author, throughout the passage, is siding with the artist against the social order. Choice D is incorrect. See lines 11–13: "Therefore he takes . . . attempt to escape from life." A person who is attempting to escape from life hardly knows how to enjoy life.

9. Choice B is correct. The author ridicules Samuel Johnson, saying that that he is as much a true artist as a kazoo player is a musician. He then says that if Johnson were alive today, he would be a Senator or a university president. The author thus implies that these positions do not merit high respect. Choice A is the opposite of Choice B. Therefore, Choice A is incorrect. Choice C is incorrect because, although the statement may be true, the author neither states nor implies that senators and university presidents are generally appreciative of the great literary classics. Choice D is incorrect. The fact that the author lumps Johnson, senators, and university presidents together as non-artistic people indicates that senators and university presidents do not have native writing ability. Choice E is incorrect for this reason: The author believes that Johnson lacked the qualities of an artist. Johnson, if alive today, would be a senator or a university president. We may conclude, then, that Senators and university presidents lack the qualities of an artist.

10. Choice C is correct. Although a love of beauty is a quality we usually associate with artists, that idea about artists is never mentioned in the passage. All of the other characteristics are expressly mentioned in the first two paragraphs of the passage.

11. Choice B is correct. The author's sincere sympathy is shown toward artists in lines 20–28: "From Dante to Tolstoy . . . actually fugitives from range and reprisal." There is no evidence in the passage to indicate that the author's attitude toward artists is Choice A, C, D, or E. Therefore, these choices are incorrect.

12. Choice C is correct. See the sentence in the second paragraph of Passage 2: "He and only he knows the world."

13. Choice B is correct. See the first paragraph in Passage 2.

14. Choice C is correct. From the context in Passage 2, we see that "world's eye" and "world's heart" refer to culture and wisdom, respectively. See lines 66–70, ". . . public and illustrious thoughts . . . resist the vulgar prosperity . . . by preserving communicating . . . noble biographies . . . melodious verse . . ." This is all about *culture* and *wisdom*.

15. Choice E is correct. See the first sentence in Passage 2: ". . . the self-accusation, the faint heart, the frequent uncertainty and loss of time, which are the nettles and tangling vines . . ." Here "nettles and tangling vines" refers to "self-accusation" and "uncertainty." Nettles are plants covered with stinging hairs. Tangling vines give the impression of weaving all around in no particular or certain direction. So nettles can be thought of as "self-accusation"—something "stinging." And "tangling vines" can be thought of as "uncertainty." See also **Reading Comprehension Strategy 5**.

16. Choice C is correct. See Passage 2: The most appropriate groups are the hardships of the scholar, the scholar's functions, and the scholar's justifications for disregarding the world's business, as can be seen from the structure and content of the passage.

17. Choice C is correct. Given the context of the rest of the sentence, the author uses the phrase "seems to stand" as "giving the false impression of being." See also **Reading Comprehension Strategy 5.**

18. Choice A is correct. See lines 100–108 and 64–66 in Passage 2 and lines 14–19 and 29–40 in Passage 1.

19. Choice E is correct. The statements in I can be seen to be associated with the artist in Passage 2 from lines 100–102 and 66–67 respectively. The statements in II can be seen to be associated with the artist in Passage 1 from lines 29–40 and 5, respectively. The statements in III can be seen to be associated with the artist in Passage 2 from lines 63–65 and 53–64 respectively.

What You Must Do Now to Raise Your SAT Critical Reading Score

1. a) Follow the directions on page 223 to determine your scaled score for the SAT Test you've just taken. These results will give you a good idea about whether or not you ought to study hard in order to achieve a certain score on the actual SAT.

    b) Using your Test correct answer count as a basis, indicate for yourself your areas of strength and weakness as revealed by the "Chart for Self-Appraisal" on page 224.

2. Eliminate your weaknesses in each of the SAT test areas (as revealed in the "Chart for Self-Appraisal") by taking the following Giant Steps toward SAT success.

Critical Reading Part

Giant Step 1

Take advantage of the Critical Reading Strategies that begin on page 1. Read again the Explanatory Answer for each of the Critical Reading questions that you got wrong. Refer to the Critical Reading Strategy that applies to each of your incorrect answers. Learn each of these Critical Reading Strategies thoroughly. These strategies are crucial if you want to raise your SAT Critical Reading score substantially.

Giant Step 2

You can improve your vocabulary by doing the following:

1. Study "Word Building with Roots, Prefixes, and Suffixes," beginning on page 70.

2. Learn the "Hot Prefixes and Roots" on page 84.

3. Read through "A List of Words Appearing More Than Once on SAT Exams" on page 90.

4. Look through the "Most Important/Frequently Used SAT Words and Their Opposites" on page 92.

5. Take the Vocabulary Practice Tests on page 158.

6. Read as widely as possible—not only novels. Nonfiction is important too . . . and don't forget to read newspapers and magazines.

7. Listen to people who speak well. Tune in to worthwhile TV programs also.

8. Use the dictionary frequently and extensively—at home, on the bus, at work, etc.

9. Play word games—for example, crossword puzzles, anagrams, and Scrabble. Another game is to compose your own Sentence Completion questions. Try them on your friends.

Remember, if you do the job *right* and follow the steps listed above, you are likely to raise your SAT score on each of the Critical Reading parts of the test 150 points—maybe 200 points—and even more.

> I am the master of my fate;
> I am the captain of my soul.
>
> —From the poem "Invictus"
>   by William Ernest Henley